THE POWER OF SOCIAL NETWORKING

THE POWER
OF SOCIAL
NETWORKING

—

Using the Whuffie Factor

to Build Your Business

—

TARA HUNT

THREE RIVERS PRESS
NEW YORK

Originally published as *The Whuffie Factor*

Published in the United States by Three Rivers Press, an imprint of the Crown
Publishing Group, a division of Random House, Inc., New York.
www.crownpublishing.com

Three Rivers Press and the Tugboat design are registered trademarks of Random
House, Inc.

Originally published in hardcover as *The Whuffie Factor* in the United States
by Crown Business, an imprint of the Crown Publishing Group, a division of
Random House, Inc., New York, in 2009.

Library of Congress Cataloging-in-Publication Data

Hunt, Tara.
    [Whuffie factor]
    The power of social networking / Tara Hunt.—1st paperback ed.
        p. cm.
    Prev. ed. published under title: The whuffie factor.
 1. Business networks.   2. Social networks.   3. Online social networks.
4. Social capital (Sociology)   5. Success in business.   I. Title.
    HD69.S8H86 2010   2010004333
    302.3—dc22

ISBN 978-0-307-44940-5

Printed in the United States of America

Design by Level C

10 9 8 7 6 5 4 3 2 1

First Paperback Edition

To my son, Tad Hunt-Sorensen, who doesn't know it yet,
but he's the one who taught me to keep it real online, and my parents,
Marianne and Terry Hunt, who gave me all of the core lessons
and opportunities I needed to get me here

CONTENTS

1

HOW TO BE A SOCIAL CAPITALIST

If someone comes up to you and, out of the blue, asks: "How's your whuffie?" don't call security.

I'll explain why shortly, but initially I want to make a couple of assumptions: first, that, like everyone in business—from a Fortune 500 company to the start-up just opening its doors—you want to be more hands-on, grassroots, and interactive to maintain a continuous flow of information to and from your customers; and, second, that you've seen a steady rise in the money you spend for marketing and promotion but a decline in the return on that investment. Yet every time you turn around, there seems to be a story about a business that's grown a huge customer base at little or no cost by catching the Web 2.0 wave—the world of mass collaboration and social networking—using blogs, Facebook, MySpace, Twitter, and other social networking tools. But when you go online and check them out, all you see is a bunch of chatter and noise. So, you think to yourself, "How do I make sense of it all?"

The question is how to do it. Catching the social networking wave of Web 2.0 is neither as easy nor as straightforward as it might seem at first blush. Simply spending money and trying to buy your way into online communities works about as well as a dude in a Brooks Brothers suit trying to fit in at the skateboard park.

To succeed in this Web 2.0 world, you have to turn conventional wisdom on its head and become a social capitalist. A social capitalist is as ravenous as corporate titans like John D. Rockefeller and Bill Gates for success, but the coin of the realm is different. People are on social networks to connect and build relationships. Relationships and connections over time lead to trust, which is the key to capital formation. The capital I'm talking about, though, is not of the monetary variety. It is social capital, aka whuffie, and a social capitalist is one who builds and nutures a community, thereby increasing whuffie.

Once whuffie is "in the bank," monetary capital then starts to flow from social capital. It used to work the other way around. Of course, rich individuals and big companies still have lots of influence, but we're talking here about an emerging world where the rules for success are truly different. If a company tries to buy its way into social networks, the law of unintended consequences kicks in and its social capital starts to diminish. Without social capital, connections in online communities are lost and any recommendation made will be seen as spam, met with negative reactions and a further loss of social capital. So, if someone asks about your whuffie, what she's really getting at is how well you are dealing with the tricky proposition of growing your business in the Web 2.0 world of social networking.

HOW WHUFFIE CAN BUILD YOUR BUSINESS

What it comes down to, in this Web 2.0 world, is that there really are *only* three ways to build a business and make money online: porn, luck, and whuffie.

Pornography, of course, needs no introduction, but I can neither endorse it nor advise you on it. I'll cringe, though, and admit that we owe it a debt of gratitude. The online porn industry pushed the adoption of much of the technology we know, use, and love today. Video and audio streaming, geo-location software,[1] and interactive-type content, such as cookies (used today by sites like Amazon.com and Google), help you find exactly what you need by recording data and storing it each time you return, then returning better and better results. Of course, porn also gave us despicable black-hat tactics like pop-ups and spam. Although effective, they're not tactics I encourage you to use, unless alienating customers and muddying your reputation is your end goal.

Getting extremely bloody lucky is the second way to make money online. I have been working in online marketing for close to a decade and have seen people who struck it rich by being in the right place at the right time. There are, however, rarely consistent patterns for these lucky folk.

Okay, so porn is out and luck is a crapshoot. That leaves whuffie, the *only* predictable way to both build a business and make money online.

The term "whuffie" was coined by Cory Doctorow, creator of the popular blog Boing Boing, to describe social capital in his futuristic science fiction novel *Down and Out in the Magic Kingdom.*[2] In the future as envisioned by Doctorow, whuffie is the only currency used. Other currencies—dollars, euros, renminbi, whatever—will simply disappear.

WHAT IS WHUFFIE, ANYWAY?

Whuffie is the residual outcome—the currency—of your reputation. You lose or gain it based on positive or negative actions, your contributions to the community, and what people think of you. The measurement of your whuffie is weighted according to your interactions with communities and individuals. So, for example, in my own neighborhood, where I have built a strong reputation for being helpful, my whuffie is higher than when I travel to another neighborhood where nobody knows me. There, members of *that* community "ping" my whuffie to find out whether I can be trusted. But for me to be fully welcomed, I can't simply use my whuffie account; I need to be helpful there as well. And I can do that, as Cory Doctorow points out in *Down and Out in the Magic Kingdom,* in three ways: be nice, be networked, or be notable. I'll explain the how-tos of all three whuffie-building strategies over the course of the book.

In this futuristic world, if you need a hotel room, a car, or fare for a ride on the bus, you will pay with your whuffie. It isn't a card or a piece of paper; your whuffie is stored on your person and anyone can ping your internal computer to figure out how whuffie wealthy (or poor) you are.

Yes, this is an idea from science fiction. In reality, though, the importance of social capital is neither fictional nor in the future. In every online community I've been part of, whuffie is a core component of connection; in many cases it is *more* valuable than money. Since the basis of these social networks is trust, something must determine how I value the differing opinions of the 2,000-plus "friends" I have on Facebook. In online communities, a friend can't pay me to make a certain choice or have a certain preference. That would be seen as dishonest and would damage my whuffie. Financial transactions don't mean much of anything in the world of online communities. They work antithetically to it. Financial transactions are part of the market economy, whereas whuffie is part of the gift economy, where services are performed without need for direct payment.

In the gift economy the more you give away, the more whuffie you gain, which is completely opposite from currency in the market economy, where when you give away money, it's pretty much gone. Saving whuffie for a rainy day doesn't work as well as saving money for a rainy day. Whuffie increases in value as it circulates throughout the community; for instance, when I use my whuffie to help you raise yours, there will be a net increase in whuffie for both of us. As it circulates throughout the community like this, it inherently connects people. This really is the key to creating wealth online, and I'll be returning to this concept throughout the book.

You may be saying to yourself, "Well, this is very interesting but I live in the real world! What about paying my rent? Paying my employees? Saving for retirement or sending my kids to college?" Of course! Day to day, you still need $1.99 to buy that quart of milk, but in online communities that $1.99 won't do you much good. We're dealing with two parallel but valid economies here. Market capital now flows from having high social capital. For example, if you are on the job market, you are probably competing with dozens of other candidates with similar qualifications. However, having lots of social capital will put you ahead of the competition if you have good connections that can recommend you for the position (network); if you have a list of public accolades on the work you've done (notable); or if your references have glowing reviews of your ability to lead a team and your likability (viewed as being nice). Having high social capital will give you access to better positions with better pay.

The same goes for your business. There is a great deal of competition in the marketplace. Having lots of social capital will make you stand out: You've really connected with many of your customers, who spread the word to their network; people talk about your product because it is notable; or you have a record of having the best customer service, and customers who have bought elsewhere now go to you because they know they'll be treated better. Having high social capital will help you win customers and sell more product.

It used to work more in the opposite direction. Those with lots of money used to have more influence. When you had money, you could buy more advertising, which was more influential before the Internet because your message could reach a wider audience than word of mouth. Money still carries clout and you can still buy your way in front of large audiences, but this doesn't guarantee influence. The stories in this book will demonstrate, time and again, that those with social capital have enormous influence. The myriad of social media tools I introduce have given people without much money, but with lots of whuffie, the ability to broadcast messages to large audiences. And because they already have relationships with these audiences, they are more likely to have influence. Market capital and social capital are converging more than many recognize. There may even come a day that social capital is seen as viable currency in the market economy.

There are clear advantages to raising whuffie. For one, as you build whuffie, you build relationships with your customers that yield longer-term loyalty. Second, the more whuffie you have, the more people will talk about you in a positive light. The positive word of mouth carried through networks is the core advantage to involving yourself in online communities. Whuffie is also a low-cost, high-energy type of strategy, whereas buying advertising spots can be quite expensive. And although it is difficult to track the impact of, say, a billboard on the side of a building, the impact of your involvement in online communities is almost immediate. Many of the tools used to connect communities, like blogs and wikis, have direct ways to collect feedback from community members.

But the most immediate reason why raising whuffie is essential for your business is that your competitors are either doing it or thinking about doing it right now. As online communities become a stronger and stronger source of consumer information, your sales will be driven by how well you are received in those communities.

THIS BOOK IS BUILT ON WHUFFIE

Let me give you an example from my personal experience: this book. It exists because of my whuffie, the sum of my reputation, influence, bridging and bonding capital, access to ideas and talent, access to resources, potential access to further resources, saved-up favors, accomplishments, and the whuffie of those I have relationships with. Neither the opportunity nor the adventure of writing it would have happened without the many years I spent building my reputation, contributing to communities, meeting amazing people, and openly giving away my ideas.

I started blogging about my theories on social networks and using them for community marketing and the growing popularity of social technologies such as wikis, blogging, and photo sharing in 2004 on Horsepigcow.com. At first my blog was just a place for me to throw ideas against a wall and see if they would stick. I didn't expect many people to actually read it besides close friends and my mom. What was surprising to me is that people did start reading my blog and commenting on posts, giving me feedback and encouraging my way of thinking about marketing. As my ideas evolved and as I interacted with other bloggers writing about marketing and technology, more and more people found my blog posts and started to respond.

After about a year of blogging, I got my first opportunity to try out my theories about the influence of social capital when I was hired by a start-up in the San Francisco Bay Area, an opportunity that came to me because of the contacts I was making through my blogging. This allowed me to test my ideas "in the wild"; that is, with a company developing a product and preparing to launch it into the marketplace. The results were phenomenal. Riya.com, a photo-searching website that uses artificial intelligence technology to search inside of the photos for faces, was the start-up I helped launch with community marketing. Within a day of the launch of the website, 20,000 people signed up and uploaded more than 1 million photos to be searched.

This success won the attention of a wider audience, and conference organizers started to ask me to come and speak in front of live audiences. Although I had little experience as a public speaker, I quickly found out that I loved it. It was through these speaking engagements that I got the opportunity to meet more people face-to-face and exchange ideas and case studies. I continued to write my blog, speak, and record all of my progress along the way by sharing photos, ideas, research, gaffes, and successes. My audience kept growing until a partner and I were able to launch our very own consultancy in 2006. From day one, we had clients and multiple opportunities. As others learned from my adventures, they would refer back to me and my work, extending my network even further.

Then one day I received an e-mail from a longtime reader of my blog who happened to be a literary agent. She wrote, "I like your original ideas and stories. Have you thought about writing a book?" I had many times, but I didn't expect to be approached about it so soon. I put my research and stories into a proposal for this book and was writing it by the end of 2007.

The fact that I openly shared my stories of success and fail-ure led to this opportunity, but the benefits of whuffie didn't end there. As I wrote, people shared interesting case studies, gave me feedback, told me their own stories, and even helped design the cover! Many of those who helped are people I met through my travels, but there were also some whom I've never met face-to-face and who live all over the world. Some are friends of friends, and others have stumbled upon my work through referrals from other bloggers.

When my publisher sent me an e-mail with an image of the proposed book cover attached, I opened it with great anticipa-tion. This would be the cover I would see on bookshelves everywhere! However, when I took a look at what he sent me, it wasn't what I had imagined. Although the designer is a pro-fessional and did a lovely job, I felt it lacked warmth. I couldn't quite put my finger on what bothered me, so I posted the image to Flickr, a popular photo-sharing website where many people follow the images I post every day. Then I posted a message to a group text-messaging service called Twitter, where I had over 5,000 people following me, and asked people for their feedback. What happened next was overwhelming.

First, I was just incredibly excited that dozens of people com-mented on the image and gave feedback on how to improve it. These comments helped confirm to me that the cover didn't communicate the content of the book. Then some submitted cover ideas of their own! The first was sent to me via Flickr from Cesar and Angela Castro, a design team couple from Kailua, Hawaii, who run a website called Standard Society. It included images of people interacting on the cover, which was much closer to the human aspect of the book. After that, a Flickr member who goes by the name of Jellyfish24 sent me another design. Via e-mail, I had ten people send their own redesigned covers. An art professor from Graceland University, Zane Vredenburg, even e-mailed me to ask me if he could assign my cover redesign to his class, to which I replied an enthusiastic, "OMG! Yes, please!" This produced over a dozen fantastic and fun covers—one even featured a rooster as the focal point and became my favorite creatively. Meanwhile, I had a conversation with one of my favorite designers in the world, Cindy Li, about my dilemma, after which she offered to submit something into the pool of growing alternatives. In the end, more than thirty people, many of them complete strangers, took the time to submit new cover art for this book. I loved them all, but the final decision went to Cindy Li's submission. What you see today is a book cover designed by whuffie itself.

Although the whuffie accumulated from the positive use of social networking tools is obviously valuable for individual projects such as writing a book, it is also vital for big companies in maintaining contact and rapport with customers and for small-business owners trying to build a customer base to create demand, increase the size of a market, and build a business. The importance of whuffie for a business can easily be seen in the sad tale of the music industry, which I discuss next. Although it squandered its whuffie, it's important to know that there are ways to use social networking tools to recover.

TEACHING AN OLD (BIG) DOG NEW TRICKS

The music business is a global industry, with a few big companies as dominant players. That the industry is in serious trouble isn't really news. CD sales continue to plummet. In 2007, they dropped 19 percent, an acceleration of the previous declines. Of course, digital music sales are doing well and growing by more than 40 percent each year. But since CDs have constituted 80 percent of the revenue of the recording industry, the digital sales numbers aren't quite making up the difference. Between 2002 and 2006, overall music revenues declined by 11.6 percent. Everyone in the business is feeling the hit.

In January 2008, *The Economist* summed up the changes in customer behavior:

In 2006 EMI, the world's fourth-biggest recorded-music company, invited some teenagers into its headquarters in London to talk to its top managers about their listening habits. At the end of the session the EMI bosses thanked them for their comments and told them to help them-selves to a big pile of CDs sitting on a table. But none of the teens took any of the CDs, even though they were free. "That was the moment we realised the game was completely up," says a person who was there.[3]

Sales units for albums that are big hits today—block-busters—are much smaller than those from just a few years back. It isn't the case, however, that people are listening to less music. They are buying more music than ever, but because of the added ability to discover new artists as well as the ability for more artists to emerge via various online channels, people have more choices and they are making them.

The decline of the blockbuster isn't just limited to the music industry. The myriad of consumer choices compounded with buyers being able to personalize their shopping experiences has led to a wider range of smaller sales. It's a phenomenon that Chris Anderson, the editor of *Wired* magazine, calls "the long tail": The rise of the Internet has spawned the phenomenon of selling "less of more." Companies like Amazon.com that offer a wide array of choice to suit any taste are successful because they cater to this desire to personalize. The idea that there are products that appeal to the mass market—that is, most everyone—is more and more questionable as consumers exercise this ability to personalize their shopping experience. The growth of the long tail demonstrates that customers have individual tastes that they will opt for over generic choices once available.

The game for the music industry is not only up, it moved on a while ago. Unfortunately, music companies continue to struggle with how to respond. Their approach has been reactionary and hostile: suing their own customers, adding levels of complexity to gaining access to music, adding levies on MP3 players, and generally hemorrhaging their whuffie by bullying music lovers. The result of years of this type of behavior has left a wake of anti-music-industry sentiment among consumers, which breeds more apathy toward the decline of the record labels. Many people are more than happy to contribute to that decline as well, supporting independents wherever they can, logging into file-sharing networks, and opening up their own music collections for others to download. These people are inclined to blog negatively about the behavior of the music industry and spend time in online communities spreading their anti-music-label sentiments. I look around at what is happening and it feels like an all-out war.

An example of how this war between the music industry and music listeners is playing out took place recently in Canada. The Canadian government, urged by the Canadian music industry and the U.S. government, proposed legislation to put digital rights—preventing the sharing of music between friends—into audio files. In early 2008, a professor at the University of Ottawa, Michael Geist, started a Facebook group that protested the introduction of potential legislation in Canada: the mirroring of the U.S. Digital Millennium Copyright Act. In the description of the Facebook group page, Geist wrote:

> In December 2007, it became apparent that the Canadian government was about to introduce new copyright legislation that would have been a complete sell-out to U.S. government and lobbyist demands. The new Canadian legislation was to have mirrored the U.S. Digital Millennium Copyright Act with strong anti-circumvention legislation that goes far beyond what is needed to comply with the World Intellectual Property Organization's Internet treaties.[4]

The group attracted more than 40,000 members in the first couple of weeks, helped by prominent bloggers like Cory Doctorow of Boing Boing pointing people toward it. Local "chapters" of Fair Copyright for Canada sprang up across the country and met regularly to discuss pressuring local government representatives to revisit this legislation.

The same tools that are used to share the music in the first place have provided people with the ability to hurt the recording industry by mobilizing to exert counterpressure to the well-paid lobbyists. No wonder the record industry is trying to pressure the ISPs (Internet service providers) to choke bandwidth! Every time someone goes online, it seems, a record label takes a hit.

But this doesn't have to be a war. Not at all. Tools like Facebook and file sharing could also help the labels create demand and find more music lovers, talent, and new revenue sources. They could be using Facebook to do things like the following:

- Connecting with music fans, musician by musician

- Enabling musicians to engage in conversations

- Finding out where the fans live so that they can bring music to them

- Using the groups to have a discussion about what digital rights management is and get feedback on what could make it better for both the labels and the fans

- Creating pages so that fans can share new musicians with their friends

File-sharing services are really simple ways to distribute music. Several methods could be used to let this sharing happen and still allow the labels to make money. Instead of tracking down people downloading the music and suing them, find out where they live and bring their favorite bands to them to play live; or learn from this and build in easier ways for fans to download and share music on their own websites, putting a donate button next to the song, urging fans to donate if they enjoy the music, or letting them download lower-fidelity versions for free and selling higher-fidelity versions alongside the free versions. They could also create a music subscription community for people to buy music in bulk, paying a monthly fee for unlimited downloads.

There are a multitude of tools online that artists and labels alike can learn to use to engage their audience. One example is Eventful Demand.

CREATING DEMAND

Brian Dear, founder of Eventful, gets really jazzed when he thinks about the exciting array of online community tools available, including his own, for musicians, artists, speakers, entertainers, and many other businesses. He sees opportunities where the labels see threats. And he should know.

Dear launched Eventful in 2004 to help people discover events more easily and has served over 6 million people (growing by 100,000 users per week). Having spent many years in the intersection of music and technology, he was frustrated by the lack of resources that enabled people to discover music and social events. Eventful allows you to track your favorite artists, authors, and speakers; find out when they are appearing in your area; and give you recommendations for similar acts. But Dear goes a step beyond this. He has created Eventful Demand, a service that allows fans to create *demand* for their favorite artists, authors, and speakers to come to them, instead of passively waiting.

Dear sees this as a win-win-win situation for fans and performers. The fans get to feel like they are part of the process and that they have some say in a concert schedule, and artists can be confident that they will play at sold-out venues. Currently, millions of fans are demanding shows, and thousands of events have been scheduled. Entire tours for thousands of independent artists have been planned using this system. A band just has to post an Eventful Demand widget on its blog, MySpace page, or band website and promote it to their fans, letting them know that they will come to the places where their fans are.

One of these artists is Jonathan Coulton, a former software developer who was able to "quit his day job" in order to pursue his love of music. Independent of any record label or traditional trajectory of growth, he has grown an amazing international fan base over a few years because of tools like Eventful, YouTube, CDBaby, Wordpress, and iTunes. In a blog post trying to figure out where to plan his fall 2008 tour, Coulton wrote:

> I need your help planning this thing. I know how London is going to go, because I saw how it went, but where else shall I play? Where are you, audience? And don't just leave a comment saying "Briglytonne!" or whatever crazy town you live in, we actually have a system for this: [Eventful Demand].

This really works; it's the only reason I had any confidence that London would be a well-attended show. So if you haven't already, add your name to a demand in the place you'd like to see me play, and that will help me plan the trip.[5]

In a couple of weeks, he received over 1,500 demands from places all over the world. By the time the fall rolled around, he had a good idea of exactly where he should schedule his tour. But that isn't the extent of it. As Brian Dear points out, much like the gift exchange of the gift economy, these sorts of interactions also create special bonds between performers and their audience. Dear talked about this in an interview:

Jonathan is a great example of the mixture of reputation and influence not only that he has over his audience, but that his audience has over him. It's a two way street. First of all, he's very authentic and he is using all of the social media tools to tell his story . . . which is an interesting story to begin with. But then the audience is invited to be part of that story, which makes it even more interesting. This exchange makes for this very positive cycle that just makes the story richer and richer and more interesting.

When artists like Jonathan use tools like Eventful Demand and end up playing in places they wouldn't have formerly thought of playing, that becomes part of the story, not only for the life of the performer, but also for the life of the fans. Everyone feels this very strong sense of ownership that you don't get when so-and-so is just coming to play at the local amphitheatre. When you feel that you helped cause the concert to happen and you actually had an exchange with the artist through social media, that is incredibly compelling.

This is really only a small slice of the potential that lies in the use of these tools.

In fact, Coulton has built his entire career using social networking tools. He encourages people to record him and take photos of him at his concerts. This has led to hundreds of music videos being created and posted on YouTube, which drive millions of people to his website to check out his music. He gives away his music for free, something he's done from the beginning when he created a podcast called "A Thing a Week," where he would post an MP3 of a song he wrote that week. He also put Creative Commons licensing on his music, thus encouraging many podcasters to reuse his content, pointing back to him and driving even *more* traffic to his website and music.

How does he make money? He sells merchandise, as well as the CDs and MP3s he gives away. What is interesting is that people enjoy his music so much they will come back and pay for it after they've gotten it for free. He also collects donations for his work, through selling virtual gifts—monkeys, robots, and bananas—in the form of cartoon images that, when purchased, show up on Coulton's website with the donor's name attached. A sponsorship of $5 will buy a virtual banana, $10 will buy a virtual monkey, and $25 will buy a virtual robot.

Coulton told me, "My secret? Just try everything. It's free or cheap. And you never know where you will find your audience." He's found his audience in very odd and amazing places. A fan of his creates Machinima videos, video screen captures from interactive 3-D games that are dubbed over with music or voice. He created a few from Jonathan's work. These became highly successful among World of Warcraft players and . . . it drove even *more* traffic to Jonathan's work.

"Security is your greatest enemy. You need to be as frictionless as possible," Coulton explained to me as he described all of the serendipitous ways his music has been discovered just because he removed all control and, instead, made it incredibly easy for people to take it and use it in various ways. "Malcolm Gladwell's book *The Tipping Point* is out of date, because everyone is an influencer now. Most people have cameraphones and can record video and send it to the Net right away for their friends to see, who will blog about it and pass it along to more friends. I just encourage it and it figures itself out."

Coulton's use of all of the tools is exactly what Brian Dear encourages. And not just for musicians.

Dear also pointed out a couple of other examples of people using Eventful Demand alongside other online tools—such as Facebook, MySpace, YouTube, Flickr, and Twitter—to really connect with their audience and figure out where they should be appearing.

Wil Wheaton, known to many as Wesley Crusher on *Star Trek: The Next Generation,* and currently an author and speaker, announced in a video that he would go to any city and speak where there were more than 200 "Demands." One of those fulfilled demands was in Boston at a local bookstore. As the news got out about Wil's visit, the store had to book the theater across the street. After the theater filled up, people poured into the street and back and forth between the bookstore and the theater just to be part of it. Even more impressive is that the crowd was attracted even though an admission fee was charged.

These social networking tools helped both Jonathan Coulton and Wil Wheaton build whuffie and an audience without spending much money. When used by people who already have a following and a built-up whuffie account, they can take them to another level. If one musician without a staff can build a worldwide audience like this by engaging people online, a company with a team of people can do this on a larger scale.

I like to imagine a recording industry that could step back and realize that the war that is being waged is a losing battle for all, with nothing but casualties on all sides. In this fantasy, I see a new ability to embrace the chaos and explore the opportunities for new forms of revenue, which *are* out there because people are spending more money than ever on the products and services that connect them. I also see a recording industry using the social media tools to be proactive with their customers, using feedback collected in real-time conversations to redesign the music experience to fit the needs of their customers. For this to happen, recording industry executives will have to become part of the community in significant ways. They will need to understand the benefits of interaction between musicians, fans, and music companies and become incredibly innovative and proactive in recognizing the needs of the customer. And in the end, they would realize that their true purpose is to lift people to new heights through their experience and sharing of music.

Yes, it's a fantasy. But it is also really the only hope the music industry has of surviving this major cultural shift in the long run. And it isn't just the music industry. This cultural shift is happening everywhere, and applying the principles I develop throughout this book will help your business survive that shift as well.

SOCIAL NETWORKS AND THE SMALL-BUSINESS OWNER

People often ask me: "I'm a small-business owner. How can online communities possibly help me?"

One way the idea for this book gelled for me was talking with a flower enthusiast whose business is growing dahlias. In late summer of 2006, my friend Christopher Allen asked me if I would take an hour one afternoon to give some advice to a friend of his, Deborah Dietz, who was interested in how online communities could help her dahlia business. I was intrigued. I hadn't thought about how such a niche industry could benefit from these tools, so of course I sat down with her.

Christopher had already helped Deborah set up a blog and showed her the major online community sites, like YouTube, Twitter, and Flickr, where she could post content to promote her business. She was very interested but didn't seem quite convinced that taking the time to do this would help her business. So we started searching around and found multiple groups of floral enthusiasts and growers on the Internet. The people in these communities were exchanging tips and advice and generally supporting one another. The interaction within these groups reminded me a great deal of one of my most beloved communities: coworking. So I told Deborah the coworking story as a way of demonstrating the benefits that accrued from being whuffie rich.

Coworking is an idea that turned into a movement when we applied online community tools. The idea itself came from Brad Neuberg, a friend who worked on multiple open-source programs, using code that is openly available to the wider community of software developers. Bored with working alone in his home office, Brad started taking his laptop to coffee shops to have more social interaction. But there were many issues with the shops. They were loud, and he was expected to buy multiple coffees and pastries if he sat there for long periods of time. The Wi-Fi was unreliable, and even though he was surrounded by people, it wasn't the kind of social interaction he was looking for. So he decided to rent a space in a community center in the Mission area of San Francisco for two days a week and advertise to other independent workers to come by and pay $15 to have a collaborative work experience. He called his idea "coworking."

When I met Brad, he was finding it a bit difficult to get the word out and handle his workload at the same time. Chris Messina, my business partner, had the idea that a more permanent space would help develop more interest and asked Brad if he would mind if we used his coworking idea to describe our concept. Brad agreed. We started posting events on event site Upcoming.org to see if there was interest from other local people in the shared-space concept. We were floored when dozens of people came to these meetings.

We started looking around at spaces after a couple of meetings. We hadn't done any budgets or business plans but wanted to explore nonetheless. Several people shot videos of our adventure and put them up online; others took photos and posted them to Flickr with the tag "coworking." We started a Google group to help us communicate more effectively and fired up a wiki at PBWiki.com to organize our thoughts.

Even before we found a space, an odd phenomenon occurred. People from around the United States and the world started to join the Google group and post their interest in setting up their own coworking space in their local community. Because we were posting all of our discussions, deliberations, decisions, and media openly, people were able to follow along and learn from us as we went. They would take our lessons and use them in their own pursuits.

Since then Chris and I have founded two coworking spaces in San Francisco: the Hat Factory in Portrero Hill, and Citizen Space near South Park, close to many of the technology start-ups in San Francisco. One of my connections with Christopher Allen, who introduced me to Deborah, is through the coworking space he cofounded in Berkeley, across the bay from San Francisco.

All these spaces are wonderful microcommunities in themselves, but the big, worldwide community of coworking is amazing. The Google group has over 1,600 members supporting one another's efforts. There are levels of "experience" in our community: coworker, catalyst, and space owner. The coworkers are people who are supporters, either through spreading the idea by word of mouth or working out of a space itself. Catalysts are people who are in the process of opening a space. Maybe they've put their proverbial stake in the ground and stated their interest or they are well on their way to opening their own space. Space owners are like the sage elders in our community. They've opened a space and are willing to share the experience with coworkers and catalysts to help them out. Because this community is so supportive, within a year over thirty spaces emerged with hundreds more in the process. Most of the spaces have been opened by independent consultants and small-business owners who just want to work with others like themselves. They didn't require much monetary investment up front, but did require lots of energy and advice.

The coworking movement has been featured in dozens of major publications, including the *New York Times, Business-Week, Wired,* and *Entrepreneur* magazine; on CNN a couple of times; and in thousands of blog posts. It's given me an even greater gift, though—a worldwide family. Almost everywhere that I travel now, there is a coworking space or a space in progress. So when the space owners know I'm coming to town, they help me find good, reliable Wi-Fi and a nice group of people to work with.

Spaces like ours existed well before the Internet. But the movement was only possible because of the Internet and the plethora of amazing collaborative and community tools.

After I had told Deborah the story, she realized she needed to tap into these supportive networks to help her gain more knowledge and contacts within her industry. She also needed to start publishing more about her ideas and activities in various places, like Flickr and her blog and Twitter, so that the people she met could see what she was all about. It would also help people find her online. The more content she produced, the more people would know about her floral business. This would open up more potential opportunities. As her network grew, so would her business. The results? Deborah has connected with many dahlia enthusiasts and has grown interest and membership in the organizations she is passionate about, SF Dahlia and the Dahlia Society of California. She continues to meet interesting new business contacts, who help her grow her business as well as her whuffie in the dahlia growing community.

She also came back to Citizen Space a couple days after our conversation and delivered us the most beautiful dahlias I have ever seen.

HOW TRUST BUILDS WHUFFIE

I was sitting down for a haircut when my stylist, Gilbert, who co-owns the salon Honeycomb in Noe Valley, a neighborhood in the central part of San Francisco, said to me, "I don't know what you say to people about me, but my business has doubled since you started coming. People keep calling in and saying, 'I heard about you through Tara.'"

I smiled. There are advantages and disadvantages for the people in your life if you live it incredibly openly.

I explained to Gilbert that when I come to him, I usually

tweet out that I am visiting Gilbert at the Honeycomb Salon. Then I explained that I usually have some question as to what I should do with my hair, so I post a photo or two of some ideas on Flickr, then point to it via Twitter to get people's "votes." During the process, I usually take my camera phone and snap the progressive stages of where I'm at and then point people to it via Twitter as well. People go and comment on the progress, especially if I have foils in my hair. After everything is done and I'm all beautified, I take a higher-resolution photo of myself, post it on Flickr, and get the reaction.

Because of this and because he is a darn good stylist, people start thinking of Gilbert as the person to see about their hair in San Francisco. Through me, whom they trust, they begin to trust Gilbert. And, because I have a good number of people in my network, there is a good chance that a few people will be calling him up.

Now when I go see Gilbert, he gives me cues on when to take a photo and reminds me to tweet out questions. He's gotten into Yelp.com, the local review site, and has encouraged many of his happy customers to go post a review for him. He's even considered opening up his own Twitter account. But even if he doesn't, being aware of the online tools and community help his business a great deal. He definitely understands the amplified power of word of mouth on the Internet.

There are multiple levels on which to be aware and to interact with online communities for small businesses. Gilbert's salon is a good example of the potential that social networking tools provide small, local operators to improve and innovate in their competitive space. Gilbert now has an advantage over other hairstylists in his neighborhood. There are all sorts of ways that local businesses, the proverbial corner stores, could improve their interactions with their local neighborhood by being online. They could put up a wiki and encourage their customers to add requests for carrying certain products so they know how to plan inventory. They could post photos, tweet, or blog about store events and changes. Corner stores rely on people nipping in for those one or two things that they forgot to get during their big grocery trip. But they could increase the frequency of visits by interacting and connecting with their customers.

USING SOCIAL NETWORKS TO DO GOOD

Online social networking tools have especially powerful potential for individuals trying to solve community issues and for nonprofit organizations.

Many nonprofits have limited resources, so their campaigns are absolutely dependent on word of mouth. Since people in online communities are incredibly enthusiastic about helping others out, nonprofit and tech seem to go hand in hand. Whether you are a large, well-funded organization or a small, local, cash-strapped organization, you will benefit from interacting with online communities and building your whuffie. Large, well-funded organizations can build whuffie by connecting to their supporters and building trust. Smaller, cash-strapped organizations will benefit through spreading awareness of their work in the community.

TechSoup is an organization in the San Francisco Bay Area that assists nonprofits in using new technology through its NetSquared project. NetSquared shows people how to use the power of Web 2.0 technologies to fund-raise and build awareness for nonprofits. At one of its events, NetSquared had Nate Ritter, a blogger and consultant from San Diego, talk about using Twitter to spread information about the fires in San Diego during the fall of 2007.

Nate's foray into heroism started simply by reading other people's tweets on what was happening, picking up a few items from local news sources, and going outside to talk to people affected by the fire. He would then tweet out what he could gather, mostly updates on where the fire was moving, who was being evacuated, the roads that were closed, and the neighborhoods to be cautious about. Many people started noticing what Nate was doing and encouraged their friends to follow him for usable, up-to-date news on the fires.

They even started sending him news themselves. People would direct message Nate with requests for reposting about shelter needs, well water contamination and availability, shelter openings and closings, people who were okay or looking to see if others were okay, Red Cross sites and meal kitchens, and so on. He was posting several pieces of information each minute after a while, becoming a human news aggregator for anyone interested in what was going on with the fires.

By the time it was over, he had ten times the followers he started with and a hundred times the whuffie. People were reaching out to him to thank him and offer their help with anything he needed. He was interviewed by *Wired* magazine and asked to come speak to several organizations on how he used Twitter as a way to get the word out about the fires.

Nate built a great deal of trust and goodwill through his use of Twitter, so when he came to speak at the NetSquared event, he discussed how nonprofits shouldn't use just Twitter to send out updates, but other online community tools to create a full picture of what the organization is doing. Twitter is great for giving updates on things like your progress and victories, and for having public conversations that help inform people on the issues. Flickr, the photo-sharing site, is another tool that can be used effectively to give people a visual reference as people post their photos. He is also using his whuffie to gather volunteers to build a nonprofit tool, Crisiswire.com, to track conversation online around issues and events.

Many nonprofits are using online community tools for awareness building and fund-raising. Interplast, the nonprofit that provides free life-changing surgery for children and adults with clefts and disabling burns and hand injuries in Asia, Africa, and Latin America, posts before and after photos of its patients' surgeries. By posting photos on Flickr of the good work Interplast is doing, it has gained many supporters, raised awareness about the insufficient access to these types of surgeries, found doctors to volunteer their time and expertise, and raised money.

Beth Kanter, a social media consultant for nonprofit organizations and a fund-raiser for Cambodian Orphans, has successfully raised a great deal of money and awareness through her interaction in online communities. Beth has e-mailed, messaged, poked, tweeted, blogged, Flickred, YouTubed, and

SlideShared her way into mobilizing a large number of supporters for her pet cause, sending Cambodian orphans to school. In 2008, Beth's efforts won her the number one spot, and $50,000, out of 606 organizations that participated in the Global Causes for America's Giving Challenge, an initiative that employs social media and technology to inspire people to support causes. Beth's success comes from her ability to build whuffie one relationship at a time through the various online networks.

I first encountered Beth Kanter through Vox.com, a blogging social network that allows individuals to form blog "neighborhoods"—groups of people who blog on similar issues or are part of a friend network. In late July 2006, I was experimenting with Vox.com and received a friend request from Beth, after which I read some of her posts. Her passion and commitment to Cambodian orphans was instantly apparent in her writing and I was really impressed with how she was reaching out to other people working in the nonprofit space, offering tips as well as asking for feedback. So I accepted her friend request. Within a couple of hours, Beth sent me a private message, introducing herself. She explained that she had been following my blog posts and activities on other social networks for some time and told me my suggestions had been really helpful for her work. She also explained a little more about what she was working on. As we talked back and forth, we sought out each other on other social networks such as Flickr, Upcoming (event sharing), and Twitter.

As we got to know each other, Beth told me about her two adopted children from Cambodia and her background. Within about an hour, Beth built an amazing amount of whuffie with me. I was ready to support just about anything she believed in. And I wasn't the only one. It grew more and more apparent to me that Beth took that time with everyone in her impressive network. She didn't grow her audience through buying e-mail lists or sending people flyers—both frequently used techniques for nonprofits; she grew it through meeting people, one at a time, once removed from her current network. And she has met almost everyone in her network by using social media tools. She got interested in my work through another person in her network, then followed what I was doing until she felt confident enough that I was the type of person who would actually be interested in her work. And she was right. I'm a big fan.

Beth is just one person with seemingly boundless energy, but a team of one nonetheless. But much like Jonathan Coulton, Beth understands that there is great whuffie-building power in online social networks, so she tries them all, making new friends and supporters everywhere she goes. Beth now gets invited to speak at conferences all over the world about how she effectively builds her network—and her whuffie—with these online tools. Seeing that Beth is a single person making all sorts of impact, I can only imagine the impact an organization would have if it used the tools.

Beyond the tools, involvement in online communities can raise awareness about an issue, give people a peek into the good work you are doing, and create trust. With so many charitable organizations around, it's harder and harder to get people's attention and support. But the more people you can collaborate with and build relationships with online, the better off your organization will be.

Whuffie, then, is the culmination of your reputation, influence, bridging and bonding capital, current and potential access to ideas, talent and resources, saved-up favors, and accomplishments. Small businesses, nonprofits, musicians, speakers, and even authors are using social networks to build whuffie and grow their businesses. But what about you? How is this going to help you grow your business? The next chapter covers how much word of mouth—the oldest and most powerful form of marketing—is growing through the use of these social networks, and it outlines five steps to help you build whuffie and amplify that word of mouth.

2

THE POWER OF COMMUNITY MARKETING

As we saw in chapter 1, people are building whuffie for personal projects and for developing a stronger audience and customer base for their businesses. They are using the tools of social networking to connect to people in online communities and engaging in a process I call "community marketing."

Community marketing enables you to go beyond traditional marketing tactics to reach potential customers. Perhaps you are part of a corporation that wants to increase sales and the number of repeat customers, or you run a start-up that needs to attract members in a busy market, or you are a solo practitioner who just wants to have a steady stream of clients. Maybe you are frustrated because your business is ignored. You have placed ads, hired a PR firm, bought expensive research, started a blog to share your news announcements, but nobody seems to be paying any attention. Perhaps you are finding out for yourself that it is getting easier and easier for customers to ignore you. In fact, maybe it seems that the louder you yell, the more they tune you out. There are several reasons why this is happening:

- **THE AIRWAVES ARE POLLUTED.** Everywhere you go, online and off, someone or something is trying to get your attention. Pop-ups, spam, banner ads, text ads, sales pitches, posters, billboards, thirty-second television spots, bus ads, business cards, sandwich boards, and so on. If you are like most people, you tune these messages out to just get through the day.
- **PEOPLE HAVE BEEN BURNED TOO MANY TIMES.** Dishonest advertising and false promises lead to mistrust. You could be offering the face cream that actually does take twenty years off someone's skin, but very few people will believe you because they have a cupboard full of expensive creams that made the same claim and failed.
- **THE PARADOX OF CHOICE.** If you haven't read Barry Schwartz's book, entitled *The Paradox of Choice*,[1] take a quick break and order it now. Too much choice without clear differentiation makes customers miserable. With every message you send them, their misery deepens. Barry reports on studies that show that more choice equals less satisfaction.

The consequence of being inundated, the lack of trust, and too many choices is that people just don't listen to ads, salespeople, or important messages anymore. They don't care what you have to say, sell, or even give away. But the number one reason that people don't listen to you is because they are too busy listening to their friends! The people they *trust*. The people *they care about*.

At first blush, this seems like yet another take on word of mouth, the strongest influencer of all of our buying decisions. It's true, and in one sense this is not news. It's a well-documented truth that the majority of our buying decisions have *always* been through word of mouth. However, what *has* changed is that, thanks to the proliferation of online communities, our personal networks have gotten *bigger,* much bigger. This means that we can shape the opinions of others, and our opinions are shaped by people we trust more than ever. Everything from what we purchase to how we parent to whom we vote for is influenced through our interactions in communities.

A few years ago, if I wanted to make a big purchase, I would have gotten recommendations from a fairly small number of people at the office or, say, friends at a dinner party. But now I have over 2,500 friends on Facebook. I follow over 1,500 people on Twitter and am followed by over 20,000 people. On Flickr, I have over 300 friends, 600 contacts, and 900 followers. On Last.fm, 200 friends. Now, I truly know and regularly contact only a portion of these friends; in short, some have more influence over my buying decisions than others. But what is important to note here is that even the most distant "friend" on one of these networks has more influence over my buying decisions than any ad or salesperson I encounter.

Earlier this year, when I wanted to find out which SLR camera to buy to replace my stolen Fuji, I first searched through the photos of my friends and contacts on Flickr, making note of the camera used for the photos I really liked. I narrowed my decision down to two cameras, but was still finding it difficult to decide, so I sent the question out to my Twitter friends. "I can't decide between the Canon EOS and the Nikon D40. Pros and cons of both?" For those of you who don't know, Twitter is a simple text-messaging service (also available via web or instant messaging), where you have 140 characters or less to tell anyone subscribed to you what you are doing at that moment. As mentioned earlier, I have over 20,000 people "listening" to me, so I had lots of feedback to choose from. My final decision came down to the opinion of someone whose photography I love and whose advice I trust to be absolutely sincere. If you are wondering, I chose the EOS. I'm incredibly happy with my decision.

Having 20,000 people listening also gives me a great deal of power to influence the buying decisions of other people. Any site, article, or product I come across that I think is worth posting, I will send the link out via Twitter. For instance, I ran across a great blog post that gave ten easy tips for being more environmentally friendly in day-to-day life and sent that link out over Twitter. Chris Baskind, who runs the blog Lighter Footstep, which posted that article, sent me a thank-you note later that day and told me his web traffic went up because of the mention. He gained almost 100 new subscribers in a couple of minutes! Similarly, my frequent tweeting about my new dog, Ridley, a rescue pug, resulted in at least twenty people telling me that I convinced them to go to Pug Pros, the rescue service where I found my dog, and apply.

Citizen Agency, my former company, ran an event called Bar-

CampBlock—"BarCamp" being the name for events where nothing is preplanned and the attendees create the schedule, and "Block" meaning that it took place in multiple venues over a city block—in August of 2007. Most of the 700 attendees signed up because I sent tweets out from the early planning stages on what to expect at the event, from what kind of food I was ordering to the number of people who were signing up daily. When I tweeted out a call for sponsors, 106 responded—both because of my constant updating of the progress of the event, and because other people started tweeting about how excited they were to be part of it. Over a period of three months, using Twitter almost exclusively for keeping people up-to-date on the event and building excitement, we went from zero to 700 sign-ups, mostly technologists and social media professionals, and from zero dollars to support the event to collecting over $25,000 from 106 sponsors,[2] mainly from Silicon Valley start-ups and venture capitalists. We were then able to hold the event free of charge for the participants.

This kind of influence through online connections is powerful, and I'm small potatoes compared with the likes of Michael Arrington, Guy Kawasaki, Veronica Belmont, Rick Sanchez (CNN), and other members of the digerati—the elite of the computer industry and online communities—who have many times the Twitter followers I have.

Twitter wasn't intended to create a bullhorn effect for its members. In fact, Twitter wasn't intended for anything but to be a really lightweight, portable status indicator (much like those people were already using in communities like LiveJournal, a blogging community), but it has become one of the core social networks of Web 2.0. Later on, I will tell more of the story behind Twitter and unveil its awesome growth, but for now what is important about Twitter is that it is a great example of a simple but powerful online community where *thousands of buying decisions are made every single day.* The point is that 140-character plain-text messages can be *so much* more powerful than million-dollar ads.

And don't fool yourself into thinking that only a certain segment of the population is plugged into these communities. It isn't just me or the digerati or the next generation (i.e., "the kids"). It's everybody.

THE GROWING UBIQUITY OF ONLINE COMMUNITIES

From a New York Craigslist.com personals ad on Sunday, January 25, 2004:

WANTED:
PERSONAL SOCIAL NETWORK COORDINATOR

Permanent full-time position for a personal social coordinator for a New York–based web designer.

Your primary responsibility will be managing my accounts with various online social networking sites including, but not limited to, Friendster, LinkedIn, Tribe, Orkut, Ryze, Spoke, ZeroDegrees, Ecademy, RealContacts, Ringo, MySpace, Yafro, EveryonesConnected, Friendzy, FriendSurfer, Tickle, Evite, Plaxo, Squiby, and WhizSpark.

Specific duties include:

- approving or rejecting invitations of friendship

- managing a database of usernames and passwords for each of the social networking sites

- sending out friendship invitations
- keeping my social network synchronized; that is, invite friends from one social networking site to be friends in all of the other social networking sites
- handling requests by friends to be introduced to another friend that they might not know
- keeping track of my current likes and dislikes and updating my personal information within each service accordingly
- writing testimonials for friends
- various "damage control" functions when rebuffed "non-friends" become upset due to non-acceptance of their offers of friendship
- continually browsing my friends' 1st and 2nd degrees for potential new friends and business contacts
- participating on any of the sites' message boards on my behalf

Future duties may include discouraging companies and individuals from starting new social networking sites so that additional staff won't be necessary in the future. Past employment as a bouncer, "heavy," or hired goon may be helpful in this regard.

Benefits include addition as my friend in all of the social networking sites I belong to.

This hilarious personal ad was placed over a year and a half before the term "Web 2.0" was used and before social networks were so common. Social networks are the framework in which communities operate; that is, the technology or the platform. Communities are the results of the interactions between individuals who are using the social networks. The person who wrote the post was obviously making more of a statement about the number of social networks to manage than seriously offering a job and was already feeling the effects of being so involved in online communities. The most striking part of this ad, for me, is that it was placed in 2004, five years ago. It was pre-Facebook, pre-Twitter, pre-Last.fm, and all of the other social networks that have become so ubiquitous.

In 2008, Cone LLC, a strategy and research firm with over twenty-five years of marketing research experience, conducted a survey of more than 1,100 men and women and found that over 60 percent of them interacted with brands they buy online and one-quarter of them interact more than once per week. They also found that 93 percent of the respondents *expect* the companies they buy from to have some sort of presence in social networks, and 85 percent believe they should interact on a regular basis with their customers through these social networks. The strongest interaction desired is the use of social networks to provide customer support and involving customers in developing or adapting products (43 percent). The least desirable interaction is to use these social networks to market to them (25 percent). Fifty-six percent of respondents reported a stronger connection and loyalty to a brand that they can interact with through online communities.[3]

So, how have all of these online communities changed the way we relate? Who are the people using them and how are they using them? Different generations are using the technology differently, but with similar impact.

The older generation is adopting online media like social networks at a surprisingly fast rate. In my family alone, I was surprised when my fifty-eight-year-old father created a profile and a private blog on Facebook. My mother, also in her late fifties, follows me religiously on Twitter. She also joined Facebook for the instant benefit of keeping in touch with her children, nieces, and nephews. My family members are early adopters, but Click-Z Online Research reports that the fifty-plus generation is a fast-growing adoption segment online, with 50 percent of them making purchases online.[4]

It's not just buying things, though, and my research revealed much more activity in the fifty-plus age bracket than conventional wisdom assumes. Take Les Loken, a ninety-four-year-old World War II veteran who passed away on Valentine's Day of 2007 and was mourned by tens of thousands of viewers of his World War II video stories on YouTube. Although Les was assisted in posting to YouTube by his daughter, Ginger, he inspired many others to follow in his footsteps. Peter—last name unknown—who is seventy-nine and goes by the screen name Geriatric1927, has been a member of YouTube since August 2006, and his videos have had many millions of views.

Peter's first video, entitled "First Try," has been viewed over 2.5 million times. In it, he reveals his reason for being on YouTube:

> I got addicted to YouTube, it's a fascinating place to go and see all of the videos you young people have produced, so I thought I'd have a go at doing one myself. But as you can see, if this ever does get uploaded to YouTube, I need a lot of help.
>
> Oh yes, and incidentally, the picture—I really am as old as I look and therefore, I think I'm in a unique position. What I hope I'll even be able to do is bitch and grumble

about life in general from the perspective of an old person who has been there and done that, and hopefully you will respond in some way by your comments and then I might be able to do other videos to follow up your comments. I do hope so.

Peter recognizes the advantages to being on YouTube. He understands the medium is powerful, but even in his first video, he speaks to the community, not the technology.

In the next age bracket of thirty- to fifty-year-olds, where I fall, online activity is growing steadily as well. The range of usage in this group is broad. Friends of mine who resisted online communities for years have now succumbed to the lure of more professionally focused websites like LinkedIn, and, more recently, have bravely ventured into Facebook. Each step they take reveals another layer of potential whuffie, so they dig deeper. Before she used Facebook, my best friend, who just celebrated her fortieth birthday, didn't think much of online communities. However, by joining she started to reacquaint herself with many of her old friends from college and even grade school. She met new people and joined some groups based on common interests. Now I get invitations from her to communities I've never heard of.

My involvement in these communities has increased over time as I've discovered the clear business benefits to participation. The more publicly I publish what I am doing online, the more people become interested in what I'm doing and support me through feedback and referrals. Almost all of the clients of Citizen Agency came from discovering our work online—not through our website, but because I blog openly about the work we do and the philosophy we engender. Even personal and social networks increase the reach of our business since we have discovered that the world of online communities does not separate personal from business relationships. Career is a key driving force for the people in the thirty- to fifty-year-old age bracket. Online social networking has become a strong way to connect with other business professionals we may not have had access to before online communities were so widely adopted.

In the younger generation, the under-thirty set, the tendency is toward even greater openness. In February of 2007, *New York* magazine published a feature article, titled "Say Everything," that describes the massive shift in philosophy by the generation called digital natives, or the millennials, whose main characteristics included:

- Thinking of themselves as having an audience

- Archiving the moments of adolescence openly

- Having a thicker skin than previous generations

In regard to thinking of themselves as having an audience, they aren't wrong. It's been said about blogging that Andy Warhol's saying that everyone will be famous for fifteen minutes has been changed so that everyone will be famous for fifteen people. When anyone publishes a photo, a video, an article, or a tweet online, it is available to be found by others and responded to. A friend once recounted to me how she became hooked on blogging. At first she wrote a few personal articles, thinking of her blog as an open diary that would be read by close friends and family in lieu of a yearly newsletter; however, after about a month of posting, she started to get comments from people she didn't know, thanking her for her funny stories and sharing their own. After about ten strangers started to regularly comment, her writing changed to "entertain" her unexpected readers. Six months later, she built an audience of over 200 regular readers who she worked hard to keep engaged. No longer was she writing for herself and family members, she was writing for an audience that she hoped to steadily grow.

I once heard David Weinberger, Harvard fellow and author of *Small Pieces Loosely Joined* and *The Cluetrain Manifesto*—two canonical books about the growth of digital communication— tell an audience, "We are recording our histories, one blog post at a time." This is a concept that is natural to digital natives, who have been online, recording their histories, for the past fifteen years—some of them since before they could spell. My fifteen-year-old son has been online since he turned seven years old, meeting other kids his age while trading virtual creatures on a website called Neopets. I sat down with him for half an hour to show him the ropes before he could take over. In two days, he was more advanced than I was. He has long forgotten the login to Neopets, but I ran across his account in an old e-mail of mine the other day, logged in, and found an impressive amount of activity, showing his ability to collaborate and share at a young age. My son and his peers will leave a digital trail of their adolescent lives as they grow up. Are they concerned about looking back and being embarrassed? According to the author of a recent *New York* magazine article about online privacy, the digital natives aren't too concerned about being embarrassed by this naked history:

> When I ask [Kitty Ostapowicz] how she thinks she'll feel at 35, when her postings are a Google search away, she's okay with that. "I'll be proud!" she says. "It's a documentation of my youth, in a way. Even if it's just me, going back and Googling myself in 25 or 30 years. It's my self—what I used to be, what I used to do."[5]

As for having "thicker skin"—in other words, the ability to shrug off negative comments and bullying—most digital natives have learned to take the criticism in stride. The people interviewed in the article had been raised with the realization that they can't control what other people post on the Internet, so the answer is to rise above it. In one case, a woman found herself all over the Internet in a provocative video she made for her ex-boyfriend's eyes only. At first, she tried to get it taken down, but realized quickly that as soon as she took it down in one place, it would pop up in three more. Her answer was to drown out the appearance of her name as an erotic star by posting her own videos and blog entries that portrayed her as smart and together. Soon after she started posting, another erotic video posted by an ex-boyfriend became more popular and the spread of hers died down. Her mantra was to choose to not be upset because she knew it was unproductive. Digital natives know that what is news today will be forgotten by tomorrow.

Who does that leave out of online communities? Not many. Online communities are crossing the chasm between the early adopters just described and the next, larger group of people on the path toward widespread adoption, the early majority. Your job: to reach them all.

A WORD OF CAUTION

You may be at a company that's gotten smart to the power of online communities to reach more people, build your customer base, and increase your revenue. You and others you work with have started joining these social networks. But a word of caution. Make sure you join these communities and networks as people, not as a business solely trying to build sales. You could find yourself with a problem like Wal-Mart back in 2007.

During the 2007 back-to-school season, Wal-Mart started using Facebook groups as a way to reach the college audience. Wal-Mart, however, was greeted with more "members" who wanted to discuss the company's treatment of sweatshop workers than those interested in learning how to decorate their dorm rooms (the intended purpose of the group).[6] The size of the Facebook group, though, was disappointingly low, yielding around 2,000 fans, far fewer members than many of other groups, such as Victoria's Secret PINK line, whose back-to-school campaign brought in over 550,000 group members. Even those created for silly fun on Facebook garnered a bigger audience; the "If 100,000 people join I'll legally change my name to McLovin" group—a fan-driven group for the movie *SuperBad*—gained 119,420 people.

PayPerPost is a business with clients who want to tap into social networks and the power of blogging. Its creators have tried, unsuccessfully so far, to build word of mouth for their clients by paying bloggers. PayPerPost's assumption has been that whuffie can easily be converted into monetary currency. However, instead of being a popular way to make money for bloggers, PayPerPost has been negatively received in the blogosphere. Bloggers who use it are publicly flogged as sellouts and accused of being no better than spammers. BuzzMachine, a popular blog by Jeff Jarvis, a journalist and associate professor of interactive journalism at City University New York (CUNY), reported a blogger who posted a recording of her kids smashing a camera that was not an HP for PayPerPost, calling it "appalling." His problem wasn't that the blogger in question was paid for the post, it was that the relationship was unclear, and that trust between the blogger and her audience had been called into question. As Jarvis wrote about his own advertising, "It's about someone buying space on my page, not about buying my endorsement. . . . Simply put, the rule is that no one can buy my voice and with it my credibility."[7]

First and foremost, the reason people are on these networks is to connect and build relationships. Relationships and connections over time lead to trust. And trust is *the basis* of whuffie—aka credibility.

When a company tries to pay for whuffie, it extinguishes it. Simple as that. Without whuffie you lose your connections, and any recommendations you make are questioned as spam and met with negative reactions (and a further loss of whuffie).

In June of 2007, Valleywag, a group blog dedicated to

reporting on rumors and tech gossip from Silicon Valley, discovered that several well-respected bloggers, including Om Malik of popular technology coverage blog GigaOm, had taken money from Federated Media, an advertising network, to embed a Microsoft slogan into their posts—a covert planting of an idea. Readers of GigaOm as well as the other popular technology blogs, such as TechCrunch and ReadWriteWeb, were enraged and demanded an explanation. Om Malik responded instantly with his apology, "So without making any excuses, to my readers, if participation in Microsoft's advertising campaign has made you doubt my integrity even for a second, then I apologize."[8] The reaction led to Federated Media instantly pulling the entire campaign. The same type of covert planting of messages has not been repeated with these influencers. Their whuffie loss was temporary, and they were able to build up trust with their readers again, but the message was clear: If you are paid to post something, then it is not to be trusted.

So if you want to be an influencer, someone who is whuffie rich, the first order of business is to make connections and establish credibility. Then you need to maintain and build those connections and continue to build whuffie. And, finally, do not do anything that will destroy your whuffie account. It's really dead simple, if you ask me. It is the most natural thing in the world. It just requires you to build, keep, and maintain *authentic* relationships.

Customers and potential customers will tune you out if you are not authentic. They would much rather listen to recommendations from their friends, who they trust have their best interests at heart. Those who think they are clever, and try to pose as friends, will be greeted with outright rejection. Really, the only way to avoid that reaction is to make genuine connections and establish trust.

This leads me right into the heart of how this is done. Instead of thinking about it in terms of being a business wanting to tap into communities, I prefer to put it in the following terms: You are embarking on the process of shifting from being a market capitalist into a social capitalist. That is, one who is more concerned about raising social capital than market capital (although the latter will come as a result of the former).

FIVE STEPS TO BECOMING WHUFFIE RICH

When I first moved to San Francisco several years ago, I was whuffie poor. I had a teensy social network. I had accomplished quite a bit in my marketing career, winning some national and international awards for campaigns I led, but all of this had been a couple of years previous and most of it happened in western Canada. I had been living in Toronto for three years and had a few newspaper articles and a small blog following to show for it. In San Francisco, people cared less about my Canadian accomplishments, so it felt as if I was starting from scratch.

What I did have was the ear of a few really great people in the Bay Area and a job at a really interesting start-up, Riya .com, the digital photo-searching application. I knew that my handful of connections could give me a leg up to start building that valuable whuffie I needed in order to do a really great marketing job for my new employer. In the first couple of months, I spent every second of every day searching out good opportunities to meet people and build trust. I must have gone to an event every night and sometimes multiple events in one night. Although I was burning the candle at both ends (getting into the office early in order to be part of the team product meetings, blog, participate in social networks, and work on incorporating alpha tester feedback into the product), it was necessary that I get out and meet everyone I could face-to-face. There is nothing as bonding as face-to-face meetings, as I discuss in later chapters.

In less than six months, I was able to grow my personal whuffie enough, as well as that of Riya.com, through employing my then-experimental ideas of community marketing. I set up a support wiki, where early testers of Riya.com, found through following the blog posts that expressed interest in Riya, could give their feedback on how well the facial recognition was working on their own photos. I openly posted photos and news as we struggled as well as achieved milestones and victories as a start-up along the way. I helped the CEO, Munjal Shah, set up his own blog and coached him to become more open about his own experience as a CEO of a start-up in Silicon Valley. I made sure that everyone in the company, including the software engineers, had a direct line of feedback from the early testers so that they could directly implement solutions to issues that arose even before the public launch. I worked closely with the user experience and design members of the Riya team to show them the best practices emerging in photo-sharing and -searching websites. I joined work groups of tech-nologists looking to bridge the gaps between the various social networks to make certain that Riya.com employed the latest web standards, also forging connections along the way with the other influencers in the start-up market. I read blogs reli-giously, making contact with everyone who was curious about Riya, whether they had five followers or five thousand follow-ers, to make certain they had all of their questions answered. I met with photographers and others with large photo collec-tions, finding out what their core needs were and asking them what their ideas were on the solutions to organizing their large photo sets. I then brought this information back to the others at Riya.com, blogged about it openly, and helped to make Riya a better site. I also continued to attend many conferences, meetups, and discussions about technology and digital pho-tography, meeting as many people as I could.

The results of this labor paid off handsomely. As mentioned earlier, in the first twenty-four hours of Riya's product launch, there were over 1 million photos uploaded and over 20,000 people joined up. And this was a very "beta" product—beta in the sense that facial recognition in images is still about ten years from becoming powerful enough to search and identify photos correctly. Photos of people are taken from various angles and in an array of different lighting situations. The arti-ficial intelligence of searching in images is currently only good enough to identify faces in controlled situations. Still, I had built a great deal of whuffie for Riya.com so that the people who were signing up were enthusiastic about being part of the advancement of this technology.

The process I used to grow the interest and, ultimately, the user base of Riya.com was complex and individual to Riya. I didn't really have a formula and still don't. But my experience led me to develop five general principles that I used for Riya.com as well as every subsequent community marketing project I've worked on.

1. Turn the bullhorn around: Stop talking and start listening.

2. Become part of the community you serve and figure out who it is you are serving. It isn't everyone. Then get out of your office and into the community.

3. Be notable and create amazing experiences for your customers. It isn't enough to design something that works. You need to design remarkable products that people love.

4. Embrace the chaos. Don't overplan. Learn to be more agile and recognize everyday magic.

5. Find your higher purpose. Social capital only gains in value as you give it away. Figure out how you are going to give back to the community and do it . . . often.

The following chapters will explain each principle and show how you can execute each one to create your own whuffie and build your business by participating in online communities. Throughout I'll use examples of companies that have put these principles to work, so that you can see real-world implementations of whuffie in action.

However, before I go into those lessons for companies, the

most powerful example of all is the whuffie-building campaign for the forty-forth president of the United States of America.

WHUFFIE IN POLITICS

November 4, 2008, will go down as a historically significant day. On that date, a majority of Americans elected Barack Obama as the forty-forth president of the United States. Obama's campaign and his victory were significant not only because he is the first African American to be elected to the presidency, but because of the way he ran his campaign. Or rather the way his *supporters* ran his campaign.

While politicians running for office, such as Howard Dean in 2004, have used online community tools to mobilize voters, this campaign was different. One of the main differences is the sheer number of people who are more comfortable with the online medium. Another is how close Barack Obama's message matched the medium: *change*. That one word, coupled with a campaign that mobilized a large number of young, first-time voters, said it all: The world has changed and the Obama machine was at the bleeding edge of it.

In the days after the election came the dozens of newspaper and magazine articles proclaiming, "It's the network, stupid!"[9] and "A Victory for Social Media, Too."[10] Even those who pushed back and proclaimed that it was Obama himself that rallied the support of so many fervent volunteers had to admit that the use of the social media tools by the campaign was impressive.[11] The combination of a strong message that millions of voting Americans were open to plus the appearance of that message on every channel of communication available—from YouTube and Facebook to XBox games to our text message in-boxes to televisions and T-shirts—drove that message home. When communications studies pioneer Marshall McLuhan wrote, "The medium is the message," in 1964, he probably had no idea how perfectly a future president would demonstrate his theory. The medium was the Internet and the message was change. If any medium communicates change, it is the Internet, not to mention the placement of Obama advertising in multiplayer game platforms on the Xbox. Obama's campaign team was not afraid to try unconventional approaches.

The level of tech savvy exhibited by the Obama campaign was significant. They seemed to cover every possible tool online with a clear understanding of how to get the most out of it. They posted personal and intimate photos along the campaign trail on Flickr. They ran campaigns and events through the Facebook group. They tweeted out both personal anecdotes and serious political messages through Twitter. YouTube was regularly updated with ads and addresses from Barack Obama. They used Ustream.tv to stream live events, rallies, and speeches so people could tune into Barack TV twenty-four hours a day, seven days a week. They created all sorts of ways that people could really feel involved at the My.barackobama.com website (lovingly referred to as MyBO). This is just the tip of it. By giving their supporters tools—like lists of people to call in their spare time; access to promotional materials to wear, display, give away, and wave; various web and mobile applications to show and spread their support; oodles of content with easy ways to share it with others; and loads of transparent information so that his supporters were armed with answers when challenged—they were able to grow a venerable force of campaigners grassroots style. Because the Obama campaign trusted their supporters with their message, it spread like wildfire. They also broke records in raising money, bringing in over $640 million, mostly from individual donors who donated, on average, under $100 each.

So, yes, the Obama campaign wielded those online tools with precision; however, as much as they were savvy about the tools, they were also savvy about the very most important part of engaging with online communities. They raised whuffie.

An article published on the *Harvard Business Review*'s website the day after the election by Umair Haque listed seven lessons that innovators could learn from the success of the Obama campaign.[12] As I read those lessons, I knew I had to recount the case study because the seven lessons Haque outlined perfectly aligned with the core principles of this book:

1. Have self-organized design

2. Seek elasticity of resilience

3. Minimize strategy

4. Maximize purpose

5. Broaden unity

6. Thicken power

7. Remember that there is nothing more asymmetrical than an ideal

The first of the principles of raising your whuffie factor is to turn the bullhorn around. By broadening unity and thickening power, the Obama campaign opened itself up for great feedback and broad interpretation. One of the core messages of the campaign and a big exclamation mark of Barack Obama's acceptance speech was that the future wasn't about him, it was about the citizens pitching in to make change happen. Within days of his acceptance, the Barack Obama/Joe Biden administration launched Change.gov. Change.gov has several ways for citizens to give feedback, tell stories, and even apply for a position in the new government. The organizational chart shows the citizens of the United States as being higher in rank than the president himself. On November 14, 2008, President-Elect Barack Obama launched the first of his weekly presidential addresses . . . from YouTube.[13] These are clear indications that the change that was part of the campaign message is serious and that the new administration is serious about listening and engaging citizens and were not merely using the online tools for promotional purposes.

The second principle of raising whuffie is to become part of the community you serve. Having a self-organized design was key to engaging and becoming part of the community the campaign was serving. Obama's campaign didn't dumb down a message to be "one with the people," but it did get involved in every online community possible to learn from and engage with its supporters. There were actually times during the campaign that I could not decipher what was coming directly from the Obama campaign headquarters and what was being created by his supporters. One example was Obamatravel.org, a website that raised funds to fly volunteers to swing states to help campaign. The organization states on its frequently asked questions page that it was an independent effort. However, the Obama campaign did not step in to change or control the message-only support of the mission.

The third principle of whuffie is to create amazing experiences, which closely aligns to remembering that there is nothing more asymmetrical than an ideal. Change is a highly powerful ideal and Obama himself delivered that message in an amazing way. I watched many people become enraptured with hope for a brighter future in the United States. The Obama campaign's message of change brought hope and excitement that millions were compelled to get behind.

Embrace the chaos is the fourth principle of building whuffie and captures two of Haque's lessons: seek elasticity of resilience and minimize strategy. I truly believe that the Obama campaign's ability to ignore the constant strategizing and strong-arming deployed by the Republicans and stay resilient in the face of the attacks was incredibly powerful. It showed an ability to roll with the punches. Postcampaign editorials talked about the importance of the "No Drama Obama" attitude of the campaign.[14] They continued with a focus on their purpose and didn't get derailed by attempts to throw them off course while at the same time being ready for opportunities like the stock market meltdown that played so well into the campaign's core message of the need for change and the focus on economy.

Finally, both the lesson of maximizing purpose as well as the idealism is exactly what I will describe in chapter 9 when I talk about how to find your higher purpose. The Obama campaign was strong on purpose and did not falter from not only delivering, but living that message. Change, nonpartisan unity, and providing hope to the middle class were just some of the messages that were delivered and lived during the campaign. Even when Joe the Plumber was making headlines for challenging Barack Obama's commitment to the middle class, the campaign did not falter. In unity, Barack Obama showed in his acceptance speech that he would remain committed to crossing party lines to solve the issues the country faced when he said, "We have never been a collection of red states and blue states: We are, and always will be, the United States of America." And, as evidenced by the way Obama ran his campaign as well as the launch of Change.gov, change is not merely a campaign slogan, but a true underlying purpose to this new administration.

Barack Obama's campaign gained election-winning whuffie because it listened to voters, got involved in grassroots community, offered a message that was compelling and engaging, embraced the chaos, and kept its focus on their higher purpose. Now that this administration has settled into Washington, I expect that the bar will be raised even higher for not only political, but all other campaigns in the future.

The world will be focused on raising whuffie to similar ends. Now you can find out how to do it yourself.

3

TURN THE BULLHORN AROUND AND CREATE CONTINUOUS CONVERSATIONS WITH CUSTOMERS

Have you ever had one of those conversations at a party where you feel like the person you are talking with isn't listening to a word you are saying, but instead is just waiting to jump in and tell you how great he is? How did it make you feel? Did you leave that conversation wanting to get to know more about him? Probably not.

Contrast that with the other person you met at the same party who asked you questions about yourself and then genuinely listened to your answers. Of course, you got into the conversation more and more, asking your own questions and having a great connection. She made you feel listened to and important. You walked away from the conversation feeling good. She is the one you follow up with the next day to go for coffee with.

You get the picture. This is also the difference between the old bullhorn style of marketer—who doesn't care about what you have to say, what you want, or why you are even there—and the community marketer. By turning the bullhorn around, the community marketer becomes interested in knowing about you, in fulfilling your needs, and incorporating whatever input you have into improving his or her product or service.

Turning the bullhorn around is about changing your interaction with customers from trying to get them to listen and pay attention to *you,* to listening and paying attention to *them.* Companies spend billions of dollars each year on sending out messages through advertising and promotion to the marketplace, attempting to get people to notice them and buy more of what they are selling. By only talking and not listening, though, these companies miss out on the essential benefits of listening: customer-driven innovation, relationship building, proactive problem solving, and making customers feel good about themselves so that they tell others how good you made them feel. And all of these benefits equal more whuffie.

Turning the bullhorn around and listening builds whuffie and is the key to Gary Vaynerchuk's success with the Wine Library, discussed next. As CEO of this large distributor of wine, he has set the bar high in the way he listens to customers and builds whuffie for his company through his video podcast, Wine Library TV.

GARYVEE IS WHUFFIE RICH

As Gary waits to be called on the set of the Conan O'Brien show, he types a message into his phone that reads: *conan is tallllll* 04:39 PM August 01, 2007.

The message was sent out to more than 1,000 people who follow him as garyvee on Twitter, a group SMS or text-message service where users answer the key question, "What are you doing right now?" What Gary is doing right at this moment happens to be something that is very exciting to his followers, who have been supporting his remarkable career growth. And remarkable it is.

In less than a decade, Gary helped turn his family's small New Jersey wine store with 10 employees into a global business with 100 employees and annual sales in multiples of 10 million dollars. Gary did it with his whuffie, which he grew by "turning the bullhorn around." Instead of broadcasting his sales message as loudly and widely as possible through multiple media channels—the traditional marketing approach—he used emerging social media to listen to his customers and create a continuous conversation with them.

Gary started working at the family's Wine Library store at the age of fifteen. "For two bucks an hour I made ice and cleaned shelves and I was miserable," he says. "I hated it and it was just very difficult. But finally, about a year in I started getting a little more comfortable, and I started realizing people got into wine to collect it. And once I realized collecting wine was like collecting baseball cards, it became 'Is there a huge difference between Kirby Puckett and Canlis Cabernet?' I really started to get into it."

Gary's passion for wine started before he was legally able to drink it, and his knack for creating passionate wine lovers out of everyday people soon became clear. He had this uncanny way of making wine accessible without dumbing it down for his customers. The most novice wine shoppers could leave his store feeling like experts, armed with colorful and interesting descriptions of the wine they purchased. Gary would give his customers both an excellent product and the ability to look good to their dinner guests (or hosts), so customers began returning to the store again and again.

In 1997, Gary decided that his family's brick-and-mortar company needed to supplement its business with an online component and launched Winelibrary.com. The online business steadily grew for the next eight years. Gary relied on a great web team to help him merchandise and sell wine, but in November of 2005 and on his thirtieth birthday, he realized the online store was missing the personalized and empowering experience his in-store customers received.

Winelibrary.com, until this point, was very much driven by price cutting, advertising, search engine optimization, coupons, and other aggressive promotions—all very traditional marketing tactics. Sales were okay but not building. Since his engagement with online customers was low, Gary didn't have a sense of how to improve results. No matter how much marketing and search engine optimization he threw at the website, there was no growth. Gary knew he needed to be building better relationships with his online customers, but he didn't know how.

Eric Kastner, the lead developer on Winelibrary.com, had been showing Gary social networking sites like Flickr, a popular photo-sharing site; MySpace, a social network built around music; and YouTube, a video-sharing site. That's when he started to formulate an idea for how he could create an empowering and engaging customer experience online. On February 21, 2006, Gary purchased a new domain and a video camera and taped the first episode of Wine Library TV—a review of three wines, none of which Gary had tasted before. It was the start of something big.

The effects of Gary's labor weren't obvious at first except for his change in lifestyle and how he worked. His job description changed drastically from being CEO of Wine Library to spending much of his days absorbed in and learning about the various tools of the new social media. As he surfed, learned, and participated, Gary realized that this was something that was going to be big for him—not just his business, but something that would help him be in better touch with his customers in general. The TV show was labor intensive. It took time to find new wines to review, shoot the episode, then edit and post it. But Gary is a natural ad-libber, so there was no scripting or rehearsing needed. It made his show much easier to produce and more natural in the end.

It didn't take long to start to see the results of this work. About two months after the first episode, Gary was getting about ten or eleven comments on each episode. He also started to get e-mails from people who would tell him that they switched from his competitor because the shows were so compelling. And of course he'd write back, building a relationship with them. A year after Gary began Wine Library TV, he had over 15,000 daily downloads and nearly 100 comments on every show. He was starting to understand his social capital. He wanted more. That's when I met him.

After a presentation on community marketing at a conference in London, England, Gary approached me to tell his story and to invite me along to a wine-tasting event some of his fans were throwing in his honor later that evening. Although I hadn't seen his show, I was impressed by the passion in his story and agreed to go along. The wine tasting was being thrown by the London group of "Vayniaks"—the name given to Gary's superfans worldwide. There were probably forty waiting eagerly for his arrival. I watched them hang on his every word as he tasted and told interesting stories about each wine. One of the listeners was wearing a wristband that can be bought on Gary's website. Clearly this went beyond an online wine store.

"Really, to be honest with you," Gary told me, "the commerce part of Wine Library TV was so irrelevant to me. All I wanted to do is build a community, and I felt the other stuff would work itself out. I just wanted to build a community of people who thought differently about wine and change the wine world."

And that is what I recognized the first time I saw Gary in action. He was changing people's relationship with wine. Everyday people. He had successfully replicated the experience he delivered in person into an equally empowering and engaging online experience. He was democratizing the wine appreciation process. This wasn't about Gary at all, but about his customers and their experience. He was merely their sidekick.

Probably the most memorable of Gary's video podcasts is

the one in which he takes the taste wheel—the range of flavors said to be found in wine—and goes through it by tasting each flavor and describing it. For anyone who knows the taste wheel, it includes tobacco and dirt, so this turned out to be an entertaining episode. For anyone who has ever had any questions as to how wine can have a tobacco nose or a peaty aftertaste, this episode is incredibly educational. It was also the episode that he re-performed on the Conan O'Brien show and later on the Ellen Degeneres show.

Although he has an informal, modest, "aw shucks" demeanor, Gary has done very well for himself. He is 100 percent genuine in his approach to community—he isn't there to exploit or just visit, he is committed and passionate about his customers and friends.

Gary is the perfect example of someone who has effectively turned the bullhorn around. He has taken a business that was largely promoted through traditional and less personal means like advertising and search engine optimization and made it highly personal with loads of opportunity for feedback and engagement with his customers. His new way of conducting business also produces great results for his bottom line and for his overall brand loyalty.

His wine business is now growing at a rate of 35 percent per year, he has published a bestselling wine book, he is flown all over the world to make appearances at conferences to help teach others in the wine world how to use social media, and he continues to make appearances on network television. He is also changing the world of wine significantly. By introducing non–wine drinkers to a more accessible version of wine reviews, he has gotten the attention of many of the larger vine-yards around the world. He is spending a great deal of time these days teaching them *the power of whuffie* and helping them connect and build relationships with a wider audience. Slowly but surely, vineyards that would only call Robert Parker, the *Wine Advocate* critic, or place an ad in a major publication when they released a new vintage, are now contacting bloggers. Gary believes that this democratization of the wine industry can only be good for everyone.

Let's take a look deeper into the process of turning the bull-horn around.

MARKETING IS DEAD, LONG LIVE MARKETING

On any given day, people in North America are exposed to an average of 1,500 to 2,500 marketing messages through e-mail, billboards, contextual ads, television, radio, and a myriad of other forms of advertising.[1] This adds up to a great deal of clut-ter. No wonder we've gotten so effective at tuning out the many things that aren't personal to us. If you let every message through, the sensory overload would be enough to drive you out of your mind.

But some messages *do* get through. The majority of these aren't marketing messages at all. They come from people we know. As I noted earlier, the number one influence on most buying decisions is word of mouth.[2] But, as with many things that require a change in behavior, there's a gap between "knowing" something and acting on it.

When researching this book I asked the question, "If the

efficacy of advertising and other forms of mass marketing are on a continuous decline, why do people continue to use them?" The answer, I found out, is simply that this "bullhorn" mode of communicating is still perceived as the most effective way to reach a large mass of people.

The bullhorn is my metaphor for mass marketing or communication that moves in a one-way direction. It includes:

- Advertising: print, radio, television, outdoor, online, banner, etc.

- E-mail marketing: newsletters, e-mail updates, e-mail coupons and offers, etc.

- Search engine optimization: tactics used to drive search engine traffic to a website

- Public relations (although there are some new techniques that I'll cover later on): press releases, cold calling, schmoozing the press, etc.

These bullhorn marketing tactics are not very interactive. They don't allow for much customer interaction and feedback. It is also very difficult to discern the true effectiveness of their messaging. Neither click-throughs on banner ads nor the volume of traffic passing a billboard helps you understand the reaction of the customer. I was trained to create strategic plans that included bullhorn marketing tactics, but as I became more and more involved in online communities, I started to realize the power of two-way conversations. That is when I discovered *The Cluetrain Manifesto*.

One of the first writings about the power of becoming part of conversations online, *The Cluetrain Manifesto* was written by Doc Searls, Christopher Locke, David Weinberger, and Rick Levine in 1998. Prior to widespread use of the Internet, carefully crafting marketing messages and delivering them through mass media was a strong influencer on how people made their buying decisions. Brand building, the process of creating an image around your product or service, was very important to the success of your company.

But as *Cluetrain* pointed out, the Internet changed things. Its manifesto listed "new truths"—ironically called the 95 Theses—outlining the fundamental changes brought about by the Web. The first and most-often cited is: *Markets are conversations*.

In other words, conversations exist in the marketplace whether you like it or not. People are talking more and more and ignoring crafted messages. The Internet is a medium that multiplied word of mouth to create hundreds of thousands (and now millions) of smaller bullhorns that belonged to customers, not the company.

IT GETS WORSE BEFORE IT GETS BETTER

When *Cluetrain* was published, the authors didn't even mention another phenomenon that was starting to brew and would lead to a further decline of the bullhorn style and an amplification of word of mouth: blogging.

The era in which *Cluetrain* was written is referred to today as Web 1.0 (as compared with the current Internet era, commonly referred to as Web 2.0). In the era of Web 1.0, most websites, save for the forums and discussion boards, were launched and written by people with higher-level technical skills. To have a website you had to know HTML and understand protocols like FTP to post your opinions on the Web. If not, you needed the money to hire someone with the skills to create it. This limited the participation of nontechnical people in conversations.

Then came Web 2.0. The launch of the publishing tools that led to the explosion of blogs happened between 1998 and 1999 with applications like Open Diary, LiveJournal, and Blogger. These tools made it much simpler for nontechnical users to publish content, offering both a simple content management interface and a hosting environment. And, even better, they were free, making them technically and financially accessible. The barriers to entry were down. In April 2007, Technorati.com was tracking more than 70 million blogs worldwide, one-third of them written in English.[3] But the really important statistic hides behind that one. Publishers of blogs were a minority compared with those reading and commenting on their blogging sites. In 2004, 8 percent of Americans were blogging, compared with 27 percent of Americans who said they read blogs and 17 percent who said they regularly commented on posts.[4] The top blogs today each have over 1 million daily subscribers, but the majority of blogs, which make up the largest part of the readership online, have a smaller, niche audience of loyal readers. All of this adds up to a great deal of word-of-mouth transfer that didn't exist pre-Internet.

THE BULLHORN STILL WORKS . . . KINDA

Surely, you're saying to yourself, with all of the money that goes into the advertising industry and the size of the media outlets that it still commands, doesn't the bullhorn still have a great deal of clout? Doesn't a clever campaign launched far and wide and executed professionally still affect more people than a post on even the most popular blog?

The short answer is yes. But the long answer is more complicated.

In 2005, Om Malik, online journalist and blogger, reported that Vonage, the Voice-over Internet Protocol (VoIP) communication alternative to traditional telecommunications solutions, was spending over $21 million per month on Internet advertising alone and acquiring 60,000 new customers per month as a result of this campaign. Since Vonage was not tracking the customers gained through nonadvertising means, this number is an estimate. Malik estimated that the marketing price for each customer acquisition was about $363. Customers would have to stick around for at least two years in order for the company to earn back what it had spent on advertising, according to Malik's calculations.[5]

Vonage was bringing in a large number of new customers from its bullhorn efforts, but the company was also spending a great deal of money to do so. It wasn't reported whether Vonage was putting the same sort of effort into the retention of customers as it was to their acquisition. But two and a half years later, Om Malik reported that Vonage was struggling and its customer attrition rate was quite high,[6] not surprising to me after reading through a series of blog posts complaining of bad customer experiences with Vonage. This left the company especially vulnerable a couple of months later when Sprint filed a lawsuit against Vonage on VoIP technology patents that they held and won, making Vonage pay out $80 million in licensing and damages.[7] It's unclear what this means for the company's long-term survival, but it probably won't have the same kind of financial capital to throw into acquiring new customers in the future. As late as October 2008, Vonage was still treading water and looking for loans on the $253 million in debt it had accumulated.

The mistake that many companies make in today's marketplace is throwing all of their energy into mass customer acquisition. What they should be doing is putting more money into reducing attrition rates. If they allocate dollars and energy to better customer service, they create happy customers who will then talk about their happiness online, thereby paving the way to more solid customer acquisition.

The bullhorn alone will not enable you to meet long-term goals of customer retention.

If Vonage spent more time working on building up whuffie with its customers, the amount of financial capital it spent would have been lower, the attrition rate would have dropped, and profits would be much healthier. By not concentrating on building whuffie and listening to existing customers, Vonage missed essential feedback from its customers on how to improve its services. Of course, setbacks like the patent lawsuit from Sprint were unexpected and contributed a great deal to the problems, but the results wouldn't have been nearly as crippling with a stronger customer base and the resulting income to lean on as times got tougher.

"Customer service is the best form of marketing," says Thor Muller, the cofounder of Internet start-up Satisfaction,[8] a website where customers are empowered to post questions, ideas, issues, and general discussion to share with other customers as well as representatives of companies. "The more that people talk and share stories of their experiences with companies, the more companies are going to need to focus on making sure those stories are positive. The only way they can ensure they are positive is to deliver positive experiences."

This is not a novel idea, either. It's been proven that it costs less to retain a customer than to acquire a new one, and the step beyond that—turning those satisfied customers into supersatisfied customers who will spread the word to other potential customers—has been around as long as markets have.

What has changed is the media through which these messages travel. And, in my estimation, this provides an excellent opportunity to shift our strategy from a high-spend, low-loyalty bullhorn approach to a low-spend, high-loyalty approach by building whuffie—which is what Dell has been doing ever since it stared disaster in the face.

HOW DELL TURNED THE BULLHORN AROUND

Jeff Jarvis, a prominent blogger and Dell computer owner, wrote in a blog post on June 21, 2005:

I just got a new Dell laptop and paid a fortune for the four-year, in-home service. . . . The machine is a lemon and the service is a lie. . . . I'm having all kinds of trouble with the hardware: overheats, network doesn't work, maxes out on CPU usage. It's a lemon.

But what really irks me is that they say if they [send] someone to my home—[a service] I paid for—he wouldn't have the parts, so I might as well just send the machine in and lose it for 7–10 days—plus the time going through this crap. So I have this new machine and paid for them to FUCKING FIX IT IN MY HOUSE and they don't and I lose it for two weeks.

DELL SUCKS. DELL LIES. Put that in your Google and smoke it, Dell.[9]

To the people complaining, including Jarvis, the company seemed to be completely oblivious to the bad press it was receiving, which merely fanned the flames. Around 50 percent of the comments posted online about Dell were negative in nature, and websites like Ihatedell.com, which included hundreds of anecdotes from angry Dell and former Dell customers about the terrible customer service they received, were being passed around the Internet.

To make matters worse, the news media were having a field day with the complaints. *BusinessWeek* wrote on October 10, 2005:

Could such sentiment lead to trouble for the world's largest PC company? Over the past decade, Dell's dependable support, combined with competitive prices and build-to-order convenience, made it the default choice for millions of consumers. Its market share continues to rise overall, and it holds 28.8% of the U.S. consumer market, up from 28.2% a year ago, according to researcher IDC. However, a sagging reputation could slow sales, jeopardizing the company's plan to reach $80 billion in revenues by 2008. In the most recent quarter, Dell missed its sales target, one reason its stock has dropped 18%, to $34, since the start of the year.[10]

As *BusinessWeek* predicted, it wasn't long before Dell lost its prestigious position as the number one personal computer manufacturer. To turn that situation around, the founder, Michael Dell, who once again assumed the job of CEO, seized the opportunity to use the new social media to turn the bullhorn around. "He approached the digital media team with the idea that Dell needed to have more of a conversation with our customers," says Lionel Menchaca, chief blogger on Direct2Dell. "The blog was part of the strategy that we unveiled to Michael. He liked the idea and said 'instead of taking two and a half to three months [to develop the blog], let's do it in three weeks.'" Four weeks later the blog was launched.

The initial period was rough. The team at Dell not only opened up a conversation, but a can of worms as well. Customers were not happy and finally had a "direct to Dell" way of telling the company. Lionel and the rest of his team were prepared for this. They had been doing their homework and knew about the issues and were prepared to face the wrath.

"Because we had done our research, we knew the core issues that we needed to address and that we needed to address these issues transparently. If we mess up, we need to say that and then we need to show the community what we are doing to fix it," Menchaca recalled.

This humility paid off in spades and, after a period of time, they started winning back the trust of certain customers. In fact, they started to win back so much trust that customers were participating in the forums and the comments sections of the blogs in incredibly helpful ways, giving all sorts of valuable ideas for changing things up at Dell.

But it wasn't until the Consumer Electronics Show (CES) in Las Vegas in January of 2007 that the company realized it needed to open up the conversation to foster more of this idea generation. Communications Manager Caroline Dietz had helped to organize a blogger/forum member get-together with Michael Dell during CES. In a roundtable discussion, Dell was struck by the number of good ideas that came up and gave Caroline the job of finding a way to encourage and support the generation of new ideas as well as the implementation of them.

Caroline and her team found an interesting tool called CrispyIdeas, a personalizable web tool that allowed customers to submit ideas about new products and service improvements to the company. Other customers could then read these ideas and comment and vote according to what they liked and didn't like. CrispyIdeas seemed like a perfect tool for executing what Michael Dell asked them to accomplish. Dell agreed to use the customizable CrispyIdeas and told the team to implement it at breakneck speed. Dellideastorm.com was launched two weeks later. In the first week after launch it brought in 1,700 ideas, a staggering response for any company, but Dietz attributes the numbers to the community inreach that Lionel and his team had been doing for quite some time.

"We didn't do any initial promotions around Dell Idea Storm, it was spread entirely by word of mouth through the existing community that the Direct2Dell team had been fostering. We picked a handful of active participants in the community to beta test it before it went out to the public and seeded it through the forums and blogs, but otherwise, it was spread by word of mouth," Caroline recalls.

Most of the initial outpouring of ideas came from the open-source software community. Perhaps not surprisingly then, the top ideas on Idea Storm were the request for a Dell computer with Linux, not Microsoft Windows, preinstalled. Although Dell had offered a Linux-based computer to its business clients, a consumer-based Linux machine had not been available.

The Dell Idea Storm team took this request directly to its product development department. The people there went straight to the forums to get more information like what "flavor" of Linux people wanted preinstalled. Ubuntu was the number one choice. Within a couple of months, the Linux Dell was available for purchase. Although the company wouldn't release exact numbers, Caroline told me that the sales far exceeded their projections and Dell plans to continue the program.

The ideas didn't stop there. From product ideas to process ideas, Dell has implemented dozens of suggestions from its customer community, who, fueled by their ability to be heard by the corporate giant, return to offer more and more. Dell is even planning to officially invite top innovators on Dell Idea Storm to the Dell offices to work with its product teams and executive staff directly.

By taking the community feedback seriously, Dell has moved the needle from highly negative to highly positive feedback: from 50 percent negative feedback online to only 23 percent in a year and a half. The company intends to keep working hard to drop that number even more and regain the trust of its customers permanently. Although Dell has yet to regain lost ground—it lost the number one spot in the personal computer market to competitor Hewlett-Packard—it gives the company more impetus to continue growing its whuffie with customers. Positive word of mouth, unfortunately, travels slower than negative word of mouth and Dell understands that this will take time. Even so, the positive results of its gains in whuffie are starting to show in Dell's numbers. In 2007, Dell overtook Hewlett-Packard in customer satisfaction surveys[11] and is seeing a 21 percent gain in worldwide PC sales, outpacing its competition for multiple sales quarters.

"We've made a lot of progress, but we still have a long way to go," Lionel admits. "And one of the areas that we need to look at is how we do this globally. The reality is that even if we are talking about a largely U.S. issue, this affects our customers around the world and currently we are only offering Direct2Dell and Dell Idea Storm in English. What we're looking at now is how to take this feedback and globalize so we can respond to these issues all around the world."

The team also expressed a commitment to listening to and serving customers from all levels of accessibility and expertise through innovative and scalable solutions . . . often suggested through—what else?—Dell Idea Storm.

OPENING YOURSELF UP TO THE CONVERSATION

Both Dell and Gary Vaynerchuk have demonstrated the most basic principle of turning the bullhorn around: opening yourself up to the conversation. In Dell's case, the company opened up its research and development program, inviting its customers to submit ideas and give feedback on its current ideas so that Dell could really listen to the needs of its audience and respond quicker. In Gary's case, he opened up his wine cellar and offered accessible insight into wine selection and created a comment section for his customers to offer their own opinions and make their own requests. This helps Gary understand the preferences of his customers, which he integrates into future Wine Library TV episodes and into his online business and his book. By having that open conversation with his customers, he knows that they prefer reasonably priced yet complex wines and that they really want to learn more about wine beyond merlot, cabernet sauvignon, and chardonnay.

What both Dell and Gary figured out before opening themselves up is that the conventional business wisdom that companies need to be secretive in order to be successful is wrong. If Dell put the fear of corporate espionage before the excitement of customer-driven innovation, Dell Idea Storm wouldn't have happened. If Gary was concerned about the competitors of

Winelibrary.com gaining all of his knowledge and using it to compete with him, he wouldn't have started Wine Library TV. What both of these examples have in common is that Dell and Gary put openness and transparency before secretiveness. Because of this change in philosophy, they both gained a great deal of whuffie. They built trust with their customers, who were overjoyed to share their ideas in order to gain better service and products; they built relationships with their community members by opening themselves up to a deeper, two-way conversation; and they provided their customers with a positive story to spread via word of mouth. They also gathered the kind of market research from these interactions that would cost hundreds of thousands of dollars—the kind of personalized research that creates a deep and clear understanding of their customers. What they didn't experience was the loss of customers or stealing of ideas that is the impetus behind corporate secrecy.

This openness and transparency led to a great deal of whuffie for both Dell and Gary. However, while I celebrate the opening of the conversation, I've learned along the way that it isn't only the openness and transparency that matters. Openness and transparency is a great first step, often beyond what your competitors are doing, but it is equally important to take the results of that openness—the feedback and the market research—and integrate it into the product itself. This is more difficult than opening yourself in the first place because there will be a great number of conversations to respond to.

4

BUILDING WHUFFIE BY LISTENING TO AND INTEGRATING FEEDBACK

Opening yourself to continuous conversations with customers can lead to amazing results like Dell's Idea Storm or Gary Vaynerchuk's Wine Library TV. Gathering feedback effectively and then integrating it into making a better product is crucial to growing your whuffie. By showing customers you are listening to their concerns and improving the product based on their desires, you build trust and goodwill.

But there is a challenge in understanding what to do with those conversations when the feedback includes a variety of voices with a myriad of interests. One thread of a conversation may lead to the feedback that your product needs more features while another informs you that your product is already too complex. Listening to customer input is important, but what you do with that information is even more important. Keeping everyone happy at once may seem to be an impossible task.

The reality is that you might gain whuffie with one customer while losing it with another, so how do you maximize your whuffie with as many of your customers as possible by responding to feedback? Over the years I've developed eight guidelines for listening and responding to feedback from clients who open themselves up to these conversations. The guidelines will help you take the results from reversing the bullhorn and convert what you've learned into better experiences for your customers. **Responding effectively to feedback expands your whuffie because when you respond correctly, you demonstrate to your customers that you are truly listening and responding to what they are saying, building trust. That trust will lead to more feedback and conversation, which leads to a deeper relationship. The guidelines are as follows.**

1. Get advice and input from experts but design for the broader community.
2. Respond to all feedback, even when you respond by saying, "No, thanks." If the ideas presented are not right for your entire customer community, it is important to acknowledge these ideas and explain why you cannot use them.
3. Do not take negative feedback personally; remember that when people give feedback, they are doing so because they care and have taken the time to improve their experience.
4. Give credit to those whose ideas you implement; nothing says "we are open to conversation" more than acknowledg-

ing great ideas from your customer community openly. By crediting those who help your company improve, you encourage others to submit their ideas, too.

5. When you a implement new idea, make sure that you highlight it, asking for everyone's feedback on whether it has improved their experience.

6. Make small, continuous changes rather than waiting to implement everything at once; by constantly improving your product by implementing customer feedback, it shows that you are consistently listening and working toward creating a better experience.

7. Don't just wait for feedback to come to you, go out and find it; even if you aren't receiving lots of feedback through your website or e-mail, it doesn't mean that people aren't talking about ways to improve your product.

8. No matter how many people like you, you will always have someone who doesn't; don't let the high you get from receiving positive feedback come crashing down when someone criticizes you.

DESIGN YOUR PRODUCT FOR THE BROADEST POSSIBLE COMMUNITY

Khoi Vinh, the designer of NYTimes.com and other frequently visited websites, believes that a website or any product or service

designed to beautifully map to the needs of a beginner or intermediate is very likely to delight an expert, too. . . . Products designed to map closely to the needs of experts are often turn-offs to beginners and intermediates. Users who come across features that reveal not just the complexity but also the specificity that experts need often quickly decide, "This isn't for me." Rarely will a beginner find herself delighted as to how well a product has been designed to map to a skillset she doesn't yet have.[1]

Khoi's presentation at the Future of Web Apps in London in 2007 opened my eyes to how important it is to design for "regular" users. Unless your product is for a specific high-end expert user, the lesson is clear: You increase whuffie by making it easy to implement and use by the broadest possible community. The Microformats community provides an example of how to do this well.

Microformats are used by web designers and developers as simple ways to add classifications, or a label, to the code in a webpage. They are what is known as a "web standard." Independents and multiple corporate representatives collaborate to develop microformats that are used as a general standard. Since multiple companies and individuals make up the Micoformats community, the classifications developed need to suit everyone involved. This poses a challenge because with so many interests involved there are potentially hundreds of microformats that could be developed. To keep the adoption of microformats simple, the people collaborating within the community are dedicated to keeping the number of microformats to a minimum. They achieve this by enforcing the 80/20 rule: creating classifications for the type of content that occurs 80 percent of the time. In the process of determining the most common forms of content, the person proposing the new microformat must prove that the content is present on enough pages and another classification is needed.

Because of the simplicity of microformats and the rigorous commitment of the those in the community to keep it simple, they have raised a great deal of whuffie in the wider web design community and have been able to get the practice of implementing microformats to a wide audience in a short amount of time. It is estimated that within the first two years of the invention of microformats, over 450 million pieces of content were marked up with microformats on the Web.[2]

The lesson from the Microformats community is that simplicity of design encourages use or adoption by a wider audience. The simplicity appeals to more people, helping them feel empowered when using your product, thereby raising your whuffie. The implementation of advanced features may actually overwhelm the novice user, resulting in alienation and a loss of whuffie.

Another example about designing for the broader community and using the 80/20 rule comes from consumer goods. Have you ever gone shopping for a new digital camera? If you're like me, it's easy to get confused by all of the features available and hard to determine what you really need in a camera. Many customers end up fatigued from feature overload.

In a study about consumer choice and digital cameras, people were shown a gamut of cameras and asked to make a selection.[3] Prior to using the cameras, the participants were asked if they wanted to buy a camera with only a few features or a wide variety. The participants all said that they preferred those with more features, thinking that they would come in handy and be frequently used. However, when actually *using* the cameras, they ended up preferring those with fewer features. The cameras with more features led to feature fatigue and higher dissatisfaction with the experiences. The study participants were more satisfied with a camera that was easier to use rather than feature filled.

Finding out what your customers need, then designing for the features that most of them need, while cutting the extra features that only some of them need, will help you design your product for your wider audience. This will ensure that even the most novice user of your product feels comfortable using it, which helps more of your customers feel smart because they can just pick up your product or use your website without an instruction manual. This builds more whuffie for you as those customers spread the word that they love your product because it's so easy and straightforward to use.

RESPOND TO ALL FEEDBACK, EVEN WITH "NO, THANKS"

Elisa Camahort is a leader of one of my favorite communities, BlogHer, the blogging community for women. Elisa attended a community roundtable I hosted and made the point that "responding to feedback doesn't mean that you have to implement every single thing that every single person wants. It does, however, mean acknowledging the ideas and letting people know that they are heard." Elisa told us, "Once people know that they are heard and get a sound response as to why you aren't implementing their idea, they usually accept and appreciate it."

Elisa should know. BlogHer is one of the healthiest communities I've been part of. It has an incredibly diverse group of bloggers who disagree with one another in a civil tone. One particular incidence of this was a series of complaints received after a BlogHer conference about the alienation that single female bloggers felt in the presence of what is known as *mommy bloggers*—or bloggers who write about their experience of motherhood. In 2006, the number of mommy bloggers at the conference had increased to the point at which they became the majority, or so it seemed to the other attendees. Because the topic of mommy blogging was a hot one, it seemed to many that every session brought up the experience of blogging as a mother. This became quite a contentious issue for those bloggers who didn't have kids or who didn't choose to blog about their kids. The suggestion was made to Elisa and the other organizers that they should create a separate conference for mommy bloggers. Segregation of the mommy bloggers didn't seem like the right solution for Elisa, though. She had enough experience in the community to know that the topic of mommy blogging was new and a strong part of the conversation in that year, but like any new topic, it would take its proper place and blend into the overall conference the following year. Elisa responded to the vast feedback by thanking the members for their suggestions, but explaining that BlogHer wasn't going to separate out mommy blogging into its own conference because it was important to have all points of view represented. Of

course, Elisa was right and, though mommy blogging continued to be a topic of discussion in the following years, it blended
nicely into the overall conversation of the conference, making
everyone happy. Elisa, along with her cofounders Jory Des
Jardins and Lisa Stone, make awesome efforts to strike a balance
between all parts of the BlogHer community.

Twitter has a similar approach to feedback. Since its launch
the desire was to keep Twitter as a simple short-messaging
platform, but still allow its community to present ideas about
the best way to use the platform. I was part of Twitter's early
testing group and, with some other early users, sat down with
Twitter product manager Britt Selvitelle to discuss adding a
groups feature to Twitter. Britt listened intently and wrote
notes as we spoke to him about what we desired in a groups
feature. At the end of the discussion, Britt explained that he
had gotten requests for a groups feature very different from the
one we had proposed, as well as requests for no groups feature
at all. He explained that, instead of implementing one or
another of these ideas—all of them good in his opinion—the
Twitter team had decided to keep the platform as simple as
possible for the time being and encouraged all of us to use the
tools others had built to personalize the Twitter experience.
Everyone in the group was satisfied with this answer, even
though Britt had just told us he couldn't implement our
desired feature. By explaining to us that there wasn't a single
solution that would improve the experience for all Twitter
users, and offering us an alternative solution, Britt demonstrated he was listening to our feedback and built a great deal
of whuffie with everyone in the group.

Both Elisa and Britt demonstrate that people will appreciate that they have been heard even if you don't use their feedback. If a customer feels like her feedback has been heard and you can provide her a good reason why you cannot implement her ideas, she will be encouraged to continue communicating with you. On the flip side, ideas that are presented but are neither implemented nor acknowledged sends the message you aren't listening. That's a turnoff to customers. They tell other potential customers about their negative experience, leading not only to lost whuffie with your original customer, but a reduced ability to gain whuffie with new customers. By acknowledging feedback—good or bad—you send the message that you are listening, telling your customers their feedback matters, leading to a positive gain in whuffie. By not acknowledging feedback, you run the risk of losing more than the whuffie of the customer you failed to respond to—you could also lose whuffie with his or her wider network.

DO NOT TAKE NEGATIVE FEEDBACK PERSONALLY

People wouldn't take time from their day to criticize if they didn't care. The way you respond to negative feedback is as important for building whuffie as your response to positive feedback. In fact, an open and nonconfrontational response to negative feedback can be even *more* beneficial for building whuffie than multiple responses to positive feedback. In every critic there is an opportunity to create a strong advocate for your company.

The best way to handle negative feedback is taking a step

back from it for as long as it takes to remove your emotional reaction. If you still feel pangs beyond the accepted time window (twenty-four to forty-eight hours) for an online response, pass it along to a neutral party to give you a fresh perspective.

This is especially hard for me. I take all negative feedback to heart. In the past, I could get ten positive comments and one negative comment on a blog post or article, but then focus on the one negative comment. When I obsess about a negative comment, I get defensive, react emotionally, and often heat things up with the critic much more than necessary. This is terribly damaging to my whuffie as it is not only the critic who reads my reaction, but others as well. They would then see me as defensive and closed rather than the open and thoughtful person I strive to be. It's taken a great deal of training for me to stop having this defensive reaction, but I still slip up from time to time, so it's immensely important that I step back and reflect on what I can learn from the critic rather than how I feel attacked. Once I started to do this, all of my readers, including the critics, respected me much more. Not only did I garner more support in general, but I turned many of my critics into advocates. Because my critics are quite often very active online community participants, the word spread that I have good ideas and I grew my whuffie in general.

On the other hand, if the feedback is not just negative, but "personal" and incredibly angry, immediate response is important. It is still essential for you to "step back" emotionally, but an extremely angry person needs a quick response. Dealing with the emotional context is a delicate process, but there are strategies.

The worst thing to do when responding to emotional customers is to ignore their emotions. Address their emotional state before anything else, even before responding to the core issue. Simply acknowledging and naming the emotion is a good place to begin. For example, saying "You sound frustrated" means that you've identified with the other person's state of mind and tells him you are empathetic. Doing so plays an important role in how the conversation will proceed. Once a person feels that emotional connection, he will be more likely to hear your response to the problem, even if it doesn't solve the issue.[4]

This, too, is an opportunity to build whuffie. Even if the individual remains angry with you personally, the others witnessing your empathetic response will see you as levelheaded and kind. That builds more trust and gives you a reputation for being fair. I've watched extremely effective customer service representatives dealing with volatile customer issues in front of a crowd so effectively that the crowd works with the customer service representative to calm the customer down. I've also seen the opposite occur, where the customer service representative got defensive and stopped listening, turning the other customers who weren't previously angry to the side of the irate customer.

A good example of a positive way to handle negative feedback is a recent experience I had with Virgin America. The flight was delayed by bad weather at the destination airport and passengers were told that it would be three hours until departure. I watched as one passenger, a man in a business suit, approached the counter to complain. He was frantic because the delay meant he might not make his connecting flight and he had important meetings to attend at the other end. But he wasn't just angry about this particular flight. He started raising his voice and letting everyone know that there were multiple occasions that Virgin had delayed flights, contributing to his stress. The woman at the counter listened to him carefully, then responded to him perfectly: "I hear your frustration and although there is nothing I can do about this particular delay, perhaps we can find another flight and connection that will get you to your destination on time." Not only did this calm the man down, the other passengers within earshot started to talk about the helpfulness of the Virgin America staff on other occasions. There were also horror stories exchanged from their experiences with other airlines. The nondefensive reaction of the woman at the Virgin America counter went a long way to building whuffie with the passengers who witnessed her empathetic reaction.

GIVE CREDIT TO THOSE WHOSE IDEAS YOU IMPLEMENT

When you ask for ideas and feedback and you get good ones from the community, it is utterly important to acknowledge not only their receipt, but also the people who have developed them. Not doing so is akin to taking the credit for someone else's insight. It's irresponsible and can lead to losing helpful contributors in your community and slowing its overall growth.

By one estimate, 90 percent of members of online communities are lurkers;[5] that is, they passively participate by, say, reading material available to the community, but they do not post material themselves. Another 9 percent occasionally posts comments and feedback only when they absolutely feel comfortable and knowledgeable on the subject. Most of the regular participation in a community comes from 1 percent of a user base. The majority of your feedback and comments will come from that 1 percent, so it is essential to find ways of keeping the other 99 percent engaged.

By creating the right incentives for speaking out—acknowledging and giving credit—the percentage of people participating can increase. One of the greatest motivations for more people getting involved is the opportunity for them to increase their personal whuffie. If someone posts a great idea in a community forum and you use it, you infuse her with whuffie by publicly acknowledging her great idea. Building more whuffie gives her the incentive to return and provide more ideas.

As the person posts more ideas and is publicly rewarded, others will notice. People want to spend their energy where it will be appreciated, so this will lead to more people posting more ideas. The friendlier your company is about implementing and rewarding ideas, the more people will come out of the lurker shadows to post more ideas. As your community members gain whuffie, so do you.

Of course, the opposite is true as well. If you aren't responding to or rewarding ideas, frequent posters will be discouraged and head elsewhere to contribute. The activity in your forums will decrease, leading even the lurkers to move to other forums.

Songbird is an open-source, customizable music player.[6] It functions much like iTunes, helping you discover new music, movies, and images and sync them with your listening device. It has the added value of being nonproprietary, so users can buy and download music from artists across the Web that may not be found in the iTunes store. The nonproprietary nature of Songbird also allows users to sync their music to multiple music players, whereas iTunes only allows Apple product syncing. Since Songbird is open source, third-party developers can create cool and useful new features for the player such as concert updates for your favorite artists, complete with the ability to buy tickets as you are listening to the music. This level of openness has great value for the customer and is an exciting opportunity for developers to gain a wider audience.

Songbird, however, was not attracting interest from as many outside software developers as it desired. Its competitors— similar open-source projects—had hundreds of developers contributing to the evolution of their software. A quick look at the developer forums was enough to reveal the issue: Many developers who had shown up online to contribute had been ignored. Multiple question threads were left unanswered by company representatives, such as potential release dates of new developer tools, and there were few places where the contributions that had been made were showcased. There was no clear benefit to external developers contributing to Songbird as there was little recognition for their contributions. To fix this, Songbird hired a full-time person to do developer relations and ensure that the incoming questions were being answered by company engineers in a timely fashion. The company also built a developer network that showcased and celebrated the current and future contributions by outside developers and ran a contest to attract new developers to contribute to the project. The result was a 300 percent increase in contributions over a six-month period and a healthy developer network where both external developers and internal hired developers were given incentives to work together to create better software.

A word of warning, though. Some incentives can create the wrong type of feedback.

Popular restaurant review site Yelp.com relies on the reviews of enthusiastic volunteer foodies to draw people to the site frequently enough for advertisers to justify posting ads on it. When building the reviews in their hometown of San Francisco, it was easy. The founders, Jeremy Stoppelman and Russel Simmons, were already hooked into a wide network of foodies, so the whuffie they built in the San Francisco community helped the word spread like wildfire. Yelp.com was soon the most popular restaurant review site in the area.

However, when it came to other markets, like New York and Chicago, where they didn't know very many people, growth stagnated. Yelp wasn't spreading via word of mouth, and there were very few volunteer reviewers. Restaurants weren't interested in talking to them because Stoppelman and Simmons lacked whuffie in these local markets.

To try to jump-start growth, they ran a campaign that offered people who posted comments on the Yelp.com site a dollar for each review. The results?

That filled the site with content, but not all of it was good. And it failed to give the community legs. "It didn't do anything to build an initial community," says Yelp's [COO, Geoff] Donaker. "These weren't passionate users."[7]

The comments Donaker refers to were reviews for local Starbucks and McDonald's—not exactly the same foodie market as was covered in San Francisco—as well as short, not-well-thought-out comments like, "It was good" and "It sucked." Monetary rewards motivate a different kind of behavior antithetical to the intrinsic passion of an organically grown community. It can also turn off people who are thinking about joining a community. If there is wind that some get paid and others don't, it may lead to the loss of people who are coming for the *right* reasons: those who just create reviews or post photos or give feedback because they care.

What *did* work for Yelp.com was to build relationships with local foodies in each of its desired markets. Instead of paying people for reviews, the company found out who the local food and culture bloggers were and contacted them personally to discuss contributing their expertise to Yelp.com. In some of the larger markets, Yelp.com hired full-time community managers to continue building these relationships, holding local tasting events and mixers at some of the nicer restaurants for these food and culture bloggers. The community managers also attended as many food and culture events as they could, helping promote themselves and gathering local interest in Yelp.com. After several months of building relationships person by person, there were enough reviews that people were contributing without being contacted at all.

There are times when offering cash or high-value prizes for

the generation of great ideas through a contest can work very well to bring in new interest (and boost current interest) in a community.

The Mozilla Foundation developer group frequently holds contests asking users to create new add-ons and extensions for their open-source browser, Firefox. A program that had been developed by a worldwide network of volunteers, Firefox is now the world's second-most-popular browser. Because it is open source, it relies on developers, designers, and promoters around the world to both build it and spread the word about it.

Although it is a huge success, Firefox still has to encourage people to continue to improve it so it can not only compete but also lead the marketplace in browser innovation. The foundation team has to come up with yearly campaigns to meet the goals of Firefox. They can't just go to their community and say, "Hey, can you do this and this for us?" because after a couple of years, people can feel unappreciated for their efforts. Instead they say, "Hey, we have prizes and special notoriety for anyone who wants to do this for us." It works and even brings in new interest to the project.

When Firefox 3 launched in 2008, the team at Mozilla needed to drum up interest in the newest version of the browser, so they ran a contest they called "Extend Firefox 3." The contest ran for four months and offered rewards of computer equipment, an all-expense-paid trip to California to work with Firefox developers and Firefox-branded bags, mugs, and hats. The allure of the contest also created excitement around the new features of the 3.0 version of Firefox. The contest appeared in over forty publications, online and offline, worldwide. The Firefox team was able to attract several thousand developers to contribute to the new version, making Firefox 3 even more attractive for people to download and creating good buzz around the release.

Using a monetary incentive worked for Firefox and not for Yelp because of the former's strong established community. Cash and prize incentives work a great deal better when they are introduced into the community to refresh and reinvigorate action rather than to jump-start action.

Additional ways to credit people include the following:

- **MENTION THEIR CONTRIBUTIONS IN BLOG POSTS AND VIDEOS.** Garyvee is especially good at dropping the names of his viewers who send him good ideas, a strategy that encourages people to send in even more innovative ideas, such as which wines to review and contests to run. As Gary says, "It really jazzes people up to hear their name in my show. I get tons of e-mails afterward from people who loved it."
- **NAME A PRODUCT OR A FEATURE AFTER THEM OR PUT THEIR NAME PROMINENTLY ON A PRODUCT.** Say someone comes up with an ingenious way to package your latest CD; why not prominently print their name on that packaging? Zipcar, the community car-sharing service, rewards its customers' ideas by naming cars after them.
- **SEND A MEMBER OF THE PRESS THEIR WAY.** In the summer of 2006, I blogged seventeen reasons why I love Zipcar, including the ease of booking, the convenience of the car locations, and the lack of hidden fees. Since then Zipcar has asked me if I would be a customer voice for articles in the

press, which makes me feel very important to Zipcar. I've even been quoted in the *San Francisco Chronicle* and *Wall Street Journal.* I also had the opportunity to be on *Oprah,* but was beaten out by a woman who uses Zipcar to deliver meals to the homeless. Nevertheless, these opportunities say that Zipcar trusts me to talk to its very valuable contacts, and they encourage me and other Zipcar fans to blog and talk more about the service.

- **SEND THEM A GIFT CERTIFICATE.** When it seems appropriate, send contributors an unexpected gift certificate for, say, coffee, music, or a book. Write a little note on it that says, "For no other reason than I just wanted to say how much I appreciate the valuable feedback you've given to us. Thanks so much!"

- **SEND THEM SWAG** (promotional items, like T-shirts, hats, pens, mouse pads, jackets, etc.). This is sometimes even better than a gift certificate, and it is especially valuable when it is *rare* swag. Even though Yelp.com found very little real leverage with paying people $1 per review, the company did find the promise of getting beautiful Yelp.com swag to be a great incentive. It has even posted the photos of the beautiful, limited-edition T-shirts that no one but "Yelp Elites" can have access to. One blogger who did a random questionnaire on Yelp found that a large percentage of users posted reviews to get that elite status.

- **UPGRADE THEIR ACCOUNT.** This is a pretty simple action to take if you have a subscription service or a freemium service (a pay scale where customers can use basic features for free, but if they want advanced features, they pay a subscription price). Freemium has been a successful business model for many start-ups because it allows people to "try before they buy." Lurkers can then continue to participate without personal expense. If they are already a paying member, extend their subscription or give them a subscription to give to a friend (always a popular option as it makes them look generous). In 2006, Flickr, the popular photo-sharing web community, had a bout of bad luck and was down for a couple of days. Instead of panicking, it created a coloring contest and awarded everyone who participated in the contest with a free year of subscription. The best part is that the company originally only offered the "winners" of the contest the subscription, but ultimately awarded the subscription to everyone who contributed an entry.

Another great example of this is the ongoing contest run by the founders of the time-keeping web application Harvest (Getharvest.com). Harvest is a great way to keep track of the time you spend on each project by entering it into an online form. At the end of each month, you can find out where you are spending most of your time, and if your time is billable, it makes it incredibly simple to bill clients for time spent on their work. The contest Harvest runs asks for stories from founders of businesses who use the application. The best stories are featured in the Harvest monthly newsletter and authors of the stories get a free year's subscription. The winners not only get access to a useful service, but they also get to be featured prominently, thus combining two great ways to credit community members.

- The best way to credit people is to *give them more responsibility.* Ma.gnolia.com, a social bookmarking website, has created a Ma.gnolia Gardeners program. Social bookmarking is the process of taking the websites you bookmark into your browser and making them public and portable in a web service. It becomes even more social when you follow friends' bookmarks to find out what they are taking an interest in. Social bookmarking is still, largely, a practice of heavy Internet users, but it is growing in popularity for many mainstream users.

The Gardeners are a small number of highly active and trustworthy members of the Ma.gnolia community who have been given administrative-level abilities within the site. Regular bookmarkers "flag" a user who appears to be a spammer, which sends a message to the administrators of Ma.gnolia to look into whether or not this is in fact the case. Gardeners, however, can make the "spam or not spam" decision for themselves and instantly remove the spammer from the public directory. Gardeners also get to beta test features long before anyone else and have inside knowledge of the company's future plans. Typically, when given more responsibility, Gardeners act more responsibly and spend more time making sure Ma.gnolia is spam free.

EXPLAIN THE IMPLEMENTATION OF ALL IDEAS TO EVERYONE

Even when changes are positive for the customer experience, they can be confusing when launched if not properly explained. Customers get used to the way a product works or the way your website is laid out. *Every* new feature and change is worth talking about. Not doing so can confuse and shock some who have gotten used to the layout and is also a lost opportunity to point things out and promote positive changes.

Facebook, one of the largest social networks online, learned this lesson the hard way. In 2006, the company decided to implement a really useful new feature that developers had been brainstorming behind the scenes for months: the news feed. The news feed feature alerts community members on Facebook to nearly everything their friends do. So, if I was one of your friends and I added another person as a friend, this action would show up on your news feed as something like, "Tara Hunt has added Jane Doe as a friend." If I break up with my boyfriend or start dating someone new and make this change on my profile, you will read, "Tara Hunt is now single" or "Tara Hunt has started a new relationship." Almost any action I take in Facebook, from the friends I add to the events I plan to attend, is recorded and published on my own news feed as well as that of my friends. This has turned out to be one of the most interesting and popular features on Facebook, but it started out as highly controversial because Facebook decided to launch it without educating users about it.

As soon as Facebook launched the news feed, the backlash started. Mashable.com, a popular technology review blog, wrote, "These additions might seem fairly small, but they could have a major effect on how users interact with the site: will you be more cautious if you know your friends are being updated with news of your activities? . . . I've heard complaints before about sites . . . that display the latest visitors to your profile page—in many ways, Facebook's new tools are more invasive. My guess is that if they'd allowed Facebook users to turn this feature off, most of them would have done so."[8] Others started a petition to have the news feeds removed that attracted thousands of signatures,[9] and hundreds of blogs debated the creepiness of this new "invasive" feature. One blogger, who launched his blog as a campaign to get Facebook to remove the news feeds, wrote that the news feeds "damage what privacy was left on Facebook. Before Feeds, it was already easy enough to stalk anyone at your school, and everyone on your friends list; but with the advent of Feeds, it is now nearly impossible not to be 'stalked' or to 'stalk.'"[10] It was speculated that Facebook would lose a great deal of trust in the web community and would not be able to recover from it.

Facebook founder Mark Zuckerberg responded to this outcry saying, "We really messed this one up. When we launched News Feed and Mini-Feed we were trying to provide you with a stream of information about your social world. Instead, we did a bad job of explaining what the new features were and an even worse job of giving you control of them. I'd like to try to correct those errors now."[11] Correcting those errors meant that Facebook gave community members the option to opt out of being part of the news feeds. If they chose to opt out, their activities would not be shown in their friends' feeds. Facebook also increased the amount of control community members had over their privacy settings in general.

News feeds are, indeed, useful streams of information about your social world. Today, it's one of the reasons that many love Facebook. Having that quick snapshot of what everyone in your network is doing is very useful and acts as a reminder to contact someone you may not have talked to lately. However, as the people behind Facebook have learned, it is far better to give a full explanation of the way a new feature works before it is implemented. Today, Facebook flags all changes with a clickable link for community members to follow to read more information on that feature. It also blogs about the changes and rolls them out slowly to a few members at a time. This allows the company to get feedback before it unleashes the feature to the entire community.

Facebook lost a great deal of whuffie when it launched news feeds and it took a long time to recover. But by flagging every change and being more open with the information about these changes, the company has gained that whuffie back as people have learned to trust it again.

If you want to avoid losing whuffie with your customers, you need to approach changes and newly implemented features with the same openness and transparency that Facebook has learned from its mistakes. You need to blog about the changes, flag the new features where they occur, complete with the ability for your customers to provide feedback on these changes, and, if possible, test any potentially controversial change with a smaller group before rolling it out to the entire community. By doing so, you will build the essential trust that is a big part of building whuffie with your customers and show them that you respect their opinions, which goes a long way to encouraging more feedback.

MAKE SMALL, CONTINUOUS CHANGES

Making small, continuous changes—or iterations—to your product will demonstrate to your customers that you are listening, further opening up those feedback channels, whereas holding back on changes until there are many to implement may only confuse and shock your customers. A great deal of whuffie is lost when you confuse and shock your customers who have to relearn how to use your product or find their way through your website all over again.

An example of whuffie lost through a big change is the release of Windows Vista in 2007, released six years after the previous version, Windows XP. This was problematic since many of the changes resulted in compatibility problems for XP users with devices such as cameras and printers that wouldn't connect, as well as new security issues. From release, it took Microsoft about six months to work with the consumer electronic companies to achieve compatibility. That proved to be a long time to be patient for many Microsoft customers who, in the meantime, reinstalled XP because their impression of Vista was damaged, and it resulted in a great deal of whuffie being lost for Microsoft. The six years it took to launch Vista also set big expectations for the newest version of Windows, leaving many people who were anticipating bigger improvements disappointed. Enterprise—or big business—customers, who are Microsoft's largest market, rely on security and compatibility. This launch called into question how secure and reliable using Microsoft would be in the future.

Lucky for Microsoft, it was able to stop the hemorrhaging of its whuffie with its customers by responding swiftly, implementing training, and rectifying the compatibility and security issues before too much damage was done. But what if you encountered the same issues without Microsoft's staff and budget? Miscalculating customer needs and implementing new user flows can be frustrating enough for your current customer base that they may look for an alternative company before you have a chance to respond.

On the flip side of losing whuffie because of miscalculating the larger change rollouts, there is also an opportunity to *build whuffie* by making smaller, more frequent improvements to your product. It enables you to gather feedback that can guide the broader improvements. It shows customers that you are listening and working to constantly improve their experiences, especially when you make sure to flag changes as you make them. This opens you up to more feedback and interaction with your customers. If you aren't headed in the right direction, small changes are much easier to retract and fix than larger changes and you can communicate this with your customers as well.

Many attribute the success of MySpace in its early days to small, continuous improvements. Often when asked why they are so crazy about MySpace, a site that most parents didn't grasp, kids would answer, "As soon as I can think of something that would be cool, MySpace has it." MySpace made a point of implementing continuous improvements instead of rolling out larger versions to keep its young and demanding crowd interested. It knew that if it waited every six months to implement the ideas of its community, they would lose interest. Certainly, this particular market—the digital natives, or millennials as they have been called—are notorious for having shorter attention spans. However, as customers grow more intimate with brands, all ages of users are starting to expect quick and frequent responses to their needs. Threadless, the online T-shirt company, knows this all too well. Its customer community includes everyone from teenagers to people in middle age. In 2006, I heard the founders speak at a conference, where they explained that developing a great deal of whuffie was the reason behind their success in becoming the world's second-largest T-shirt retailer. One of their "secrets" is letting their customer community know they are listening by implementing community feedback within two weeks for both the website and product line.

This practice can work for consumer goods as well as websites, as shown by Timbuk2, the laptop and courier bag manufacturer located in San Francisco. The majority of Timbuk2's product lines are manufactured in China in order to cut costs. But the company has kept some of the manufacturing local, actually right inside of its San Francisco offices, allowing it to test out new products and features and to service its customers' custom bag orders. Timbuk2 found out its customers were happy to pay more to get exactly the colors and style they wanted. Local manufacturing allows the company to prototype and test new products with local customers before committing to larger production runs and to be really flexible when it comes to responding to marketplace needs. When the Mac-Book Air came out in the spring of 2008, Timbuk2 was able to create a special glove-type laptop bag within weeks to sell in smaller local retailers. When it saw that sales on that sleeve were slow, the company knew that mass production on the product wasn't feasible.

Because Timbuk2 personnel could put out a prototype quickly, they were able to test the product without spending much. However, even more significant is that they were able to interact with customers on their blog and through their customer service site at Getsatisfaction.com during this prototyping, building deeper relationships with people in the Timbuk2 online community. This is an incredibly valuable whuffie-building exercise because it involves customers directly in the line of innovation. Most manufacturing is planned at least one year out because of the complexity of mass production, but these local and agile factories allow for an idea to prototype within days. Because of the quick turnaround, Timbuk2 can invite its customers into the conversation and get really inventive.

Being agile and rolling out smaller, more frequent changes and products shows your customers that you are ready to respond to their needs, and it also protects you against making big, expensive mistakes.

Small changes can also have a big impact by improving a customer's experience and help put more whuffie in the bank. That's been the case with the way Google uses small changes to attract more search customers.

Google is a huge company with a great deal of whuffie. It has, however, taken many small steps and a great deal of customer interaction to get there. Many of these small steps have been invisible because they were related to Google's search results. In her keynote address at the annual Google developer conference, Google I/O, in 2008, Marissa Mayer, vice president of search products and user experience, revealed some of the philosophical secrets behind the success of Google. One is that the simplest design is probably the right design. Google uses the principle of Occam's razor, based on the work of fourteenth-century English logician friar William of Occam: All other things being equal, the simplest solution is the best.

When applying Occam's razor to increasing the usability of the search engine, Google takes a look at tweaking small things like white space and colors behind advertisements rather than doing large overhauls. Split A/B testing, the process of showing users different versions of the page and recording the results of their interactions, shows that even the slightest increase in white space between the logo and the search results can affect the number of page views and that a light yellow background behind advertisements rather than the previous light blue background will increase users' satisfaction with their experience, resulting in more searches per day and more page views.

This split A/B testing is not only useful for finding out how to increase web traffic and page views, it results in figuring out what your customers need even before they know it themselves. Similar to the previous point when kids were describing what they love about MySpace, this type of small change testing could bring improvement to a customer's experience right as he or she thinks of something that could improve the site. Keeping in sync with customer needs like this builds a great deal of whuffie. A company that is in sync with the needs of its customers builds a great deal of loyalty.

Small changes are not necessarily insignificant. They include, for example, implementing features to enhance a current experience (like adding photos or chat), making the interface simpler to use (without changing it wholesale), or adjusting your product to be compatible with another one (adding an iPod plug in a car). If you were baking a pie, a big change would be to swap out the apples for plums; a small change would be to add cinnamon. If people were hoping for apple pie, the small change would be more welcomed.

GO OUT AND FIND FEEDBACK

Your website may have the world's best feedback system, but it may not be enough to get a real handle on the way people are reacting to your product, especially when there are problems. There are different tools—personal blogs, Twitter, and other forums—where people may feel more comfortable providing feedback, as the geo-location-based web app Brightkite.com recently discovered.

Early in 2008, Brightkite.com launched a service allowing people to publish their location so their friends would have the option to come and join them. But to use the program you needed to physically input your location into Brightkite rather than have it detect where you are and automatically send information to your friends. Some of the original users found it laborious and started to post criticism of the service to Twitter. There were also concerns about privacy since many users wanted to keep location details confined to their circle of friends, not broadcast more widely. A Twitter member who goes by the screen name kevnull commented online, "Brightkite doesn't seem to be honouring its privacy setting. Look at our profiles logged out."

Within minutes of posting, the team at Brightkite

responded with real concern for the issues that kevnull was raising. The conversation between the Brightkite representative and kevnull was entirely public and others started to join in, myself included. The Brightkite representative decided to open a chat room, inviting people to come and give feedback in real time.

When people saw how quickly Brightkite was responding, more and more started to post their own feedback. This created a great deal of attention for Brightkite, and it had to provide more invitations as other Twitterers were clamoring to try out and give feedback to the service.

The loop of feedback continued and Brightkite responded to everything and gave frequent updates about its progress in resolving the problem. This impressed even more people, who blogged and tweeted about Brightkite's great response, attracting even more people to use the service. Even though Brightkite has an entire feedback process created on its website, it recognized that responding where people were comfortable giving feedback was in the company's favor. Not only did it continue to get great ideas and a good sense of the most frequently requested features, but it also built a great deal of whuffie and goodwill in the wider community.

THERE WILL ALWAYS BE THOSE WHO DON'T LIKE YOU

Even when you are being showered with love and affection and your whuffie is at an all-time high, there will be *somebody* in the crowd who wants to tell you how awful you are. You may be the world's most brilliant public speaker, bringing 99 percent of the crowd to a standing ovation at the end of your talk, and there will inevitably be that one guy who decides to write a blog post about how full of hot air you are and how little value you offer. You may be one of the hottest companies around, with your product flying off the shelves of every store in the nation and people writing endless letters of thanks for positively changing their lives, and there will be one woman writing a blog dedicated to exposing all of the ways you damage the environment with your office policies.

My advice in these cases is to stop just short of ignoring them. The best way to erode your whuffie account is to concentrate on and engage them in a fight. The fact is that some negative feedback is *not* constructive, it is purely disruptive. In online communities, we have a name for these types of critics: haters. Haters are people who love to disrupt a conversation. And if you let the haters disrupt, you will look like a loser in the eyes of your community, damaging the whuffie you have with the people who respect and trust you. Haters are often just people who want a bit of attention and, in the midst of your success, they see an opportunity to stand out as the naysayers. They view your whuffie as something that they can use to gain their own by pulling you down a notch or two. The key is to not let that happen and to either neutralize the haters' quest for attention or find a way to turn them into your biggest champions.

How can you tell when the criticism is disruptive versus constructive? It's not always cut and dried, but here are a few indicators that someone is showing off instead of just upset because he or she had a poor experience with your product:

- The tone is "snarky" instead of angry. Instead of complaining about real issues, jokes are made at your expense.

- The comments are dismissive. It's pretty obvious that the person making the comments has never tried your product or has approached it with a preconceived notion that she wouldn't like it and found every reason to back this notion up.

- If asked to elaborate on how you could improve his experience, the critic is either silent or diverts attention from any real answer.

- Not always, but quite often, these disruptive comments are made in forums where the critic feels you aren't present or won't read it—for instance, in the comment section on another person's blog post about a positive experience with your product.

- Quite often, but not always, disruptive comments are made anonymously or under a pseudonym.

The way to handle haters depends on the context of their comments. If the person has written a blog post making fun of your product, the best thing to do is leave a neutral but humorous comment, showing that it doesn't bother you. Something to the tune of, "Hahaha. This is a great poke at my widget! Thanks for taking the time to write this. You are very funny." If the hater sees you aren't bothered and recognizes that he is being watched, it will usually tone things down. But if he responds with more snark and meanness, ignoring these further comments is highly advisable unless you can match his sardonic wit. If the comments were left on someone else's blog post, do not respond to the hater at all. Instead, thank the blogger for her feedback and answer any questions outlined in the post itself. Don't even mention that you've noticed the hater. The same treatment goes for a forum or a tweet. Don't engage. If the hater addresses you personally, ask him to elaborate on his experience and explain what he needs from you to help him feel better about your product. If he responds, he's probably not a hater at all, just a very angry customer.

The situation in which you've encountered a disruptive angry customer is one in which you can really make a difference. Although you don't want to spend all of your energy on one person who feels negatively about you or your product, you will want to employ the tips given on not taking negative feedback personally. Find out what the issue is and whether there is a way you can help rectify it. Sometimes just taking the time will turn a heavy critic into one of your biggest fans.

There is a great deal of whuffie to be gained from how you handle these tough, negative situations. That holds true even for those you ignore. People will observe your actions and will applaud your professional handling of the situation if you rise above the fight. A surefire whuffie surge results from being the "bigger person" in an online community.

Turning around the bullhorn, and responding to feedback in

particular, doesn't have to be confusing or scary. It merely requires being a good listener as well as an astute implementer. Maintaining the balance of openness and vision is the toughest part, but the good news is that merely being aware of it will help you hone your balancing skills along the way.

Merely opening the doors of communication doesn't mean that someone will talk about you.

One of my recurring nightmares is throwing a party and no one shows up. I've set the table, baked the cookies, poured the wine, and set the mood perfectly. The invitations have been sent, the RSVPs have been collected, and the porch light is on. For hours, I sit there alone in my party dress, constantly peeking out from behind the curtains to see if anyone is coming. I practice my forgiving face in the mirror as I imagine the guests pouring in late. But nobody comes. (Ack!) Just imagining it leaves me in a cold sweat. Awful as this seems, it happens all of the time. People try to build communities without giving enough thought as to *why* anyone would come to the party. Next thing they know they have built a very expensive ghost town. "How do you attract people to your community?" is the most consistently asked question I've heard at various community conferences. It sounds a great deal like another classic question, "How do I attract customers to my product?" This brings us to the next of the five principles to becoming whuffie rich: the need to participate in the community you serve.

5

BECOME PART OF THE COMMUNITY YOU SERVE

Whuffie is built through forming strong relationships with your customers and potential customers. But who are your customers and where are they found? As noted earlier (chapter 2), your customers are gathering more and more online, expressing themselves through the myriad tools in online communities. They are forming their own strong relationships with new friends, some of whom they have never met offline. They are reaching out to these new friends for recommendations on everything from what kind of dog food to buy to where to take their next vacation. They are exchanging tips on skin care, restaurants, diets, and careers. And they are exchanging this information with the people they trust—real people they are meeting online who have gained enough whuffie in their eyes to be trusted with these recommendations. More and more people are looking to online communities to make new friends who can help them succeed at whatever they are doing. Many companies that want to use social networks to sell products make a crucial mistake. They join them in order to study the members of these communities or to "collect" them. Done the wrong way, your foray into online communities can lead to a loss rather than gain of whuffie if you enter the space and become suspected of not being a trusted friend.

Becoming part of the community you serve is not as simple as merely joining social networks and adding a bunch of friends. Your interactions *have* to be meaningful and authentic. You need to join online communities as a true participant, one who contributes as much as gains from interactions there. You need to balance your interests with the interests of the other members of these communities, oftentimes with your interests needing to take a backseat. Your participation needs to be grounded in the desire to be part of the community you serve, engaging fully in the conversations and being a full-fledged peer to the group you are part of.

This being said, building whuffie by becoming part of the community you serve is not impossible. It is something that many companies are doing successfully, and the people participating are nearly impossible to identify as company representatives. The successful company representatives in an online community are seamlessly integrated, with only a hint that their company is part of the package. The whuffie these companies have gained from being such an integral part of these communities is invaluable because, as a peer, their tips and recommendations are as valuable in the cycle of word of mouth as that of another trusted peer.

A really great example of this is Threadless, a company that makes custom T-shirts. It has not only become part of the community it serves, but it has also built a strong art community online that it is merely a part of.

THREADLESS HAS MORE WHUFFIE THAN IT KNOWS WHAT TO DO WITH

Threadless is a vibrant online community of artists with nearly half a million registered members. It's also a company of thirty-five people, working out of übercool offices and running a brick-and-mortar retail store in Chicago's Lakeview district. Its revenue has doubled every year since it started in 2000, all because its founders understood the second principle of the whuffie factor: **Whuffie only grows when you participate genuinely in a community, listening and integrating feedback.**

Art students Jake Nickell and Jacob DeHart met in 1999 after entering an online T-shirt submission contest. They decided it was such a great idea for promoting blooming artists that they should launch a website that held weekly contests: They would pay the winning artist $500 in cash and sell the winning T-shirt designs to pay for the website. The idea caught on so rapidly that there are now six weekly winners chosen out of an average of seven hundred weekly submissions. Each winner receives up to $12,500.

The artist submits an original design through the website, Threadless.com, then other community members vote on all of the submitted designs until the most popular ones bubble up to the top. Once the best are chosen, the winning designs are manufactured in limited quantities. Everyone seems to win in the Threadless community: Winning artists get money and notoriety, T-shirt lovers get to choose the designs they want, and Threadless makes money and continues to grow.

Sitting down with Jeffrey Kalmikoff, the head of operations, and Jake Nickell, the cofounder and CEO, to talk about the Threadless community is like sitting down with two of the thousands of members of the Threadless community. There is no air of importance or sign of their extreme rocking success. They are just a couple of really nice, humble guys who love what they are doing. Oh . . . and they happen to run one of the coolest companies on the planet. But Jeffrey and Jake aren't too concerned about being popular or making a bunch of money. That's not what they focus on. They don't like to disclose numbers. They don't talk about growth. Instead, everywhere I've witnessed them talk about Threadless.com, they have focused on their community. They are more concerned with the health and happiness of their customers and community than with being one of the coolest companies on the planet.

A healthy community for Jeffrey and Jake means that the members of Threadless continue to benefit from their interaction with the company. At the South by Southwest Interactive conference in 2006, Jake said it all: "The community could kill Threadless. If the community thinks we deserve to die, we probably deserve to die." In other words, if the members of the community are no longer benefiting from their interactions, they will go elsewhere and Threadless will no longer exist.

The folks at Threadless understand that the success of their business is predicated on the happiness of their community. So they put the happiness of their community first. As they have grown the company, the prize money for winning designs has increased. They've added all sorts of ways for people to participate. Rewards don't just go to winning designers but to a much wider part of the community. Those who submit photos of themselves wearing Threadless T-shirts get discounts on future purchases. Threadless also prints limited runs of T-shirts with a gold label; if you're lucky enough to get one, then your next T-shirt is free. There is also a club that you can subscribe to where you get a very limited edition tee every month for twelve months.

Why is being part of the Threadless community so addictive? Because of the time and attention Jake and Jeffrey spend on the details of community, which stems from their being part of the community they serve. They interact in the Threadless.com forums, read blog posts and comments from community members (both on the Threadless.com site and off), submit designs to be voted on, answer support e-mails, and throw in-person events and meetups to get to know their community members face-to-face. They are obsessed with getting to know as many of their community members as possible. They don't just speak to the community, they *live* in the community.

Threadless is the epitome of a company that is part of the community it serves. Jeff and Jake personify the central lessons about community at the heart of this chapter: They understand their community innately, they work to build relationships with it, and they are forever obsessing about being the kind of company that delivers on their promises (their internal motto is *Our project is not good enough,* which means to them that they should always be seeking to improve the customer experience in order to stay relevant). They get out of the office to experience the world, continue to build the whuffie of others by providing a tool for artists to display their work, avoid promoting themselves, and deposit more than they withdraw from their community interactions.

Threadless has more whuffie than it knows what to do with, so its founders keep giving it away by transferring their success to their community members through bigger prizes, offering more exposure for artists, and lowering the prices of T-shirts.

THE KEY TO BUILDING A COMMUNITY

Identifying who your community is isn't easy. The key, as Jeff and Jake demonstrate, is to build it from the ground up. There are no guidebooks for developing communities or maps for locating them. Even more confusing, there is rarely one "community." Your customers come from a variety of backgrounds, interests, and experiences and gather in multiple communities related to how they interact with your business.

If, for example, you make a running shoe for long-distance runners, some customers will participate in world triathlons, and others will be members of casual running clubs. Your most influential customers might be professional athletes or trainers. Perhaps you even have a large group of teenage customers who like your shoe for style. Obviously, each of these groups of customers hangs out in very different communities. The way you build relationships is very different for each group.

Don't think about a bigger demographic group as you begin to figure out who you serve. Instead, think about individual customers with real feelings, interests, interactions, relationships, likes, dislikes, hopes, dreams, and struggles. It might be someone close to you or even *be* you.

Thinking this way is counterintuitive to what is taught in business school about psychographic market segmenting and mass marketing. It may be frightening to think about having only one customer! If you only think about one customer, will you run the risk of alienating all of the rest? You don't want to limit your options, right?

Well, yes, in fact, you do.

Remember that what we are talking about here are *relationships,* and it is hard enough to have a relationship with one person, let alone a market segment of people. Plus, there is plenty of research that backs up the success of companies focused on solving a problem for one customer.

Author, researcher, and speaker Marcus Buckingham points out that Wal-Mart focuses on one person—she lives paycheck to paycheck and has her hands full with kids. She requires an inexpensive and efficient shopping experience.[1] Buckingham says that this customer is a real person, not a profile. This allows Wal-Mart to hone and focus its operations, marketing, and even the way that it lays out its store on that one customer. Wal-Mart employs greeters to help point the busy customer in the right direction. It focuses on buying bulk at the lowest price possible in order to offer savings for its cost-conscious customers. The company's marketing focuses on its low prices and the ability of this discerning customer to do price comparisons and shop smarter.

Many other big companies readily identify their core customer and core focus. The core customer for Virgin Mobile is focused on fun and wants value for her money because she is just entering her career. Consequently, Virgin offers products like low-price, pay-as-you-go phones with really cool ringtones rather than BlackBerry-like business devices. Google is focused on the searcher who needs to find something fast. Because of that, the company concentrates on processing power and getting more accurate results. The other search engines, like Yahoo!, focus on ad revenue in order to maximize space for their advertising customers, but Google strives to satisfy the core searchers by keeping the results targeted on their needs and ensuring quick page loads.

Even for those companies that ultimately became everything for everyone—in other words, their audience is now broad enough to be defined as mainstream—if you took a step back in time, you would discover a core offering to a core customer. Amazon.com, the online retailer that now offers makeup, clothing, cars, and electronics, started out focused on the book aficionado who is interested in more than just current "bestsellers." As the number of Amazon customers grew, so did what they wanted to buy online. Amazon's product lines expanded as its customers grew more comfortable with ordering online and started to demand a wider selection of products. Amazon did an excellent job meeting the needs of the book community, building whuffie—earning trust through lower prices and good service—so asking this community to trust Amazon to deliver the same service on an expanding number of categories was an easy leap.

Amazon zeroed in on the individual first, getting to know

more about his or her needs over time as the relationship deepened. Amazon built whuffie with its core audience of book lovers—many of them influencers—and as the word spread that Amazon had great service and selection, more came. As more customers visited the site to buy books, Amazon started testing other items like movies and electronics, categories that appealed to this expanding community. The company involved its community in helping one another make better buying decisions by implementing peer reviews of books and products. As Amazon gained more and more whuffie in the marketplace, attracting a wider audience, it could add more categories to its offerings. By starting with a strong core and moving outward, Amazon has built one of the strongest online businesses today.

Trying to figure out who your potential customer is used to be measured through demographics—or segments of the population narrowed by age, sex, religion, geography, income, and other slices and dices of personal data—narrowing your potential market to a demographic such as eighteen- to thirty-four-year-old single women in urban areas with an income of over $50,000 per year. Then in the mid-1990s, market research got more sophisticated and started to turn toward psychographics—concentrating more on the attributes relating to personality, values, interests, or lifestyles of people—which recognized that not all eighteen- to thirty-four-year-old women enjoy yoga and that companies were looking for people with certain tastes rather than government statistics. However, today we can narrow our markets down to an even more personal level because people often publish their preferences very explicitly in online social networks. Some social media consultants are calling the further narrowing of this profiling *socialgraphics*—the segmenting of people through what kind of groups they join, preferences they publish on social networks, the content of their public wish lists, and what they discuss with their friends in online communities.

Socialgraphics gets a little closer to explaining the buying preferences of a potential customer, although many of my own friends in these social networks would probably tell you that they aren't defined by the items on their Amazon wish lists. I prefer to use more of an anthropological approach to understanding the core customer; that is, taking an actual person who is a customer or for whom the product is being built and getting to know more about that person and his or her needs.

Larry Halff at Ma.gnolia, a social bookmarking website, once presented me with a demographic/psychographic profiling document prepared by a marketing consultant describing the four character types who were Ma.gnolia's core customers: a white male who liked sports and drove an SUV; a white female who liked to shop on- and offline and had a white-collar job; a teenage boy who spent a lot of time on MySpace and liked to skateboard; and a middle-aged white male whose family had grown, who had time to explore the Internet again. I had a good giggle. Basically, this online company had "narrowed" its customers down to nearly everyone who uses the Internet regularly.

I suggested using a more anthropological approach. Instead of merely imagining characters, I poked around the Ma.gnolia community and found four really active customers/community members. I then spent time using social media tools to get to know them.

I first followed the links they provided in their profiles, most often to a personal blog or website. I instantly subscribed to any RSS feed that was provided. RSS stands for Really Simple Syndication and describes the act of subscribing to updated content as it appears on a blog or a webpage. You can add RSS feed links to a news reader like Google Reader, Bloglines, or Net Newswire to be notified of new content on any webpage with an RSS feed. You can also read the content right there in the news reader without ever having to go back and visit the original webpage or blog. Some of the individuals I followed had photos on Flickr, a social-networking tool I also subscribe to. By reading through the backgrounds of the individuals, I discovered that two of the community members were graphic designers who really loved Mac products. They followed blogs like Engadget and tended to post blog entries that described new Mac programs. One of these designers was also a fan of websites built on Rails, a programming language. Our client ran a site built on Rails. The other two community members were also fans of Mac products, but one was a celebrity gossip blogger (as well as frequent restaurant reviewer, fashion hound, and foodie) and the other one was very involved in nonprofit fund-raising. Both blogs revealed tons about these members' passions.

I "friended" these four community members of the Ma.gnolia site and started to interact with them through the content they were producing. We started to chat back and forth and found that we had a lot in common—we all used Mac computers and enjoyed good design online. I also found out that three of them were foodies and shared my taste in restaurants. I introduced all four to Larry and Todd of Ma.gnolia so they could direct any feedback directly to the source, which all of them really appreciated. I explained transparently that I was on a hunt to find out more about the members of the community and how the site could better suit their needs. I got a flood of enthusiastic suggestions, all of which I copied the site owners on, who started to interact personally with the community members. Larry and Todd were able to build strong relationships with all four of these community members, giving them roles as administrators on Ma.gnolia and making them featured linkers to help them connect to other members in the community. The four of them not only blogged about this interaction with Ma.gnolia, but they also continued to tell the story to their networks of contacts online—in chat rooms, wikis, and e-mail—and in person at events, bringing these new contacts into the Ma.gnolia community.

I didn't create a new document that described these new character types because these were people, not characters, who Larry could interact with directly, and who were providing great feedback and had unique needs. Once Larry made that connection, he started to make more, building up individual relationships within his community. As Larry got more involved, Ma.gnolia's whuffie grew.

By building relationships with individuals—real people— you don't aim at a target, you make a connection. A target doesn't build your whuffie, but a real connection does. A target doesn't tell friends to try out your website, but a real connection does. You build these connections one at a time, which will turn into four and then forty and then four hundred and so on. Creating profiles and sweeping generalizations about people doesn't lead to positive interactions, it leads to impersonal, top-down transactions. Finding and meeting your real community members will help you understand and serve your community and build you the kind of whuffie you need to succeed.

USING SOCIAL MEDIA TO CREATE WHUFFIE AND SERVE YOUR COMMUNITY

Once you've identified your community, being part of it means interacting on a peer level, not as a corporate evangelist or sales professional. It also means that you interact on a day-to-day basis with that peer, building individual relationships for the purpose of learning, experiencing, and bonding in positive ways. It means that you drop all agendas from your interactions; you are not waiting for the perfect moment to pitch your product or close a deal. You are just another community member. You, therefore, have to take off your business hat and put on your customer hat. You need to be a customer evangelist, not a corporate evangelist. What this doesn't mean is evangelizing your company to your customers. It does mean evangelizing your customers to your company by intimately knowing their concerns and needs.

Blogging, vlogging, and podcasting, Twitter, wikis, social bookmarking, forums, and face-to-face events are some of the best ways to use the new social media to interact with and serve your community.

BLOGGING

To blog or not to blog, that is the question. A corporate blog can, of course, be a really amazing way for your customers and potential customers to find out about you and your team. It can also be a great way to highlight community members who are raising the social capital of others, furthering good causes, and providing useful information for your customers and making deposits in their whuffie bank. A really great example of this is the blog by NetSquared, a company that helps nonprofit organizations leverage Web 2.0 tools for building community and raising money and awareness. Its blog concentrates on highlighting the great work of those nonprofits using the tools effectively, as well as the Web 2.0 companies that are helping nonprofits.

A blog requires dedication. And it is much better if it is posted to by multiple members of the company and not just the marketing department. General Motors has its vice chairman of global product development, Bob Lutz, blogging, even though he describes himself as merely a seasoned "car guy" who understands people who love cars. If you can't keep up with a post every day or so, and very few team members make a commitment to regular posting, you are better off not doing it. However, there is real value in blogging; if you make the leap, here are some tips for you:

- **CHOOSE A PLATFORM.** There are several blogging platforms you can use. Some of the most popular ones are Blogger (hosted), Wordpress (hosted or installable), Typepad (hosted), and Drupal (installable). The benefits of a hosted blog platform are that you don't need to learn how to install software to a web server and there are usually multiple templates to choose from. Hosted blog platforms, therefore, are the simplest to use. The installable platforms, however, allow for more customization and control of your blog. You can get a designer to customize the look of your blog and add any features you need to make it more interesting. Wordpress and Drupal are also both open-source software, which gives you the option of having plug-ins, widgets, and add-ons—additional programs done by third-party developers that can pull in information from other websites like Flickr, Facebook, and Twitter. Using the open-source platforms, such as Wordpress and Drupal, gives you the advantage of having a large community of support available for building your blog. Because so many independent software developers have worked in the code already, it is easier to find someone to help you develop your blog template.

- **SET UP YOUR RSS FEED.** People reading your content will most likely be subscribing to your RSS feed. Feedburner, an online tool that helps you manage and keep track of your RSS feed, is a great tool for "pimping out" or adding features to your RSS feed with social bookmarks, photos, and other tools. You can also use Feedburner to track excellent RSS feed statistics.

- **TRACK THE CONVERSATION.** Follow those who talk about your company and/or link to your blog through Technorati, a blog tracking and searching site, and Google Blogsearch. Just type your blog or company URL into the search box.

You can also track these updates as they come in by subscribing to the RSS feed from the search results.

- **HAVE A CORPORATE BLOGGING POLICY.** This should include loose guidelines and tips for everyone in your company who is blogging. Try not to be too rule heavy, but make it clear what should not be written about on the blog. Remember that you need to be open and authentic on the blog, so some self-critical analysis may be in order. Don't stifle "bad news." One of the earliest templates that many people use as a model is the Sun Microsystems blog. Its blog guidelines can be found on its website at http://www.sun.com/communities/guidelines.jsp.

- **LINK TO OTHER BLOGS.** Blogging is more about raising the whuffie of others rather than you. The more you link to other blogs and drive traffic to them, the better you will be received by the wider blogging community. Instead of just talking about what you and your company are doing, talk about interesting things you have found on other blogs. Point out other companies that illustrate what you believe in, and if you find customers with blogs, highlight them. Links equal love in the blogosphere and the more love you give, the more you will receive.

- **READ AND INTERACT WITH OTHER BLOGS FREQUENTLY.** Really effective bloggers read and comment frequently on other blogs. Subscribe to and read as many blogs as you possibly can. Use a blog reader like Bloglines, Netvibes, Google Blogreader, or the like to fill your feeds with blogs by your community members, competitors, people who write about your industry, blogs that cover topics that are ancillary to your work, blogs that are just interesting, and so on. When people comment on your blog, they will often leave a blog address. Subscribe to them, too.

Oodles of great books are available to get more in-depth tips on blogging. *Naked Conversations* by Shel Israel and Robert Scoble and *The Corporate Blogging Book* by Debbie Weil are good primers.

VLOGGING AND PODCASTING

Vlogging or videoblogging can be an even more interesting and in-depth way to show the real personality of you and your company. But they are time-consuming to produce and edit, as is podcasting. The results, however, can be very rewarding. Being able to see and hear brings people closer to you.

Gary Vaynerchuk, for example, gets excellent results from the Wine Library TV video blog. Gary is entertaining, provides useful content, and keeps the videos nice and short for easy consumption. They help grow his whuffie and drive the success of his business.

Another terrific execution can be found at Willitblend.com, the video blog of commercial and home blender manufacturer Blendtec, Inc. Each episode surrounds the question "Will it blend?" and is a humorous test of the company's blenders' capabilities. Blendtec has blended everything from glow sticks to a video camera, but the company's popularity really shot up when it blended an iPhone, putting it in its industrial-strength blender and hitting puree shortly after its market release, which was a great way to create buzz. Blendtec does an excellent job showcasing its product and makes the videos memorable by adding humor to the mix (no pun intended).

Figuring out what content to produce is the fun part. Making it compelling is hard. Some suggestions for what content to produce for your videoblog or podcast are:

- Interviews with interesting people in your industry.

- Interviews with and stories about people from your customer community.

- Tips and tricks. For example, if you are a company producing outdoor gear, you could do a weekly show on good trails or tips for outdoor survival.

- Screencasts. Produce instructional videos that show the activity on your desktop or how-tos for your product lines.

- Generic advice. If you are a business consultant, you could do a show a week on topics like improving presentation skills, getting things done, or handling difficult professional situations. You will begin establishing yourself as an expert and then be better positioned to charge more for personal coaching when people hire you.

- Tours of your office and facilities. If you have multiple locations, interview the employees at each location.

- Support local community events or raise money for charity. If you are doing great stuff that changes the world, use your videoblog or podcast to explore this area and promote others doing great work. Videoblogs can be very instrumental in movement making.

Generally, viewers don't have much more than three to six minutes' worth of attention to give to any videoblog or podcast. Good editing and transitions help get people to become subscribers.

As you open and close, the video or podcast needs to include credits and some music. Great royalty-free music (i.e., music that you can use for a one-time fee or for free with attribution), can be found online at Magnatune, Mobygratis.com, Stockmusic.net, and MP3.com. If you want to use photography, you can search Creativecommons.org or Flickr for photos licensed by Creative Commons. It's also a good idea to contact the photographers to confirm it is cool with them if you use their work commercially. iStockphoto.com also has great photography that you can license for use cheaply and without hassle. The trick is to be as creative as possible.

For video production, I use iMovie on my Mac to edit, but many people swear by FinalCutPro. iMovie is ideal because it is inexpensive and quite simple to learn, but FinalCutPro has more features if you want to create highly produced videos. It may be worth the investment to learn how to use both of them if you are serious about video. Garage Band on the Mac is great for editing and producing podcasts. On the PC, Audacity is great for editing and producing.

For distribution, Apple's iTunes allows for anyone to add their podcasts or videocasts so that people can transfer your content to their iPods. You can also host your videos on a myriad of free websites including Youtube.com, Google Video, Blip.tv, Viddler.com, Vimeo.com, and Revver.com.

Once again, there are loads of great resources both in print and online for learning how to videoblog or podcast. I would highly recommend the book *Secrets of Videoblogging* by Michael Verdi, Ryanne Hodson, Diana Weynand, and Shirley Craig.

TWITTER

Twitter, a tool for sending short messages, can be an amazingly powerful platform for connecting with your community and driving traffic to websites. Having an event? Tweet it out! Launching a new product? Tweet it out!

The key to Twitter is that the level of listening you do in addition to talking helps you build your whuffie (aka social capital). The more you interact on Twitter, the more people will interact with you, which attracts other users to you as well. Tony Hsieh, CEO of Zappos, one of the biggest online shoe stores in the United States, discusses his use of Twitter:

> You send an SMS text message to Twitter with your note, and your message will be automatically broadcast (like CB radio) to whoever is choosing to follow you (your friends). If people don't care what you're doing, they won't follow you, so don't worry about sending out trivial messages.
>
> At first, it will seem really weird and unnatural for you to do this, but just trust me on this one. You will find

that it's actually a really good way to stay in touch with all your friends and know what's going on in their lives.

... I was flying in to the Vegas airport, and I twittered "Just landed in Vegas airport." I would have never texted anyone that message, but in the Twitter culture, that's exactly what you're supposed to do. It just so happened that someone on my Twitter network was about to fly out of Vegas, so we met up at the airport bar and had a drink. I would have never known otherwise that this person was at the airport, nor would I have ever sent him a text message or called him that I had just landed.[2]

I love this story because it shows exactly what Twitter can do for you: accelerate serendipity. Tony has embraced Twitter in the way that I described as becoming part of the community—to become a peer whom people can trust and connect with on a deeper level. Tony connects with his Twitter friends beyond creating a company/customer relationship. He actually relates to others on a human level, building his whuffie a great deal.

There are no "rules" about what you should tweet out. It is important that you balance the "outbound" with the "inbound"; in other words, the announcements with the conversations. Zappos and JetBlue are two companies that are popular tweeters. Here are some ways that you can build your whuffie through Twitter, based on the methods that these companies have employed:

- Share personal reflections about your company, product, service, and brand. When you offer your personal thoughts, you open yourself up to real conversations with customers and create trust.

- Discuss events—both your own and other events your audience may find interesting. By talking about your own events as well as others, you provide a service to your followers that finds events that will interest them and if they interest you as well, this provides a way to meet your followers.

- Contests ("The first three people who answer this trivia question get . . .") drive more followers and interest in what you tweet.

- One of the conventions of having a conversation in public is to reply to someone's comment by using @twittername at the beginning of a message. For instance, Tony at Zappos could say to me, "@missrogue I found that episode of Mad Men to be the best." This indicates that Tony is actually following what I say and makes me feel important.

- Another Twitter convention is to use direct replies that are sent privately. You do this by using "d twittername" at the beginning of a message. So JetBlue could respond to me by saying "d missrogue I'm sorry to hear you are having a bad day. So am I." This helps me feel even more important to the company and creates deeper bonds because Morgan at Jet-Blue has taken the time out of his day to respond to me privately. This is helpful to answer people when the response is a private matter or when you want to show concern (i.e., someone reports an accident, etc.).

- Keep new blog posts to one per day at the very most, and you should also promote other people's blog posts that are of interest.

- Announcements—if it is interesting, tweet it.
- OHs, which stands for overheards. If someone says something funny that could be entertaining if repeated, type "OH: 'Repeat the funny message here.'" For instance, one of my favorite overheards was, "OH: 'Teamwork is coated in BBQ winsauce.'"
- Help spread fun Internet memes or jokes. Quite often, people will post links to funny videos and photos for people to follow. Just because you are tweeting from a corporate account doesn't mean you lack a sense of humor. These tweets are entertaining and show your fun side. Feel free to be playful. It's a playful medium.
- Lyrics and quotes—famous quotes are entertaining for your followers. Picking good quotes from industry leaders that align with your company philosophy is a double bonus.
- Links to media you create—video is fun, podcasts, perhaps interviews that are posted online about you, and so on.
- Shout-outs—@twittername rocks! Thanks for the great link: http://insertlink.com. These make people feel great, too.
- Tweets that make people laugh are awesome, but tweets that make people think are even better.

Zappos and JetBlue are very good at providing all of the preceding types of tweets. Both companies do a great job of balancing promotional tweets ("View this month's selection of first-run movies from Fox InFlight Premium Entertainment" and "Got lots of twitters about our new beta site http://zeta.zappos.com") with personal ones ("The term 'Interwebular Chronicle' makes me laugh" and "At Vegas airport now, waiting a couple of hours until my flight to San Jose, CA") with conversational tweets ("@laughingsquid Thanks! Just wait until our new terminal at JFK opens!" and "@wisekaren I'm wearing Donald Pliner shoes to the wedding"). They also have fun contests ("I want to meet more customers. On Monday, I will select a random @zappos follower for free trip for 2 to Vegas" and "Two days left to win two trips on JetBlue to 'The Simpsons Movie' premiere in LA") to help increase their follower numbers and keep people reading.

Much like blogging, Twitter takes time. You have to pay attention to what your followers are saying and show that you are listening. There *are* ways to minimize the work and keep up-to-date, though:

- Run a Twitter application on your desktop that helps manage and track your incoming and outgoing tweets. For desktop clients, go to the Twitter support wiki at http://twitter.pbwiki.com/Apps. My favorites are Twhirl, TweetDeck, and Twitterific. All three of these automatically stream incoming tweets from the people you follow and alert you when someone sends a public @yourtwittername as well as a private d yourtwittername to you. They run on your desktop so you don't have to keep going back and refreshing your Twitter page in your web browser.
- Take Twitter on the road! If you have an iPhone, there are great sites like Pockettweets or the Twitter mobile site. You can also just send your text messages to 40404. That's pretty simple. Check out the apps page again for more options on other phones like BlackBerries.

- Keep track of who is talking about you, so you can reply back! With Tweetscan you can track all sorts of keywords there as well as watch who is replying to you (there is also a tab on the main website for your replies). You can even plug the results into your RSS feeds.
- Put a Twitter widget on your blog. A widget is a small application that pulls in the content from one website, in this case Twitter, and displays it on another website, in this case your blog. Widgets usually look like small boxes that can be posted in your sidebar along with your website menu.
- Hook up a Twitter widget to your Facebook page. Only update your status in one place and have it show in multiple places. You can find details on Explore.twitter.com, where there is also a great listing of fun apps to use with Twitter. Watch out, though. It's totally addictive!
- Use Twitter's track feature to find people who may be an interesting match for your community outreach. Some companies, like Dell, track keywords like "Dell" to make sure they follow the concerns posted by anyone who mentions their brand name on Twitter. Other companies will track the feedback about their competitors to see how they measure up.

Talking "Twitter" is another layer of learning when it comes to using this complex but rewarding tool. There is a glossary of terms on the Twitter support wiki at twitter.pbwiki.com/ Twitter+Glossary, where you will find that *most* terms used on Twitter start, not surprisingly, with "Tw." Like tweet, meaning one post on Twitter, and TweetUp, which is a Twitter Meetup. But the basic terms you need to know are the commands to put in front of what you are saying:

- D twittername—direct message (not public, goes right to the tweeter in question)

- @twittername—public reply

- Follow twittername—start following someone

- Leave twittername—stop following someone

- On—turns your general Twitter notifications on (on your phone or however you are receiving tweets)

- Off—turns notifications off

- Help—accesses the other commands as you may need them

There are more tips on Twitter lingo on the Twitter website.[3] Last, here are a few other "Tweet like a pro" ideas:

- When you tweet out a link, you can shorten the length of that link with a tool called Tweetburner. Instead of using a long URL such as http://en.wikipedia.org/wiki/The_Fifth_Discipline, which takes up 49 of your 140 character allowance, Tweetburner will shorten it to http://twurl.nl/wpdwy4, which forwards to the longer URL. This gives you more room to type an explanation of the link you are sending out.

- The mother of all places to find everything awesome for Twitter is the Twitter support wiki, http://twitter.pbwiki.com, which was set up by Twitter fans.
- Want to set up a "group" tweet—or the ability for more than one person to send a tweet from a single account? Grouptweet is a great tool to set up. Open up a new account, then go to Grouptweet.com and enter the details for that account. After you set this up, anyone you follow from that account can send a direct message to post. For example, I can send up @whuffiebook on Grouptweet.com, then follow @person1. When @person1 sends d whuffiebook to my account, the tweet will show up like *"person1: content of the tweet person1 sent."*

Now you are ready to tweet like a pro!

WIKIS

Wikis are wonderful tools for encouraging collaboration. They are webpages with an edit button that anyone can click on to change the content of the page. One of the largest and most popular wikis in the world is Wikipedia, the free online encyclopedia. It was built by hundreds of thousands of people clicking on edit buttons and adding their knowledge to the pages and creating a comprehensive resource.

Some basic uses for wikis could include the following:

- Collaborating on documentation

- Information sharing between community members

- Organizing events and thoughts

- Brainstorming with community members

Wikis are best used once you have a bit of a momentum with a customer community, but they are an amazing way to build stronger bonds and get more in-depth input.

Various wiki solutions are available to suit your needs. You can use a hosted wiki like PBWiki, Wikispaces, or SocialText, all of which provide free versions to try out but charge a fee when you want to personalize or add features like multiple private authors. The advantage to a hosted wiki is that it is quick and easy to set up. Installed wikis such as MediaWiki (the wiki software Wikipedia uses) allow you to totally personalize the experience, but advanced programming skills are required to set these up and you have to pay for your own hosting. You can also choose between open-source and proprietary wiki software. The advantage to the open-source versions is that, much like open-source blogging platforms, there are often many wiki designers and developers to choose from if you need to get advanced work done. To make certain you get the right solution, try the Wikimatrix.org website to find the right wiki for your needs.

SOCIAL BOOKMARKING

Delicious was the site that made publicly bookmarking links popular. Previous to Delicious, a person would save a website as a bookmark in his or her local web browser. For people who spent a great deal of time online, creating bookmarks became an arduous task of creating folders and trying to organize all of the sites they wanted to save. If they wanted to share any of the links with other people, they would have to open the page and e-mail each link separately to their contacts. Delicious revolutionized the idea of bookmarking websites. When you bookmark a website in Delicious, it is saved on a website under a user's account name, not in the person's browser. If an individual wants to share bookmarks, he or she only has to point people to a web url. This way, anyone can follow what his or her friends and contacts are reading just by subscribing to their bookmark page.

Delicious also introduced the idea of tagging to organizing information. Instead of putting bookmarks into single folders to organize them, a user can assign tags, otherwise known as labels, to the bookmark. If I like the Zappos.com website, I can save it to my bookmarks and tag it with shoes, shopping, favorite, handbags, and freeshipping. I can also save Nordstrom .com (another shoe-shopping site) and tag it as shoes, shopping, departmentstore, clothes, handbags, and favorite. This saves both Zappos.com and Nordstrom.com in the categories of shoes, handbags, shopping, and favorite, but when I just want to see shoe websites that offer free shipping, I can search under the tags shoes and freeshipping and only see Zappos.com.

Other sites like Digg and StumbleUpon are different versions of social bookmarking. They allow steps beyond merely bookmarking, tagging, and sharing. Digg allows users to vote on (or "digg") bookmarks that members submit so that the most popular ones rise to the front page and can be more easily found. StumbleUpon is a discovery tool that randomly picks user-submitted bookmarks. You just keep clicking on "stumble" and website after interesting website appears.

How can this tool help you connect to your customer community? Well, first, you can find out what interests them by following their bookmarks. I set up a bookmarking group for my client Scrapblog where people could post interesting online scrapbooking tools. Scrapblog readers can now discover new resources as well as the latest news in the scrapbooking community. Many Scrapblog members joined the group and added their own bookmarks, which gives Scrapblog a glimpse into what interests their users.

Second, you can use Delicious to publish relevant bookmarks on your blog. If you are finding really interesting stuff, this is a good way to provide value. Chris Baskind is a blogger who runs a group called Lighter Footstep where members post bookmarks about green living and green business. He feeds the bookmarks collected into his blog, Lighterfootstep.com, where his blog readers can enjoy the many resources collected by his community.

Third, you can add links to the bottom of all of your posts, videos, and podcasts that say, "Share this." People can submit your website to any or all of the bookmarking sites automatically, creating more opportunities for your site to be discovered and read. There are really simple plug-ins, like Sharethis.com, for Wordpress that do this easily. Plug-ins are little computer programs that you install along with your blog—sort of like adding a template or a macro to Microsoft Word to enhance your experience with the main program. These plug-ins, once installed, add extra functionality to your blogging software, such as adding the ability to hook up your photos from Flickr or your tweets from Twitter so they display on your website.

You can also start a bookmarking group for your customer community to post related links they want to share with you and one another. Use StumbleUpon to find interesting sites for ideas and help your customers get their own posts "dugg" by submitting them to Digg for recognition.

FORUMS, CHAT, AND VOICE

Forums have been around for years and are highly useful for customer communication. Over the years, forums have evolved and one of my favorites for customer service is a modified forum called Getsatisfaction.com. My former company, Citizen Agency, implemented GetSatisfaction for Timbuk2 (the San Francisco bag company) in lieu of traditional support forums, and it has been a great success. Timbuk2 uses GetSatisfaction for the majority of its customer support now. The reason it works so well for Timbuk2 is that, previously, the company's customer service was all done via e-mail and over the phone. This led to its customer service team answering the same questions over and over. Even though it had a page on its website dedicated to frequently asked questions, customers wanted to call in. Because GetSatisfaction is an interactive customer service board that displays the questions and answers of all previous inquiries, many of the customers who previously called in now find their answers online. The customer service phone calls have decreased, and the positive feedback on getting answers has increased.

On traditional forum sites such as discussion boards, some conversations may get buried or repeated, leading to company representatives answering the same question or having the same discussion over and over. GetSatisfaction, on the other hand, brings the most recent discussions to the top, which helps people discover the most common topics. GetSatisfaction also lets community members vote questions and answers up higher in the results, so the most popular questions get the most attention. They also use threaded conversations, which are conversations within conversations, and "emotions" to define the general feeling of the discussion taking place. If contentious customer issues arise, a company like Timbuk2 can watch these to keep an eye on the customer mood level in the discussion. Another highly useful feature of the modified forum is the search function built into the question box. If someone types a question that has already been asked, the previous thread will then be presented. Duplication is thereby reduced and answers are found more quickly. Work for customer service people is reduced since they don't have to answer the same question twice.

Chat can be incredibly useful for building relationships with your customers. Many companies are incorporating live chat into their websites so that customers and potential customers can instantly ask questions and have more confidence in their decision process. There are many lightweight, inexpensive (or free) solutions such as Meebo.com, Campfire (Campfirenow.com), and Skype.com, which allow you to publish a link to invite people to come and chat with you. People can click on the link to open the application or website and join the chat in progress. Many start-ups use Campfire to hold weekly open discussions, inviting people through publishing a link to the chat on Twitter and on their blogs for anyone who has questions or concerns to join a company representative in the group chatroom.

Video discussions are also available through companies such as Ustream.tv, Live.Yahoo.com, Qik.com, and Seesmic.com. Users can publish a link through any medium—such as Twitter, their blog, via e-mail, and so on—to a live (Qik.com, Ustream.tv, Live.Yahoo.com) or prerecorded (Seesmic.com) video and invite others to chat either through video response (Live.Yahoo.com, Seesmic.com) or chat room (Ustream.tv, Qik.com). Ryan Carson, CEO of Carsonified, an event production company, likes to tell the story of how he used Seesmic.com to get feedback on his company. He posted a short video asking the simple question, "How are we at Carsonified doing in keeping up with producing relevant events?" Almost instantly, Ryan received several video responses from people giving him positive feedback as well as really interesting ideas for future events.

Being able to reach a company representative on the phone makes customers feel more secure with a company. Wesabe.com, an online community for people to collaborate and share their financial goals, found voice incredibly useful in establishing trust in a very touchy area: personal finance. Cofounder and CEO Marc Hedlund is proud of the fact that his phone number is in plain sight on the website for people to use between the hours of

12:00 and 4:00 P.M. PST in case they have any questions or concerns about the company. He believes publishing his number and being readily available has helped in the growth of Wesabe. Because he is dealing with personal finance, his openness is crucial since people need to trust him if they are going to give him their financial data to manage.

If you're worried about the cost of a customer service line, there are many inexpensive online solutions for receiving and making calls that can be embedded into your website. Open Wengo and Gizmo are two open-source projects that allow you to send and receive phone calls inexpensively online. Skype and Jajah are equally inexpensive to use, but they are not open source.

If you can increase the opportunity of striking up a direct conversation, it is more likely that you are going to build trust with your customers. As Marc Hedlund says, "Talking one-on-one is difficult to scale, but very important for building early relationships."

FACE-TO-FACE

Known jokingly as F2F in the Internet world, face-to-face is still the most powerful way to build connections with other people through events such as meetups, or an informal gathering around a topic; information nights, where you can advertise that you will be showing a demonstration or asking for feedback on your product; lunch meetings, where you invite people out for lunch to hold a discussion around a topic; and BarCamps, which I described before as a "plan as you go" conference.

Tim Westergren, the founder of popular online radio station Pandora—a service that you can use to create your own stations based on your favorite songs or artists—has used traveling meetups for the past two years with great results. Tim travels to places with a good number of Pandora users, rents a space, then sends out invitations and posts a public notice for people to come down and have a conversation with him. He's greeted groups of more than 300 at some of his events. The format? He takes the first thirty minutes to tell the story of Pandora and relay its commitment to helping listeners discover excellent music and the opportunity for bands to promote their music. Then he opens up the floor to questions and a discussion with the community members. He's received amazing feedback and there hasn't been a meetup he has regretted. It's been an incredible way to build bonds between Pandora and its customer community.

BarCamp will be covered in more depth in chapter 8, "Embrace the Chaos," but here's a quick overview. In 2005, a group of techie types in the San Francisco Bay Area decided to throw an event called FOOCamp (Friends of O'Reilly Camp). FOOCamp was loosely based on open-space principles of self-organization. It was a conference with a blank schedule that was to be filled in by the attendees, who would also be the speakers. The attendees filled out the blank schedule, then present their research to the other attendees in their time slot. Only "Friends of O'Reilly," his speakers and authors, were invited to the FOOCamp. BarCamp took the model but opened it up to everyone. There have been over 400 BarCamps worldwide since the first one held in 2005.

Camps can be one night, one day, a whole weekend, or as long as desired. Many of them are thematically based. My former company, Citizen Agency, has thrown camps for specific clients around specific community topics, such as public transit, or developing applications for the iPhone. For the purposes of F2F, very few other formats are as intimate and empowering as BarCamp, because everyone is given a chance to present and discuss topics important to them. Since the schedule is created by the attendees, everyone gets their say in what is presented and discussed. Collaboration is also highly encouraged at Bar-Camps, where I have seen many people sit down to discuss really big ideas.

SOCIAL NETWORKING

Facebook (general social network), MySpace (music and general social network), LinkedIn (professional social network), Flickr (photo-sharing social network), Dopplr (travel social network), and many other sites are part of the social-networking umbrella of wonderful tools for building whuffie as you join up, build a profile, meet new friends online, and start building deeper connections.

One of the values of social networking is that people can draw others to solve common problems. As Facebook founder Mark Zuckerberg pointed out, the power in these networks is their ability to exploit the "social graph," or the connections that people already have. Because of the myriad of communications tools built in, like messaging, events, photo sharing, commenting, groups, gift giving, and favoriting (or marking people's contributions as favorites), members of these networks are able to communicate more frequently and on various levels of intimacy. One can get to know another through ambient means: I can read someone's profile, watch their open dialogue, view their photographs, and track their news feeds to get to know them from a distance before finding a common bond through which to approach them. These public details create all sorts of opportunities for accelerating acquaintance between outlying members of a community.

Leisa Reichelt, who coined the term "ambient intimacy," describes it as being "about being able to keep in touch with people with a level of regularity and intimacy that you wouldn't usually have access to, because time and space conspire to make it impossible. Flickr lets me see what friends are eating for lunch, how they've redecorated their bedroom, their latest haircut. Twitter tells me when they're hungry, what technology is currently frustrating them, who they're having drinks with tonight."[4] The community members grow bridges and bonds, and the community becomes stronger through these ongoing interactions. If you share ambient intimacy with your customers, you will get to know them so well that you will be able to anticipate their needs. If you share your own details in the same way, you will build deep relationships and bonds of trust that will create incredibly strong whuffie.

Using these tools is as easy as your day-to-day offline interactions, only you are interacting virtually and through the various web tools provided, whether it is video, chat, blogging, twittering, or collaborating on a wiki.

Whuffie flows from the trust, reciprocity, information, and

cooperation that moves quickly within these social networks. And each of the networks that operate online has an incredible amount of whuffie to excavate. Of course, you have to follow the rules of the tools and interact appropriately. But by interacting positively and frequently, and following the lessons from this section, you increase your chances of making those connections that will lead to more bridging capital—and becoming part of the community you serve.

6

DEPOSITING INTO AND WITHDRAWING FROM YOUR WHUFFIE ACCOUNT

QUESTION: What do you call someone who joins communities, adds friends, and then uses social media tools to promote only his or her own interests?

ANSWER: A community freeloader. Don't be one.

Now, promoting your interests within a community isn't a bad thing per se. Having strong networks of people is a great advantage to furthering your causes, getting advice, meeting the right contacts to further your career, and getting folks out to your events. However, it becomes problematic when you lose the balance of *deposit* and *withdrawal* in that whuffie bank account of yours.

Now, I don't want to reduce every interaction we have with another person to being a transaction, but, in effect, that's what interactions are. If I ask a friend for a favor, she is bound to oblige. However, if I ask that same friend for ten favors, she may start to feel like I've depleted my "account" with her. Of course, with different people, we have more leeway. With our close friends and family, we have loads of social capital to withdraw from; as our relationships get more casual, the less influence and favor we carry with others.

For instance, have you ever heard yourself saying, "I don't want to use up my favors with him" or "It's time to cash in those chits"? Well, whether we are aware of it or not, there is a transaction—even if it isn't always direct or equally reciprocated—that happens between people. In *The Origins of Virtue: Human Instincts and the Evolution of Cooperation,* Matt Ridley points out that this isn't unique to our culture or even to us as human beings. Tit for tat (and reciprocity) is a common tool for community balance among many cultures as well as animal groups. It ensures that people both contribute as well as benefit in the community.

Transactions are actually a very positive part of our relationships, especially when we do a favor for someone without expecting an immediate return. Those favors add up to a great deal of future social capital.

What I've observed in the various communities I've been part of is the entrance of community freeloaders—the type of people who just withdraw their social capital until they are totally whuffie poor, then wonder why they aren't getting ahead. There seems to be no realization that tit for tat is a useful mechanism for long-term success within communities. These "short-sighted self-interested people are what economists call 'rational fools.' If the rational fool turns out to be taking short-sighted decisions, then he is not being rational, just short sighted. He is indeed a fool who fails to consider the (long term) effect of his actions."[1]

It is rational (economically) to take advantage of people in the short term to make gains, but as Ridley points out, it is often the generous people who turn out to be the most success-ful.[2] This is largely due to the reciprocal expectations of human beings. As support for this theory, Ridley discusses the research of Robert Frank, an economist who teaches at Cornell University and writes for the *New York Times*.[3] Frank has stud-ied the behavior of individuals in all sorts of situations where generosity is pitted against selfishness, such as in the exercise Ultimatum Bargaining Game, and reported that there is a human tendency to reward generosity and cooperation and punish selfish acts.

In the Ultimatum Bargaining Game, one player is given $100 and told that he can share any amount with the other player. The catch is that if the other player refuses the amount offered, neither player gets anything. Logically, the receiving player should accept any amount, as even $1 of the $100 is bet-ter than nothing. However, time and time again, players who are offered an "unfair" amount refuse the offer, and both players leave empty-handed. Furthermore, the most common scenario in the testing is that the player with $100 will give the other player $50. This is an economically irrational act, but shows how deep our desire for fairness runs. The generosity of the player with $100 is rewarded with both players walking out with $50. The selfishness of a player who offers a small amount is punished with both players walking out with nothing. That both players understand the value of generosity and that their performance is based on this idea in the majority of the tests is telling. Generosity is important to human interaction.

So what kinds of actions are *deposits* and what kind of actions are *withdrawals*? Well, it really depends on the community and the individuals you interact with. For instance, most people would probably feel good about helping out an even casual acquaintance with an introduction to another acquaintance. Some may put a caveat on the introduction ("I don't know him too well, but he comes highly recommended," etc.). Of course, the size of that favor also matters to whether the withdrawal is too large for the relationship.

If someone I just met asked me to recommend them to Jimmy Wales, founder of Wikipedia, I would probably feel that was a little presumptuous and would need the person to spend more time establishing his or her trustworthiness with me before I provided an introduction. A misfired intro-duction might hurt my own reputation with Jimmy. But most first favors may actually be a deposit (leaving me with the feel-ing of having done something nice for someone else, I warm up to the person), then start to become withdrawals after that point.

But to speak in general terms about what is a deposit and what is a withdrawal, I present the following table.

DEPOSIT	WITHDRAWAL
Asking for the first favor. Performing a favor for someone else.	Continuing to ask for favors without thanking for previous favors or performing your own favors.
Requesting simple advice. Implementing that advice. Giving advice. Rewarding and thanking those who gave you advice.	Requesting a great deal of advice from an associate for your personal gain.
Asking for a lateral introduction. Introducing others for no personal gain. Sending a thank-you for an introduction.	Asking for a prestigious introduction. Requesting multiple introductions without reciprocity.
Promoting your event. Throwing a great event that people really enjoy and get lots out of. Attending other people's events. Helping others promote their events. Volunteering at events.	Promoting endless events. Expecting people to come to your events when you don't go to theirs.
Telling someone casually about the work you do and your company. Asking someone else about the work they do and their company.	Only being interested in promoting the work you do and in your company.
Creating useful things and sharing them with others. Sharing the process of your work with others so that they can learn from it.	Keeping secrets and being closed.

DEPOSIT	WITHDRAWAL
Creating something with other community members for the benefit of your community.	Creating something that imposes your ideas and will on your community (even if you mean well).
Sending someone an exclusive beta test invitation to your hot new start-up (that they already know about). Rewarding beta testers for the valuable feedback they give (by being open and communicative and implementing their ideas with credit).	Sending someone a beta test invite if they don't know who you are and you haven't previously met. Requesting feedback constantly.
Giving your time to community projects. Encouraging people to get involved in your projects.	Competing with other community projects.
Offering help to a new person or someone who needs introductions.	Only hanging with and being interested in the A-listers.
Being there for the right information when someone needs to make a purchase.	Giving people unsolicited pitches when someone is busy.

Of course, this list isn't exhaustive. The withdrawals aren't all for the same amount and there are many gray areas for people, but you get the gist. What the items in the deposit column have in common is that they are reciprocal, relationship-building actions that *add value to a community,* whereas the withdrawal column is about personal gains that *only add value to your bottom line.* Now, of course, there is personal gain in the relationships, but it is a long-term gain, rather than the short-term gains of the withdrawal column.

And don't get me wrong, promoting your events, asking for connections, and telling people about your company are totally viable, real, and legitimate actions that are and should be performed within networks and communities every day. The trick is, just like a bank account, make sure you have a healthy account balance (i.e., more deposited than withdrawn). As well, much like a personal bank account, it is beneficial to carry a higher balance.

You never know when you'll have a rainy day.

IF YOU CANNOT ADD VALUE DON'T PARTICIPATE IN ONLINE COMMUNITIES

There is nothing that bloggers love more than a story of a company that has screwed up its whuffie by misusing the social media tools available to it. In a piece published in *Forbes* magazine on November 14, 2005, Daniel Lyons wrote:

No target is too mighty, or too obscure, for this new and virulent strain of oratory. Microsoft has been hammered by bloggers; so have CBS, CNN and ABC News, two research boutiques that criticized IBM's Notes software, the maker of Kryptonite bike locks, a Virginia congressman outed as a homosexual and dozens of other victims—even a right-wing blogger who dared defend a blog-mob scapegoat.[4]

Even though the piece was highly negative and questioned by many bloggers as hyperbole, its sentiment was on the money: Blogs and other forms of mass self-publishing enable a wide variety and large number of people to expose the mistakes of corporations where the established media don't always go. And the bigger the company, the more likely the gaffe will be front-page news.

There are several examples of companies whose involvement in social networks and online communities did them more damage than good and are now paying dearly. As they try to rebuild their whuffie, they do so from a deficit rather than a neutral position. Trust lost is far more difficult to regain than not having trust at all.

Dell's story from chapter 3 is one example of a community starting to successfully climb back from being whuffie poor. The community team at Dell knows they have much further to go to regain the trust of their customer community than competitors, such as IBM and Hewlett-Packard, that did not make the same mistakes.

Wal-Mart is an even better example of a company that has continuously made highly unfortunate forays into online communities. Its first attempt in 2006 was a blog supposedly run by independent customers who were traveling across America. The blog characters, it was discovered, were faked and the content written by a public relations firm. Both Wal-Mart and Edelman Public Relations were called out by popular public relations bloggers, such as Shel Holtz and Kevin O'Keefe of LexBlog, who incited a discussion within the membership of the Word of Mouth Marketing Association (WOMMA) as to whether Edelman should be thrown out of the association for its violation of the WOMMA Code of Conduct regarding the unethical practice of artificial word-of-mouth marketing through fake identity creation.[5] However, after a formal apology posted on the Edelman blog, the firm was let off the hook.

Wal-Mart, though, made another foray into social media that also ended in failure. It launched its own social network for teens called "The Hub," which was closed down ten weeks later because of negative feedback. According to TechDirt, a technology market analyst blog, the Hub was another failure that involved fake identities: "The G-rated site with limited functionality had all the makings of a politician wearing a backwards baseball cap in a bid to win the youth vote. So it's no surprise at all that the project has been abandoned. It's not clear that the site ever had any users, though the company apparently tried propagating the site with fake profiles of hip kids wearing Wal-Mart gear. The dead giveaway was that the kids were talking about Wal-Mart clothes in their profiles."[6]

Previously mentioned in chapter 2, Wal-Mart's third strike was for the 2007 group page on Facebook regarding its back-to-school campaign. It appeared that Wal-Mart was aiming this campaign at influencing students on Facebook to buy back-to-school supplies at its stores and online, but what it achieved was to draw nearly 200 posts, mostly "talking about how the retail giant 'destroys communities' and prevents unionization."[7]

Technorati, a blog search engine, tracks over 120,000 blog posts written about Wal-Mart, the majority of which criticize the company's many moves. In fact, Wal-Mart's failed attempts at online community interaction have made it *more* of a target for negative feedback than if it hadn't tried at all. Many of the posts I reviewed seemed to indicate that Wal-Mart's efforts in social media were driving people to its main competitor, Target.

So, to truly become part of the community you serve, you must add value. Using social media to fabricate stories is *not* the same as being part of the community you serve. Wal-Mart missed out on the opportunity to really engage a wider audience and even address the concerns of its critics. By opening itself by being more transparent and letting people speak for themselves, Wal-Mart could have engaged in real conversations and built real relationships with potential customers and, potentially, the influencers in these social networks.

YOU CAN DRIVE A HORSE TO WATER . . .

Wouldn't it suck if you put tons of work into building relationships and everyone flooded to your site or store to check out your product and then *never came back*? Well, it happens. You can be the nicest, most networked social capitalist in the universe, but if you aren't offering anything remarkable, usable, or lovable, your business will probably go nowhere. Of course, you can look on the bright side and enjoy your amazing new support network or you could avoid all of that and work to create amazing experiences for your customers, which leads us right into the third surefire way to become whuffie rich.

7

BE NOTABLE: ELEVEN WAYS TO CREATE AMAZING CUSTOMER EXPERIENCES

In addition to being nice and being networked, which I've outlined in previous chapters, the third way to build whuffie is to be notable. In *Down and Out in the Magic Kingdom,* whuffie is gained and lost through a person's negative or positive actions. For example, acting rude to someone will lose you whuffie points with that person and anyone else who observes your behavior, while creating a beautiful work of art or composing a symphony will gain you whuffie points with those who enjoy the work. The business equivalent of creating a symphony is creating a notable product or service—something that moves people. When you are notable, you thereby sustain and build the community you serve by offering amazing customer experiences and people will connect to you through those experiences.

This chapter builds on earlier ones by developing eleven ways to be notable. What you may find remarkable is how companies have put these ideas into practice in industries that are severely commoditized. They have become very notable and created all sorts of customer communities, raising a great deal of whuffie in their wake.

Many of these eleven can be done in tandem; in fact, the more of them you can implement, the better. By working on developing synergy between them, you'll then be able to create even more whuffie for you and your business, as you'll see about the notebook that is more than a notebook.

But first, here's an overview of eleven ways to be notable:

1. *The dazzle is in the details.* Pay attention to the special touches, the quality of the little things, and the element of surprise when designing your product.
2. *Go above and beyond.* Figure out what your customers expect and where they are getting their most amazing experiences, then go beyond that.
3. *Appeal to emotion.* The way you make your customers feel when they use your product will be the way they feel about you.
4. *Inject fun into your product.* Stop taking yourself so seriously and start having fun. Make your customers laugh and enjoy the experience.
5. *Make something mundane fashionable.* Anything that was once routine and unsexy can be made fashionable. Just ask Method home products (see page 182).

6. *Design for flow.* Integrate game development theory into customer experiences.
7. *Let people personalize.* Customers want to feel like individuals; let them make your product uniquely theirs.
8. *Be experimental.* Try new things, test out new products, involve your customers in innovation.
9. *Simplify.* The easier your product is to use, the faster your customers will be falling in love with it.
10. *Make happiness your business model.* Money can't buy you happiness, but certain companies have gone a long way to helping people achieve the basis of happiness: autonomy, competence, and relatedness.
11. *Be a social catalyst.* Help people connect through experiencing your product or service and you will build oodles of whuffie for making that connection.

THE DAZZLE IS IN THE DETAILS

There is nothing that says quality like attention to detail. Consider Moleskine, a company that makes small bound notebooks that are used by many writers, artists, technology influencers, and others to hold precious notes, ideas, inspiration, and original works of art. They inspire creativity and connection. It feels right. It opens right. Gliding one's pen across the pages just flows. It's the perfect notebook.

But it's just a notebook. Right?

Well, kind of. It is a notebook with an attention to detail that also appeals to a level of nostalgia we have around history. When you buy one, there is an insert that reads:

Moleskine is the legendary notebook used by European artists and thinkers for the past two centuries, from Van Gogh to Picasso, from Ernest Hemingway to Bruce Chatwin. This trusty, pocket-size travel companion held sketches, notes, stories and the ideas before they were turned into famous images or pages of beloved books.

I'm not sure it's the same notebook Hemingway used, but it makes for a great story; and the bound book is incredibly well made. The binding is solid. The pages are stitched in meticulously. The cover has a texture that feels great in your hands. There are tiny details, like built-in pockets and a rope to hold your current page, that make using the notebooks into a pleasurable experience rather than just a utility. It is a rock-solid product.

Moleskine has grown by and large through word of mouth. Moleskine notebooks are to be used in public places. They are objects that strike up a conversation between people. The sheer quality of Moleskine inspires inquiry from onlookers. When I use a Moleskine in a public place, it's not unusual for the following dialogue to happen:

"Nice notebook. Where did you get it?"

"It's a Moleskine. The type of notebook used by Hemingway and others."

"Really? Where can I get one?"

When two people open their Moleskines, the dialogue is even more remarkable:

"Nice Moleskine! I don't know about you, but I can't use anything else now."

"Yeah. The whole thing about Hemingway is probably just bunk, but the quality is hard to beat."

There is a bonding that happens over these simple notebooks that is unprecedented and is what has led to the incredible word of mouth Moleskine has enjoyed from its introduction, captured in the following news article on "The Cult of Moleskine":

> . . . the image of artistic geniuses sketching and scratching at some Parisian cafe appealed to a certain personality type. The word-of-mouth from these memo-making mavens spread. I found my first Moleskine, for example, at an art gallery in Sydney, Australia, in 2002. When that book was filled, I tried to find a replacement in Toronto, but had no luck. When I found a store in New York that stocked them, I was so worried I might never find them again I bought eight.[1]

More proof that Moleskine has gained cult status is in its many fan-produced websites (otherwise known as fansites) that the fervor behind the notebooks has created. There is Moleskinerie, "acquired" by Moleskine in 2008, but started by a fan of Moleskine from Milan, Armand Frasco, and dedicated to connecting people through the creative uses of their Moleskines. Google Blogsearch reports over 334,000 blog entries about Moleskine, and there are multiple Flickr groups for Moleskine, several MySpace pages, a Facebook group, a Google discussion group, a LiveJournal page, and multiple Moleskine sightings in YouTube videos.

Moleskine has done a terrific job embracing the community,

too. The makers are frequently found commenting in response to blog posts, sending fans free samples, posting their own shots to Flickr groups, and participating in online forums in a respectful, peerlike fashion. In other words, they don't sound corporate or have a PR voice; they post using their very own personalities and enthusiasm. They celebrate the "hacking" of their books (people deconstructing them and putting them to uses other than the intended note taking) and even feature these customers daily on Moleskinerie.com.

They also play nicely in the wider web community, posting links to interesting websites by artists, creative types, and writers. Even though Moleskinerie.com was acquired by Moleskine, it still reads like a fan blog, complete with objective posts and the heavy promotion of the work of other people. It has a section that is separate from the main blog for corporate announcements and press releases.

So, no, Moleskine is not just another notebook. It is a living, breathing example of a beautiful product and a company that is embracing community and growing its whuffie along the way.

You really must know your customer community to figure out which details to pay attention to (see chapter 5, "Become Part of the Community You Serve"). What details matter to them? Are they into funny things? Are they into nice textures? Focus on not just the obvious things but the less obvious, and put as much detail into those pieces as you do the main purpose of the product.

In addition to being detail oriented with your product,

there may be the opportunity to add interesting detail by simply changing the message on your website's error page. From time to time it is inevitable that people will encounter an error message on any given website, perhaps when they type an incorrect URL or your servers go down. Instead of having your visitors land on the usual error page—quite often represented by a 404 Error message—why not make the experience of hitting an error page more of a comic relief? Twitter did this in the early days of the service. There was a funny photo on its error page of a cat stuck in a computer with a caption that read, "im in here!!!!!!!!!!!!! . . . . but that file isn't." It worked by making people laugh when they expected to be frustrated and it created a personality for the website that was playful and fun. Lots of people took screenshots of the error message and posted it on Flickr and on their blogs, which spread the word even further about Twitter. By paying attention to that small detail, Twitter became remarkable.

GO ABOVE AND BEYOND

Take a look at the most reputable or loved company in your industry or market to figure out what it does to serve its customers. Then take it another notch up. In the conference world, that's what TED (Technology, Entertainment, Design) did for people interested in the future of technology.

With literally thousands of conferences every year to choose from, people clamor to get into TED. You have to be chosen for the privilege of paying $6,000 to attend. Some would say that making people apply in order to pay all that money takes chutzpah. But I have never heard anyone say they felt TED is not worth the effort or money.

TED is more than simply an experience. It is akin to a religious retreat for the community lovingly referred to as TEDsters.

Unlike other conferences, which choose seasoned speakers and safe topics, TED takes painstaking care in making certain its content is original, that ideas are woven together to uncover more questions, and that these questions are provocative and mind-blowing. There are speakers and subjects diametrically opposed to each other so that the speakers are people doing unique and exciting research that is yet to be discovered by the mainstream. And the speakers rarely disappoint. For instance, at the same conference that Nancy Etcoff presented on the limits and worth of happiness, Martin Seligman, the founder of the study of positive psychology, did a presentation on how to create a happier life. During another TED, Paul Stamets presented a talk on how mushrooms are going to save the planet opposed to Al Gore's presentation on why humans need to save the planet. This variety of explanations for who and how we are creates in-depth discussions that last long past the end of the conference.

How do they do this? Chris Anderson, the curator of the conference, and his team scour YouTube, blogs, posted research, and upcoming books to weave together these speakers and topics. TED's own community, which is robust on TED.com, often provides this content, and its network allows for ideas to percolate among the already turned on and educated minds of TEDsters.

Even more interesting is the way in which TED is able to

achieve this while actually giving away much of its content online. On TED.com, you can watch video of many of the past speakers at TED for absolutely free. How does this work? The TED team recognizes that, although the content is amazing, the value conference attendees get goes way above and beyond the content: It's the powerful network of attending TED. Because of the invite-only status of the attendees, TED organizers get to choose those whom they think will be able to really help one another achieve more whuffie. Sure enough, when people recount their TED experiences, they usually talk about the crazy amount of amazingly smart people they meet and the exciting ideas and projects that have come out of these meetings.

TED also has a scholarship fund to sponsor participation by various grassroots thinkers for whom the $6,000 fee is too high a barrier. The paying members get the advantage of meeting people doing really interesting work that will most likely be the big successes of the future, and the TED conference adds diversity to its lineup.

I was lucky enough to attend TED for the first time in 2008. It truly is an experience and eclipses any conference I've ever been to. The speakers at TED are doing top-notch research, some of it yet to be unveiled, and seemingly unrelated subject areas, such as the psychology of good and evil and particle theory, are woven together in such an interesting way in order to answer a bigger question. At my first TED, the interdisciplinary lineup led to the bigger question, "Why are we here? What is our higher purpose?" The talks were so compelling that I have continued the conversation with other attendees far beyond the days of the conference, spilling into events such as HeroCamp, a gathering of individuals in Houston in October of 2008 to discuss how we can change education to create more good deeds by inciting people at a young age to ask the same questions brought up at TED. This type of depth of discussion and commitment to questions doesn't come out of many conferences I attend. Think about the best experience you've had in your business, then take it up a notch. You should be shooting for just above that.

APPEAL TO EMOTION

There are sights, smells, and flavors that bring on a flood of emotion. These emotions can be tied to a memory or, alongside a story, can be the result of a new experience. The song you are listening to when you fall in love will always bring back memories of how you felt at that moment. The image of the Eiffel Tower may always remind you of that joyous summer spent with your best friends in Europe. The taste of peanut brittle could bring on the feeling of comfort you felt when at your grandmother's. These emotional triggers are brought on through the stories you directly experience, but many products come with stories attached. The aforementioned Moleskine is accompanied by Hemingway's story. When a new Moleskine owner opens her notebook for the first time and reads the story, she shares the emotions attached to the moment Hemingway wrote his first novel. This emotional connection to another person through his story creates a feeling of attachment. The same goes for flavor.

Vosges Haut-Chocolat excels at connecting its customers to

an emotional experience through the flavor of its chocolates. Katrina Markoff started Vosges in her San Francisco kitchen in 1998. By 2007, this creator of exotic chocolates had fifty employees and $12 million in sales. In 2005, Markoff was named one of *Inc.* magazine's Most Fascinating Entrepreneurs[2] and in 2008 American Express and *Entrepreneur Magazine* awarded her the Woman of the Year Award, noting "connection to people and community is at the heart of Vosges Haut-Chocolat. By using exotic ingredients—from wasabi to anise to ancho chile powder—in her specialty chocolate truffles and other desserts, Markoff enables her customers to taste and experience different parts of the world."[3]

Katrina Markoff's creations are meant to invoke a feeling of being part of the culture she has woven into her recipe. Her Japanese-inspired Black Pearl Exotic Candy Bar weaves together a combination of ginger, wasabi, and black sesame seeds mixed with dark chocolate that takes the taster on a journey through flavors that evoke Japan. Just eating one of these exotic bars is an experience, but if you eat one while in one of the Vosges boutiques, the staff will tell you the entire story of Katrina's journey through Japan and her experimentation with the flavors. The Vosges website also offers up the type of information that immerses the shopper in Katrina's experience as travel recommendations are provided and Katrina's inspiration for the bar is explained in depth alongside the description of the ingredients.

Vosges doesn't just pay lip service to being culturally aware, either. Its product line includes chocolates made with 100 percent organic cacao beans that are fair trade certified and checked meticulously for quality. The company's commitment to fair trade and environmentalism is something it "eats" itself, not raising the prices of the bars to achieve this feat. Vosges also partners with several organizations to support women's rights, children's charities, and other causes in the countries where it buys its ingredients.[4]

I first encountered Vosges on a business trip to New York when I was looking for a coffee shop where I could do some work. I saw Vosges at 132 Spring Street in SoHo and was enticed in by the idea of haut chocolate. The experience of buying and eating a single truffle was akin to going to a fine wine bar. The staff member helped me through my buying decision, describing the flavors and the culture each flavor came from before giving me a sample truffle. As I took a bite, I could actually imagine the scene of the marketplace where the chiles were purchased.

Shortly after I returned home, I posted a review of Vosges to my blog. About five days later, I received a thank-you note from a representative of the company offering to send me a care package of Vosges chocolate. Of course, I was thrilled and the package arrived a week later, filled with all sorts of samples.

Vosges doesn't currently work extensively in online communities, but as I found out, it doesn't ignore them, either. It has a couple of videos posted on YouTube of founder Katrina Markoff. There are a few fan groups for the chocolatier on Facebook and a MySpace page with about 1,500 friends.[5] However, it is Katrina Markoff's commitment to worldwide community issues that continues to thrust the company into the spotlight and make it a favorite topic of foodie bloggers and writers.

It matters to this group that Vosges is not only a chocolatier that makes high-quality, interesting flavored chocolate, but that it does so with a conscience. This conscience tells a story beyond the chocolate and makes it into an experience. When you buy a bar for someone else, you can tell the recipient that what she is about to eat is not only delicious, but it is also ethically golden, which means a great deal in today's post–*Inconvenient Truth* era, ushered in by Al Gore's presentation, movie, and book on the need for sustainable lifestyles.

Think about how you can immerse your customers in a nostalgic experience, taking them to another land or back in time, and build it into all of the ways that you interact with your customer community.

INJECT FUN INTO YOUR PRODUCT

As the movie explaining the safety features of Virgin America's airplanes begins, you notice it's completely different from that of other airlines: It's highly entertaining. The characters are silly and include a toreador and a bull showing you how to buckle up your seat belt. The narrator says, "If you are the 0.0005 percent of people who have never used a seat belt . . ." and the bull rolls his eyes as the toreador struggles to figure out his seat belt. I don't know about you, but I usually ignore the safety video, opting instead for my magazine or book or even a nap. Because Virgin makes the video funny and entertaining, I actually watch it. The movie accomplishes its purpose: It gets

people to watch something they already know about and reinforces behavior.

The safety film is consistent with the Virgin brand. Where
other companies put in little effort and produce standard fare,
Virgin takes it as an opportunity to make its customers smile.
Safety videos, overnight flight kits, nonemergency signage, the
safety cards in the back pockets, and even the check-in experience have much thought put into them as to how to leave the
customer with a smile.

Flickr, the online photo-sharing company, also makes fun a
core component of its business. When I log into the website,
for example, I'm greeted with: "Hola missrogue!" or "Përshën-
detje missrogue!" or "Góðan daginn missrogue!" or hello in
many other languages. For various holidays, Flickr created fun
"Easter Eggs"—surprises hidden in their software—for people
to discover. One Christmas, for example, an Easter Egg
revealed a beard on a photo when a "hohoho" tag was added
and a note box was drawn on the photo. Talk Like a Pirate Day,
which happens on September 19 of every year, was started in
1995. It is customary for participants in this unofficial holiday
to insert things like "scurvy" and "Ye" into their language in
order to sound more piratelike. There is also an official website,
Talklikeapirate.com, where you will find links to tools that
will convert websites and phrases into pirate-speak automatically. On one Talk Like a Pirate Day, Flickr hid a link that
would translate the entire site into pirate talk. Phrases like
"Yarrrr" and "Me matey!" were interspersed throughout.
When Flickr's service went down in 2006, it replaced the site
with a coloring contest:

Arrggh! Our tubes are clogged!

Because this sucks*, we thought you might like to enter an impromptu competition to win a FREE PRO ACCOUNT!

Just print out this page and color in the dots. When the site's back up, take a photo of your creation and post it to Flickr, tagged with 'Flickrcolourcontest'.

Team Flickr will pick a winner in the next couple of days, and that lucky duck will get a free year of Pro.

*Seriously, we apologise for the unannounced downtime. We're working as fast as we can to get flickr.com back online.

By entertaining its community, Flickr successfully avoided the wrath of angry customers. It also made more fans than ever as people passed around this funny page and story far and wide.

Virgin America, following the broader reputation for fun of the Virgin Group, was in a good position to enlist its lobbying support when in December 2006 the U.S. Department of Transportation threatened to suspend Virgin's operation on the grounds that the company had too much foreign control. Immediately, the company filed an appeal, outlining that it met the federal regulation that domestic airlines need to be at least 75 percent owned and controlled by U.S. citizens. The situation looked bleak because the Transportation Department isn't under any obligatory time frame to address appeals. Every day that the Virgin America fleet was grounded would be a day that it would lose a great deal of money as well as the momen-

tum and excitement the company had built up with potential
U.S. customers.

Instead of merely fighting the ruling through traditional
legal means, Virgin America took it to the grass roots. On January 17, 2007, it launched the website LetVAFly.com, where
U.S. fans of Virgin could send their e-mails of support for Virgin America to lawmakers and officials in the Transportation
Department. They drove support to LetVAFly.com by talking
to online community influencers like Boingboing.net, one of
the most popular blogs online that reaches an estimated 2 million readers per day, and Diggnation.com, a podcast by
Digg.com founders Kevin Rose and Alex Albrecht that is
watched by 250,000 fans every week. Both Diggnation and
Boing Boing had already been fans of the Virgin brand as well
as big proponents of the power of grass roots, so when presented with the opportunity to be part of this appeal, they
enthusiastically agreed. Alex Hunter, Virgin's head of group
online marketing, reported that it circulated promotional
time-lapsed videos of Virgin's airplanes being painted through
YouTube.com. The videos received over 200,000 views and
were driven to the front page of Digg, a user-voted news website. Within a week and a half, LetVAFly.com had registered
5.5 million hits and 21,000 signatures and e-mails from
supporters. The website even sold a bunch of promotional
material, such as T-shirts and mugs printed with the Let VA
Fly logo.[6]

Because its whuffie was so strong, the results of Virgin America's grassroots campaign were very positive. In March of 2007,
the U.S. Transportation Department granted Virgin America

the license to fly domestically. Even prior to launching, the response to the campaign received 30,000 signatures on a petition and resulted in over 75,000 letters of support going to the Transportation Department. The number of e-mails received at the Transportation Department were so high, the department created an auto-responder that read, "If your inquiry is in response to the Virgin America appeal for a domestic flying license, please know that we are reviewing this matter and will get back to you shortly." Keep in mind that none of the people who participated in this campaign had ever flown with Virgin America (though they may have flown Virgin Atlantic)! They achieved this remarkable goal by connecting with the wider community that knows and loves the Virgin brand of companies and giving them the tools to spread the word that they wanted to fly a Virgin-branded airline alone.

Time will tell if Virgin America will continue its edgy appeal, but the company is making many efforts in keeping its whuffie high in online communities with things like adding Boing Boing TV and the Diggnation podcasts to its free in-flight entertainment options, returning the company's support to the community that helped it win its appeal to the Transportation Department.

The lessons for you from Virgin America and Flickr are that if you ground your user's experience in fun, human language (e.g., saying "You are awesome!" instead of just "Thank you" when someone finishes filling in a form), you can make people smile through their entire experience. If you aim to make people laugh, you *will* be memorable and build whuffie.

MAKE SOMETHING MUNDANE FASHIONABLE

Moleskine and Vosges are sexy experiences: fashion, creativity, and moving across cultures. Method home products are about something a little less elevated: making, if you can believe it, cleaning the house a better experience. Scrubbing the shower tiles will never be the same.

Method is a line of environmentally conscious, fashionable cleaning products meant to sit out in the open, beautifying your home, instead of hidden away under the sink. The shapely clear bottles filled with colorful liquid are designed with minimalist labels and come in smaller sizes so that you display them proudly for all guests to see. This is a huge departure from the cleaning products your mom used with their overdesigned labeling and bulky family sizing.

It's hard to believe, but some of the reviews on People Against Dirty convinced me that people can actually find pleasure in using certain cleaning products. Not to mention that there are fan blogs, written by both men and women, around their love of Method home products. One of those blogs, Method Lust,[7] is written by a Canadian graphic designer, Nathan Aaron, who regularly does reviews of new products and is crazy about the design.

Danny Seo of the HGTV program *Red Hot & Green* actually wrote, "Working with Method is a dream come true."[8] A dream come true? Don't we say that for true love? For the birth of our children? For winning the Nobel Peace Prize?

Well, in this case, it *may* be an exaggeration, but it's a pretty strong statement nonetheless. The truth is that what's in those bottles isn't really that earth-shattering. It's nontoxic and environmentally friendly. It smells good. It looks good. It works well. But it's not worthy of a Pulitzer. What it is worthy of is a whuffie award, if there were such things to give out, because everyone I talk to who knows Method sings its praises. "I love that I don't have to hide my cleaning products under the sink any longer," and "Method makes dish soap sexy." When I first began hearing about Method products from friends, I was doubtful, but the first time I saw the Icon Dish Soap bottle behind one of my friends' sinks, I understood.

In a profile on founder Adam Lowry, Startupnation.com describes the care he took to make his products remarkable:

> You have all your domestic experiences in that house or wherever you live. And so from the furniture you buy to your kitchenware, you put a lot of thought and emotion into what you put in that space. Yet the commodity products that you use to maintain this very important space tend to be uninteresting, ugly, and toxic—and you hide them away. Why did that have to be?[9]

So Lowry and his partner, Eric Ryan, set out to change that phenomenon:

> Our idea was to turn that reality on its head and come up with products that absolutely could connect with the emotion of the home. We wanted to make these products more like "home accessories." We believed there was an opportunity to really reinvent, and in the end, change the competitive landscape.

They made these products not only objects of beauty, but also environmentally friendly, which appealed to the growing sense of earth responsibility for people. At the time, none of the major players in the home cleaning market space were doing this. They were all competing as commodities using traditional tactics like advertising, lowest prices, and buying shelf space. Sure enough, even though Method products cost more and were available in fewer outlets, they stood out as different very quickly and within five years, the company's revenues were $40 million. Method home products gained whuffie by making regular household cleaning supplies a thing of beauty.

DESIGN FOR FLOW

In his 1991 book, *Flow: The Psychology of Optimal Experience,* Mihaly Czikzentmihalyi described the state you can get into when enjoying a task. It could be playing a video game or painting, but time starts to melt away and you become absolutely focused on what you are doing. Many people get caught up for hours in social networks because of the interesting web of connections. A good book will take you away into its world, helping you forget the real world that is functioning around you. Music, especially when one experiences it live or in saturated sound, can take you away into its melody, really connecting you with the artist.

Game developers for years have read Csikszentmihalyi's book as inspiration to help them create the most addictive games possible. It's very apparent when I watch my teenage son concentrate on getting to the next levels of the games he enjoys so deeply. This level of concentration is something that I've desired him to have in many other areas of life. Just imagine if we could design a school system that achieved flow.

What creates a state of flow? As Csikszentmihalyi says:

> When describing the optimal experience in this book, we have given as examples such activities as making music, rock climbing, dancing, sailing, chess and so forth. What makes these activities conducive to flow is that they were designed to make optimal experience easier to achieve. They have rules that require the learning of skills, they set up goals, they provide feedback, they make control possible. They facilitate concentration and involvement by making the activity as distinct as possible from the so-called "paramount reality" of everyday existence.[10]

As in video games, there are levels of skills to achieve. You don't want to start out with high barriers to entry, but you also don't want to make it too easy. As a person learns the skills, you need to be ready with greater and greater challenges. As each challenge is achieved, the player feels a sense of accomplishment. The learning of skills, the goal setting, the feedback, and the ability to control one's destiny are all really powerful components.

How does this fit into creating amazing experiences? Being a Mac user for years, I have enjoyed the ability to learn skills and move to higher levels of knowledge that make my experience even better. The barrier to entry is very low for a new user, but there are lots of hidden secrets to making the experience better. For example I can find specialized applications on the Apple.com website, and there are keystrokes and shortcuts I have picked up from other Mac users along the way. This lack of frustration combined with a sense of accomplishment has made me and many others fervent Mac lovers.

Think about what in your product or service you could build the same flow into. Is there a learning curve to your product? Could you provide rewards and feedback at each level? If you can, designing flow into your product or service could create some addiction to it.

One way to add flow to your customer's experience with your product is to introduce the idea of Easter Eggs into your products. I mentioned these earlier when I talked about Flickr injecting fun into their webpages on Talk Like a Pirate Day. However, Easter Eggs aren't just for websites. Some of the most famous examples of Easter Eggs are offline, such as the example of secret messages being revealed when playing records backward. These are meant to be discovered by users accidentally and are purely for entertainment. Easter Eggs are part of the small details that make a difference for customers and are a good way to get people connecting around your product. One other one comes from Alfred Hitchcock, who made background appearances in the movies he directed. He would be seen for a brief moment doing things like crossing in front of a building in the background or appearing in a photograph. This became one of Hitchcock's signatures, and discovering his quirky appearances became a game for his many fans.

The Easter Egg of popular western U.S. burger chain In-N-Out Burger is its "secret" menu that is not posted in the various In-N-Out locations. In fact, its in-store menu is limited to three different burgers: hamburger, cheeseburger, and double cheeseburger. However, those who are in the know understand that there are many different styles of burgers to choose from, including a 4x4 (four hamburger patties and four slices of cheese), Protein Style (substitutes a bun for leaf lettuce), Animal Style (any burger with lettuce, tomato, mustard, cooked beef patty, pickle, extra spread, and grilled onions), and Grilled Cheese (a cheeseburger minus the burger part). This "secret" menu is printed on the company's website but is not in the stores; finding out about these extra options has been part of the experience of In-N-Out for years.

Easter Eggs are best when they are lighthearted and nonusability essential. They bring a challenge that can help keep your customers engaged with your product or service.

LET PEOPLE PERSONALIZE

More and more, people are demanding the ability to make something their own. To personalize and stamp it with their own brand. There is nothing worse than feeling like just one of the many. Personal differentiation is important, especially to the Generation Y group, who have been told all of their lives they are special and unique. They have also had multiple products and experiences that allow them to customize everything. Build-a-Bear workshop, custom Nikes, and customizable MySpace pages are just a few that come to mind.

Whenever I hand people one of my Moo cards, their eyes get big and they exclaim, "What a memorable card!" Why is it memorable? Because it is half the size of a regular business card. Just as wide, but half as high. Its dimensions are almost "adorable."

But the real cool factor of Moo cards is the self-design aspect the company gives you on its website. Moo uses your Flickr account to pull in your very own photos to print as the artwork on your card. When you hand it to someone, you are giving the person your very own creation. People get to peer into your world a little bit through your photos.

Moo cards are used as both business and personal cards. I've seen people use personal photographs of their family to introduce themselves. The cards look and feel less formal than full-sized business cards, so handing them to a new friend doesn't feel too impersonal. The person receiving the card can turn the card over to reveal photos of the people in your life.

The personal experience from the website carries all the way through the personal act of exchanging cards through the way they are distributed. Occasionally, I'll take a handful of different designs, spread them out in a fan, and let the recipient pick his or her favorite, like a trading card. I've not only personalized my experience, but I connect to others through letting them personalize their own by having their choice of card. Moo founder Richard Moross says this is a common way of presenting the Moo cards, a really great way for spreading the word of mouth about them. Most people instantly decide to get a set themselves.

Richard considers Moo part of the "people-powered" revolution of manufacturing that has been instrumental in getting a community of users and content-driven manufacturers together to exchange ideas and partner for better promotion and distribution and to exchange ideas with one another. People-powered manufacturing, as Richard calls it, is an emerging field in which individuals personalize products and then have them produced by agile manufacturers like Moo. Other examples are Threadless, whose community designs and chooses what is printed on the T-shirts (see pages 118–121); Ponoko, a company that accepts designs for furniture in computer-aided design (CAD) files that it will produce, ship, and even sell for the designer; and Cafe Press, which offers products like T-shirts, mugs, pens, mouse pads, and other promotional items for which people can submit their designs to purchase, print, or sell. Anyone can submit designs and the "people-powered" manufacturers produce the goods.

As people exchange these simple yet personalized creations, they are exchanging information about themselves. The combination of simple and personalizable leads to very high customer satisfaction and Moo card customers are a rabidly fanatic group that spreads the word far and wide.

This is both aided by and reflected in Moo's success in online communities. It participates frequently in Flickr, where Moo has a group where people who take photos of their cards can share them. Moo administers a Facebook fan site, where people post their love of their Moo cards and post their photos. Moo also displays mentions of Moo cards on its site, showcasing many customers' creations. The employees at Moo take great care in participating in online communities widely, commenting on blogs and photos and responding to tweets about Moo cards. It's worked greatly to the company's advantage as its participation has helped it establish deeper relationships with its customers, get quicker feedback, and come up with great new ideas for Moo products.

One of the amazing things about Moo cards is that they allow all sorts of levels of customization. You can use any number of independent artists to customize your cards or pull in photos that you took from your Flickr stream, making the cards truly unique. You also get to play around with the layout just enough to print what you need to say on the cards. Note that Moo also takes flow into account. There are lower barriers to entry for people wanting to just make nice cards, but the company also allows the option to personalize, pulling in photos from various sources. This incorporation of flow and personalization makes the Moo experience truly enjoyable.

The more you can let your customers personalize their experience with you, the more remarkable you will be and the more whuffie you will gain.

BE EXPERIMENTAL

Skinny Corp, the company that runs the T-shirt design community Threadless (see chapter 5), is all about experimentation. They use a method called "Wouldn't it be cool if . . . ," a phrase one might use to describe something that doesn't exist, but would be really great if it did, to come up with interesting new ideas to try out.

One example is the Skinny Corp I Park Like an Idiot project, invented by a staff member frustrated with people taking up multiple spaces or parking so that access to driveways is blocked.[11] One day he came into the office and proclaimed, "Wouldn't it be cool if there were a website where we could put an 'I Park Like an Idiot' bumper sticker on really bad park jobs?" They launched it within weeks. The site hit a nerve and is wildly popular. It sells the bumper stickers in packs of twenty, forty, and one hundred.

Skinny Corp is quite infamous for its many experiments, some wildly successful, some not so, but its experimentation continues to create entertainment and drive traffic to its various sites.

Moo is also an experimental company. The original idea itself was novel: make little half cards, letting people use their own Flickr photos. Founder Richard Moross had no idea how powerful that idea would become; however, because he realized the response to the cards was based on the fact that they were different and personalizable, he decided to continue to experiment in that vein. Every new product Moo comes out with is experimental; they put it on the market to see how it is received, then tweak it.

What both companies have in common here is that they are not only approaching innovation through experimentation, but also through launching smaller, more scrappy projects along the way. The key to being experimental is rapidly prototyping and launching new ideas to see how they will be received, then tweaking and updating as needed.

SIMPLIFY

Keeping it simple is tightly related to flow in that you don't have a high barrier to entry. Products that are too difficult to learn from the outset will always suffer returns and bad word of mouth.

37 Signals is a Chicago-based web design firm that is well known in technology circles for its simple but effective approach to design. In early 2000, it released a product called Basecamp that revolutionized project management software, not because of what it did, but because of what it doesn't do. Basecamp is project management software that "gets out of the way" of projects and supports, instead of overwhelming, users. The experience it gives customers, most of whom are not technologically advanced, is highly empowering.

Project management software solutions have been on the market for many years, so the concept wasn't new when 37 Signals released Basecamp. However, many of the existing software solutions were incredibly complicated to learn and use. Entire training seminars had to be built around software like Microsoft Project. As project management tools went, it had everything needed to keep right on top of a user's project. However, Microsoft Project also had hundreds of other features that made the application very complex and confusing. It took more time to run the project management software than it would to actually work on the projects themselves! Only real experts could navigate around the complex software enough to make use of it. This, as you can imagine, was completely disempowering for the customer.

37 Signals simply focused on the common needs of people running a project, such as to-do lists that could be assigned to parties, a "milestone tracker," and an organizable communications function for group members. Everything else—Gantt

charts, time tracking, complex reports, and other extra functions—seemed to be extraneous to the core needs of moving a project along. The philosophy of 37 Signals is that these functions could be handled by other programs if they were needed. Even eight years later following launch, 37 Signals has added only a few additional features to Basecamp.

The pared-down model has done very well. With over 1 million customers, it is the most popular project management tool on the market. It's very simple to learn and use the software quickly and users become efficient in no time. Basecamp creates superheroes out of regular folks. Where they were previously overwhelmed with features and interface design, leaving them feeling inept, they now get to feel smart and savvy, picking up knowledge almost instantaneously.

And because the features are simple and generic enough, many people use them creatively to suit their needs. With the software getting out of the way of the user's needs, instead of being the be-all and end-all, it becomes the useful sidekick to the newly minted superhero. The sidekick assists the superhero in then saving the day for clients and project teams.

The result is that Basecamp is well loved and oft discussed in online communities. 37 Signals has its own blog, Signal vs. Noise, which is highly popular and boasts an average of thirty-five comments per post.[12] The company's "simplify to empower customers" wisdom has been celebrated far and wide, and it has been able to apply its experience to writing books, teaching seminars, and generally being the authority on these matters. All of a sudden, basic project management software becomes a tool of empowerment and a truly amazing experience for 37 Signals customers.

The important lesson here is that the defaults are set to simple and the options are set to advanced. You should build a product or service that is easy for a beginner to use without instruction, but also allow for people to uncover more advanced options as they mature through your product.

MAKE HAPPINESS YOUR BUSINESS MODEL

I have always taken it for granted that it is the job of individuals and companies I pay to deliver products and service that enhance my experience, not take away from it, which is why I've spent my entire career as a customer advocate rather than as the type of marketer who will try to close the sale at any costs. It has been my experience that if I make customers happy, they are much more likely to come back and be return customers, and, if I continue to make them happy, they will send many others.

But what exactly *makes* people happy? Some think happiness means that you get what you want, you have all of the material things you desire, and you have ultimate freedom; but this is not true happiness. There are multiple studies proving that people who ostensibly have everything their hearts desire aren't any more happy than those who don't and who have to work hard to get a fraction of that.

Martin Seligman, author of *Learned Optimism* and founder of the study of positive psychology, asked why there was so much emphasis in psychology on what makes people unhappy and what leads to negative feelings. He thought that it would be much more powerful to look at ways to increase the occurrence of situations that lead to positive feelings. As the area has gained popularity, so has the search for the definition of happiness itself. What does it mean to be happy?

The American Psychological Association did a study across multiple cultures to piece together the core of happiness and found that four elements were consistent in moving people's feelings from unhappy to happy. They are autonomy, competence, relatedness, and self-esteem. Autonomy refers to the level of control individuals feel over their surroundings. Competence is the feeling of accomplishment that arises when people are challenged and able to meet that challenge. For many, this is evidenced when they proclaim, "I'm happy at work because I feel I'm growing." Relatedness is how connected people feel with others. The first three—autonomy, competence, and relatedness—are how humans interact with outside influences, but self-esteem is how happy they are normally. This is also called a *set point* by Jonathan Haidt in his book *The Happiness Hypothesis*. Some people are just naturally more happy than others and the only outside influences that can move a set point are cognitive behavioral therapy or drugs.

Autonomy, competence, and relatedness are good points of happiness and great places to start when discussing how a product or service can influence levels of happiness. Many companies, such as Wordpress, the blogging platform, deliver customer autonomy. Wordpress gives you autonomy by making it supersimple to publish content online and voice your opinions. Before simple online publishing tools were available, there were fewer tools for individuals to be heard by a large number of people. Online publishing tools give millions of people what they need to boost their autonomy. Wordpress gives empowerment to its users and builds whuffie through this empowerment.

Apple is very focused on helping its customers feel competent through intuitive, simple interfaces. The iPod/iTunes interaction is the easiest music downloading and listening experience available. You plug your iPod into your computer and iTunes opens up automatically, allowing you to configure your iPod playlists. If songs are missing in your playlists, you click on the iTunes store link in the application and you can search and buy music with a few clicks that is instantly synced with your iPod. If you want to load your CD collection onto your iPod, the process is as simple as popping CDs into your disc drive. iTunes has a simple-to-follow interface that loads the music into your library and onto your iPod instantaneously. Previously, MP3 music players required special software downloads to sync the player with the computer, additional software to convert the CD music format to MP3 format for the player, additional software to allow you to purchase and download MP3s from online music stores, and multiple folders on your desktop to manage it all. The simple interface that iPod/iTunes supplied made it much easier for people to manage their growing digital music libraries, and, therefore, Apple won a great deal of whuffie through it.

Online social networks like Facebook help people connect and increase relatedness. Started as a tool to help Harvard students meet one another and organize their social schedules,

Facebook has grown to well over 25 million people who are using the tool to catch up with old friends, meet new ones, and keep in touch with current friends. The company has built many components to ensure several levels of connection, including events, groups, games, blogs, walls (where people can publicly leave general messages for members of Facebook), pokes (a poke is a casual "nudge" one Facebook user can give another), videos, and photos. All of these tools are just another way to connect on Facebook, making it a very popular service for people of all ages. Facebook definitely wins whuffie by helping people connect and build their own whuffie as they meet others.

Businesses *can* and *should* play a role in making people happy since it builds whuffie. As you make people feel good, that good feeling is related to your product or service. Good feelings about your company add up to loads of whuffie. So how can your business integrate the principles of happiness into what you are offering? There are two ways in which you can help people with becoming happier:

1. Create tools or deliver services that help people proactively pursue happiness, such as in the examples of Wordpress, Facebook, and iPod/iTunes. Can you increase autonomy, competence, and relatedness through what you are offering?
2. Create tools or deliver services that *reduce the barriers* to happiness, such as fear, confusion, loneliness, and feeling disempowered and out of control of one's life and the basic struggle for survival (not being able to fulfill basic needs like hunger, security, and the need for belonging). There

are plenty of industries, such as insurance and cellular phone providers, where extra fees and forced contracts leave people feeling out of control and confused. Within the examples of industries where people feel disempowered is an opportunity to create the opposite. How about starting an insurance company that offers clear contracts and open communication and trust with your customers? Or offering a cellular phone plan that doesn't require a contract, keeping customers loyal through great service instead?

To me it seems pretty obvious that it would be simple to build a business around helping people achieve autonomy, a feeling of competence, and relatedness. In fact, many of the web companies that have been successful in the past couple of years have their business build solidly on one or all of these.

And I believe that as people discover that these things are within their reach, they will gravitate more and more toward those companies offering tools to help them achieve happiness. We need more business models built on this desire to make people happier. If you make people happy, your whuffie will grow rapidly.

BE A SOCIAL CATALYST

A social catalyst is the type of product or service that people connect around. In the early days of iPod, the white headphones helped connect fellow music lovers. There was instant recognition that you had something in common. Others would see your white headphones and ask about your level of satisfaction. Conversations would ensue. A peer-to-peer exchange would happen. Although iPods have become so ubiquitous now that this special exchange is more rare, it was one of the ways in which Apple built whuffie with its early adopters. Creating social connections between your customers builds your whuffie.

Are you offering a product or service that is a solo experience but could become shared? Moleskines and Method's beautifully designed containers that sit on your countertop are good examples of solo experiences (notebooks and house cleaning) that have become social tools.

You can catalyze social connections through what you create in multiple ways:

- *Have a compelling story.* Moleskine's story is compelling enough that it actually becomes a conversation topic among customers. When customers share the story behind a product with one another, it reinforces the positivity of their experience with the company.
- *Create something beautiful.* There is nothing like good design to invite conversation. Whether it is a piece of jewelry or interesting packaging on a beauty product, it will attract attention from others who will strike up a discussion on the design.
- *Make people laugh.* When people laugh, they connect. A funny label sewn on a pair of pants or a silly error page encourages sharing of these details. People constantly shared Twitter's aforementioned 404 Error page with a cat stuck in a computer that read: "im in ur serverz making thingz better!!!"

- *Help people look really smart.* Give them the tools to look good in front of others. Gary Vaynerchuk is a social catalyst because he helps people understand wine so that they can go to a dinner party or a soiree and share their knowledge with others.
- *Appeal to emotion.* Love, happiness, sadness, excitement, and other strong sentiments will be remembered and shared. People don't always remember the message, but they will almost always remember the way you made them feel and they will share it.

If you can connect people to one another through the sharing of your product, you will turn a chore into an experience.

THE MOST-NOTABLE-COMPANY
PRIZE GOES TO . . . APPLE

Apple is a company that has put into practice the ideas outlined in this chapter and has thus created amazing customer experiences. Apple's notability is key to its ongoing success.

- Attention to detail is impeccable, from the sounds the iPhone makes when you type on the touch screen to the high-end graphic detail Apple enables in its operating system.
- Customer service is said to go above and beyond that of its competitors with the addition of the Genius Bar at the multiple Apple Stores.
- The packaging is a thing of beauty, making opening the box to your new iPod an unveiling experience.

- Apple appeals to emotion in significant sensory ways. The touch wheel on the iPod is not merely functional, it is also a unique sensory experience. Instead of controlling or pushing the buttons on your MP3 player, you caress the touch wheel of the iPod to find the music you want. Apple's iPod ads very clearly demonstrate the emotional connection you feel with the music you love.

- Apple has injected fun by adding color, rounded corners, and happy graphics to all of its devices.

- The logo itself is a tongue-in-cheek reference to taking a bite out of life.

- Apple is one of the most fashionable companies around. The designs are stylish, and there is a certain cachet to owning an Apple computer, while many other computers are just machines. There is nothing mundane about Apple. I mentioned earlier my graduation from Mac novice to Mac expert over time. The ease of entry to using Apple products and room for my skills to advance definitely shows that the idea of flow is built into the Apple experience.

- The myriad of Apple accessories I can add to my various devices, like skins and laptop covers, allows me to personalize my Apple experience. Although many of these personalization tools come from Apple partners, I can buy them in the Apple Store at the same time I buy my MacBook.

- The only area in which Apple may not deliver as highly is in being experimental. The company is usually very cautious with its ideas, holding its cards close to the chest until it unveils them. However, the employee culture at Apple is highly encouraging to crazy and experimental ideas for future product lines. The company has a way to go to get to be as agile as the Threadless team, though.

- Apple's appeal to a wider audience is due to the simplicity of its user interface. The iPod removed the bulk of buttons that plagued previous MP3 players and streamlined the music experience by bundling the iPod with iTunes and the iTunes store. This simplified the ability to discover, download, and manage your music a great deal.

- Is happiness Apple's business model? It definitely encourages autonomy through making online publishing, video uploading, and music editing incredibly simple to do with its tools like iMovie and Garage Band. Apple also furthers a feeling of competence by creating a simple-to-use platform that slowly helps teach and challenge its users to improve their skills. Apple also scores high on relatedness with its recognizable icons like the white headphones and uniquely shaped phones that lead to many conversations being struck up, which also shows Apple as scoring high in the social catalyst department.

Because of Apple's notability, especially after the launch of the iPod, the company has slowly climbed to being well loved and whuffie rich. The Apple community of users will fervently defend their choice of hardware and software. I've even experienced the influx of angry Apple fans after posting a negative review of the iPod Nano. My comment section on that post needed to be shut down to cool off the angry tone. The iPhone has also attracted a strong developer community, producing thousands of third-party developer applications for the popular iPhone. Within a month of launching, the iPhone applications store sold 60 million applications and brought in, on average, $1 million daily.[13] This is just the tip of the iceberg on the number of home runs Apple has hit because of its focus on being remarkable and creating amazing customer experiences.

The only thing you really need to know is that without having a compelling product, none of what you do to raise whuffie will mean much at all. People will like you and want to support you, but they won't want to buy your stuff. The good news is that if you've done everything right, the feedback provided from people who like you and want to support you will help you build better stuff.

Now, of course, you may go into this blindly, having no clue what the next big idea will be. That has been the case for most of the companies that I can point to that have been big successes: They were just being experimental and came across the next big idea.

This is why it is important to embrace the chaos. Why and how would you do that? Glad you asked . . .

8

EMBRACE THE CHAOS

In my early marketing life, I wrote month-by-month rollouts of elements of the campaigns I worked on, including complex Gantt charts that assigned each step to individuals who were part of the campaigns. Once I wrote a sixty-four-page plan for a campaign for promoting a vodka-infused root beer drink. The client loved it. It was incredibly detailed and well thought out, down to what each of the salespeople would say when asked about the beverage. We ended up following about 15 percent of it in the end. Why? Because as we started out in the launch, we found better ways to execute and new ideas to integrate. We changed our path about twenty-five times before we even launched until we decided to throw out the plan altogether and open ourselves to the great ideas that were emerging along the way from potential customers and others in our supply chain. The end result was a multiaward-winning guerrilla campaign that helped the client surpass all of its goals. The plan still sits on my shelf as a reminder that overengineering a campaign adds stress and is a waste of time.

Embracing the chaos and being open and flexible is the better way to go.

That was about ten years ago, long before Web 2.0 and blogging, facebooking, twittering, and flickring became part of our everyday lives. Although there was much to learn from the marketplace then, it's increased one-hundred-fold in the past decade. The benefits we gained by creating a few dozen evangelists while interacting with customers face-to-face ten years ago have exploded because we now have the ability to interact with hundreds of customers online. Every point of contact equals an opportunity to create whuffie because every point of contact gives you access to many more points of contact.

Embracing the chaos of community means letting go of the need to plan everything and the fantasy that you can control any given situation. Instead of building up plans and structure, you should be building flexibility and environmental awareness into your campaigns. You need to be hyperaware of your surroundings and be able to tap into opportunities as they arise and that you never could have predicted.

Yes, there is great fear in uncertainty. Things could go terribly wrong on a moment's notice. Your intentions could be misread. Opportunities could take a long time to manifest, leaving you feeling afraid that you've made the wrong decision. A community in which you've invested time and energy could revolt and take everyone elsewhere in a flash. Yes, embracing the chaos is frightening. But there is a *huge* upside.

In this chapter I'll show you how four organizations each used a different social media tool to embrace the chaos of community. They didn't know what the ROI (return on investment) was going to be, and there was very little market intelligence to say that their leaps of faith were going to result in anything at all. However, their efforts resulted in amazing outcomes that surprised everyone involved and raised tremendous whuffie for themselves.

THE LIBRARY OF CONGRESS EMBRACES THE CHAOS WITH FLICKR

Beth Dulabahn and her colleagues at the Library of Congress Office of Strategic Initiatives were facing a formidable challenge. The library was sitting on warehouses full of materials— documents, memorabilia, photographs—that were meant to be shared with the public as part of the nation's historical record. But none of it could be opened to the public until it was identified and catalogued. With its limited staff resources, the library couldn't possibly do what was necessary. It was a classic catch-22 situation.

But what if the library could open its collection to the public before it was catalogued and then enlist the public in the work of cataloging? Beth and her team, including Michelle Springer, project manager of digital initiatives, and Helena Zinkham, acting chief of prints and photographs, were well aware of the power of information sharing in online communities, like Wikipedia, Amazon, and even Zappos. So they decided, as Beth puts it, "to dip our toes into the water of social networking" with a small pilot project: using Flickr to post 3,000 photographs from two collections, the Depression era in color and black-and-white shots from the Bain News Service.

Helena had simple goals for the project:

1. Put the photographs where people are—don't make them come to the library. One of the collections they would load onto Flickr had been posted online for ten years and still lacked a great deal of data.
2. Gain a better understanding of how social tagging and community input could benefit the users of collections and the library.
3. Gain experience participating in web communities interested in the kind of materials that libraries hold.

They got all that and more.

George Oates, head of special projects at Flickr, now owned by Yahoo!, immediately realized that access to Library of Congress photos would be of immediate benefit to users of Flickr. She told me, "I've always been interested in how people are creating a photographic history of themselves on Flickr. What if I could have photos of myself and friends from last summer at a beach in Adelaide and have them alongside photos of people from the early 1900s on the same beach? All sorts of really interesting opportunities emerge."

Indeed, it was just such openness to its community that led to the creation of Flickr, which began as one feature of the massive multiplayer online game The Game Neverending. Because gamers were using the Flickr component more and more frequently and wanted to see it developed, the company changed its business model from being an online game to being a photo-sharing site. Then the founders met Joshua Schachter, founder of Delicious, a social bookmarking tool (now owned by Yahoo! as well), who introduced them to tagging. It seemed like a good way to classify and sort photos, too, so they integrated tagging into the core of Flickr. Tagging is now considered one of the key differentiators that has made Flickr so wildly popular.

George Oates and Heather Champ, Flickr's community manager, called the experiment with the Library of Congress "The Commons." The webpage explaining the project was built in a day. While important, this promotional webpage paled next to the type of licensing that Flickr and the Library of Congress implemented: No Known Copyright.

Flickr's copyright levels included All Rights Reserved and the suite of Creative Commons copyrights, which are as follows:

- Attribution licensing allows others to copy, distribute, display, and perform your copyrighted work—and derivative works based upon it—but only if they give credit the way you request.

- Noncommercial licensing states that others may copy, distribute, display, and perform your work—and derivative works based upon it—but for noncommercial purposes only.

- No Derivative Works licensing states that others can copy, distribute, display, and perform only verbatim copies of your work, not derivative works based upon it.

- Share Alike licensing allows others to distribute derivative works only under a license identical to the license that governs your work.

Neither All Rights Reserved nor the Creative Commons copyrights worked for the Library of Congress. First, the Library of Congress and Flickr could not assign copyright to many of the photos because the copyrights had expired. Second, the status of some of the photographs was completely unknown. Third, both the Library of Congress and Flickr wanted people to use the photographs as they saw fit. Assigning new copyrights on behalf of the Library of Congress and/or Flickr was just not appropriate. No Known Copyright states:

1. The copyright is in the public domain because it has expired.

2. The copyright was injected into the public domain for other reasons, such as failure to adhere to required formalities or conditions.

3. The institution owns the copyright but is not interested in exercising control.

4. The institution has legal rights sufficient to authorize others to use the work without restrictions.

This is a radical shift in thinking from a museum standpoint. Many museums rely on their ability to reproduce these photographs for their own income. In the new model, "If you make use of a photo from the Commons, you are reminded to conduct an independent analysis of applicable law before proceeding with a particular new use."[1] This means that people could go about reproducing and using the images, but would

210 THE POWER OF SOCIAL NETWORKING

have to take the necessary steps on their own to track the origin of the photograph before using it for commercial purposes. This license removes the legal responsibility from Flickr and the Library of Congress and puts it in the hands of the person using the image.

There were obviously all sorts of levels of complexity, but both the Library of Congress and Flickr allowed the project to emerge organically. Members of both teams attribute much of the success of the project to their unplanned approach and set out to only learn from the experience. As Beth told me in a phone interview, "We basically made no promises to anybody about how long it was going to go on, what we were going to do with the results, and I think even if it had partly been a blip on anyone's horizon and we'd gotten very few tags, that also would have told us something. The point of the pilot was to learn something about pushing our stuff out and trying to get feedback and engaging with the community. So almost anything that would have happened I think would have had some valuable information in it."

The result was better than anyone could have predicted. When the Flickr team and the Library of Congress team posted the announcement of the Commons to their respective blogs, the flurry of excited response in the blogosphere led to January 17, 2008, press coverage in the *New York Times, Seattle Post, ZDnet, PCWorld, NPR, WebProNews, Library Journal, DieWelt, Newsweek,* and various other international publications. It drove people to the collections, and within a couple of weeks, more than 50,000 tags had been assigned to photographs and many thousands of comments, notes, links, and discussions had emerged—more facts than either team could have ever dreamed.

Nearly two years later, traffic continued to be driven to the Library of Congress Prints and Photographs Online Catalog, creating great interest in these and other collections it holds. The tagging and commenting continue to grow organically, creating rich stories around each of the photographs. Thousands of people have linked up photos to the original news stories at their source, invoking even more interest from the news media on these projects. Forty additional museums and libraries have contacted George to donate their collections to the Commons.

This story isn't complete, as all stories of people engaging communities at this level. These aren't "campaigns" that start and end; these are just the beginning of unlocking future potential.

The Library of Congress was able to build a great deal of whuffie with the Flickr community because it opened itself up and embraced the chaos. It did not know where this partnership would go or what the results of posting its photos to Flickr freely would be, but because it was willing to experiment, it made amazing connections and built a great deal of whuffie. Any future collection the library posts will be greeted with the same enthusiasm, and it now has the attention of a much broader audience than before it embraced the chaos.

THE *WASHINGTON POST* EMBRACES
THE CHAOS WITH BLOGS

The *Washington Post* is another example of a reputable organization willing to embrace the chaos, be experimental, and try out new media, but within the bounds of the brand it has already built.

In January of 2005, the *Post* launched its first blog, by humor columnist Joel Achenbach, called Achenblog. Hal Straus, vice editor for interactivity and community, recalls not really having much of an agenda or an idea of where it would lead: "It just seemed like a natural progression." His inspiration came more from political bloggers than other media companies, who weren't really doing much in the space yet. He was interested in the stylings of Andrew Sullivan (The Daily Dish) and Josh Marshall (Talking Points Memo), both of whom blogged about politics from very strong points of view, as a model for what he wanted to do, but even then, it was a bit of a shot in the dark.

The *New York Times* had launched a technology review blog by David Pogue in November of 2004, but many media companies were still wary of going into territory where conversations could get quickly heated. Questions such as "What if people can't differentiate between our columnists, who are held to strict objectivity, and commentors, who aren't?" were raised. These types of questions were absolutely valid because the market for blogs hadn't totally gone mainstream yet.

But what emerged was something that neither Hal nor his colleagues could have predicted: a strong community around Achenblog. They even had a name for themselves: the Boodle. Wikis were created to describe the emerging language,[2] including terms like Achenbloghogging (posting an inordinate number of comments) and Boddle (the Boodle gone wrong). They began meeting in other places online to discuss the *Washington Post* columnist's posts.

Hal and his team were delighted by the reaction—a reaction that Hal says he couldn't have planned. The *Washington Post* decided to let the community take its natural course as it set out to launch more blogs.

Today, the *Post* has nearly sixty blogs, many of them with healthy communities. The Fix, by political columnist Chris Cillizza, gets upwards of 250 to 300 comments on every post, many of them deep discussions about the topic he presented. Celebritology, another popular blog written by Liz Kelly on, what else, celebrities, gets 60 to 150 comments on each post. On Faith, a conversation on religion with Sally Quinn and Jon Meacham, received over 1 million comments in its first year.

"Not all of the comments are good," Hal told me. The company ends up deleting those it deems offensive. Offensive, for the Washington Post Interactive, means anything that uses hate speech or includes personal attacks. It will also delete the types of comments that could incite riots. The immigration debate brought on many of these.

This type of close attention to the mood of the community is important for setting the tone, especially in the face of hot topics such as politics and religion. The *Washington Post* also requires a login, which further discourages bad behavior. Many online communities understand all too well that when certain individuals disrupt the conversation, the signal-to-noise ratio can favor the noise. Still, there is a delicacy in maintaining the balance between allowing for free discussion and debate versus having a conversation hijacked by someone posturing for attention.

One advantage to keeping the conversation thoughtful is that it has led to a great deal of self-policing in the communities. Quite often when a commenter is getting out of hand, the other commenters will take action before any of the *Post* staff have to step in.

Nancy Kerr, assistant managing editor for futures content at the *Post,* also tells all of her bloggers, "You need to have a thick skin. Not everyone will agree."

There have been two main advantages created by engaging community for the *Washington Post:*

1. It has exposed the paper to a broader, more national audience that is engaged in its content.

2. It also increases the time spent and the frequency of the visits for the *Washington Post* online.

These are both very desirable outcomes when you consider that newspapers make money selling advertising. Higher, more frequent volumes of visitors bring in more advertising revenue for a paper. In a time where circulation is declining for the printed version of magazines and newspapers, this is very good news.

"Community and social networks are the future of business," Hal believes. "As the next generation comes up, you really have no choice but to provide community outlets."

By embracing the chaos, the *Washington Post* grew its audience and the level of engagement with readers. All of this raised its whuffie significantly. And the paper did it early on, so it has a good head start on growing that whuffie with the news-hungry audience.

JET BLUE EMBRACES THE CHAOS WITH TWITTER

I have the same fears as everyone: failure; looking incompetent; negative word of mouth; nobody coming to the party; not being able to pay the bills; being beat by the competition.

Everyone feels fear, even those whom you admire as fearless. It is the way you handle fear that determines how successful you are. The only way you truly fail is by letting fear actually hold you back from trying. Quite often, the negative outcomes from taking a risk are minimal compared with the positive outcomes, especially if those risks include opening yourself up to customers.

I use Twitter as a way to face my fear of failure. Every time I am scared, I tweet out to the more than 8,000 people who follow me. I tell them why I am afraid, but also that I won't let them down by letting my fear take over. Writing this book, my first, has produced many of these tweets. What I get in return is the following:

- People responding with support and egging me on to keep going because they have faith in me.
- People responding with empathy because they experienced similar fears, who often simultaneously respond with gratitude because hearing me voice it helps them know they are not alone.
- People responding with assistance and advice, often really useful information that I can use to get myself "unstuck."
- People responding with tough love, reminding me that I am lucky to be in the position where my greatest fear is me

screwing up an awesome opportunity. The power to succeed is in my hands.

What I don't get are the responses I fear: ones that tell me that I'm weak or that I cannot do this. By being open about facing my fears, I have created more opportunities than barriers, and I have won the trust of many who didn't know me before I tweeted.

I've been incredibly impressed by airline JetBlue's use of Twitter for similar means. It has been very human in its approach to Twitter, not being afraid to laugh at itself and occasionally making mistakes. Take, for example, this public exchange of tweets between a JetBlue employee and a customer on Twitter:

JetBlue: There's a lot of talk going around about corporate rolls in Twitter. Since this IS a conversation . . . What WOULD you like to see?

SarahM: @jetblue, did you mean "corporate roles"?

JetBlue: @SarahM sighh . . . yes first role: spelling

The JetBlue representative and community manager, whose real-life name is Morgan, was simply responding to a correction of grammar, but the fact that she responded is significant. In this exchange, Morgan came across as human because she was able to laugh at her own mistake, and this personal connection helps others feel as if JetBlue itself is more human. Most companies have a fear of seeming imperfect. I've spoken with people who are afraid of having a blog or using Twitter lest they make a mistake. What they don't understand is that it is not the mistakes that matter, it is how the company responds to those mistakes that matters. In fact, making small errors here and there and the acknowledgment of them is actually very useful for building rapport with the wider community. If Morgan spent her time refining and tweeting out only official announcements, the conversations that she is currently engaging in wouldn't happen. Instead, she spends a lot of her time on Twitter having discussions like the preceding one, from responding to small corrections in grammar all the way to responding to larger issues with customers frustrated with the service and delays, and making sure people know she is listening to the feedback.

And the positive reviews for Morgan's tweets and JetBlue's approach to Twitter are pouring in. From the blog Socialized PR:

> JetBlue is in uncharted skies. Morgan [the JetBlue employee who tweets for the Twitter account] and Jet-Blue have shown a true willingness to engage in a real conversation alongside the company's promotional tweets, and I think that's how successful corporate social media has to play out.[3]

And from the well-known social media consultants at Red-Monk:

> i'll admit to being more or less in the bag for JetBlue already, but their usage of Twitter would impress even if i hated them as much as i hate United. the fact that i can

communicate with their folks via a tool i use that's not email? huge.[4]

There are also hundreds of messages from Twitterers messaging @jetblue (the common way to begin a response to a tweeter you reply to is @username), giving them direct feedback, kudos, and ideas. By being fearless and opening themselves up to direct and honest feedback, JetBlue is winning over many people's confidence and building relationships in online communities that will spread the story of their fearlessness far and wide.

JetBlue embraces the chaos by letting Morgan be Morgan on Twitter, and it's working in the company's favor. By allowing Morgan to admit the mistakes of JetBlue and work with people to fix their concerns, Morgan shows how down-to-earth and accessible the company is. People no longer feel like numbers, they feel like peers. And this builds a great deal of trust and loyalty with the members of Twitter and JetBlue. JetBlue and Morgan have gained a great deal of whuffie by embracing the chaos on Twitter.

TRANSITCAMP BAY AREA EMBRACES THE CHAOS WITH WEB 2.0

I didn't know it, but I was about to take on one heckuva heated public services issue: public transportation in the San Francisco Bay Area in February 2008. The prior year, my colleagues in Toronto, Ontario, Canada, had put together an intriguing event called TransitCamp and were written up in the *Harvard Business Review*:

In public meetings, TTC [Toronto Transit Commission] officials cowered as angry riders protested the system's aging infrastructure, from the rolling stock to the stations to the TTC's once highly praised website. As cash-strapped officials grew defensive before a railing public, it became clear that communication was among the most badly broken parts of the system—an impediment to constructive action.

The stalemate might have persisted if not for the serendipitous convergence of social networking technologies, a growing army of technology and transit geeks, and a new, open-minded TTC chairman named Adam Giambrone. He accepted a pitch from local bloggers on how to revitalize the TTC website: Use the geeks' lively networks as conduits for ideas.

On February 4, 2007, Giambrone and other TTC officials came together in a unique live event dubbed TransitCamp. Created by members of the Toronto blogging community, the grass-roots meeting melded citizen activism with crowd-sourcing. About 120 attendees used real-time Web 2.0 collaboration tools to engage each other live and in person.[5]

The structure, or rather lack of structure, of TransitCamp is the most interesting part. This was not a town hall or a structured conference. TransitCamp was built on the BarCamp model. BarCamp is an international network of user-generated conferences. Instead of a preset schedule, an empty grid is posted in a public location with times printed on one axis and rooms posted across the other axis. The participants fill in the schedule as the day proceeds. The audience becomes the presenters and everyone is encouraged to participate. This encourages lively discussion and cutting-edge ideas to emerge. The BarCamp idea was born in 2005 in response to O'Reilly Media's FOOcamp, an invite-only event loosely based on the open-space model, where there is no preset agenda. BarCamp was launched as an open alternative to the O'Reilly Camp as those who weren't invited thought the model sounded like a good one to use. The first BarCamp took place in Palo Alto and was organized in six days between six people. Since the first BarCamp happened there have been well over 400 around the world.

The original TransitCamp took this open and democratic discussion model and applied it to a very process-driven area: government public services. The organizers thought that if they could get Toronto Transit Commission officials together with the local blogging and technology communities with this open framework for discussion, some interesting ideas may emerge. And they were right. The first TransitCamp was such a success that those involved continue to meet once a month until this day with the same unstructured meetings, opening it up to the wider public.

For TransitCamp Bay Area, I chose to do some prescheduling on day one instead of using the pure open-grid BarCamp model. This helped convince many officials that coming out would be worth their time, but the majority of the schedule was open to revision along the way.

One of the pieces that really intrigued me about the original

TransitCamp was making a big point to attendees: "This is not a complaints department. This is a solutions playground." I wondered at the time of the original camp whether this was really necessary. I thought that if the people coming out were giving their time and expertise freely, this slightly authoritative message may have been unnecessary. As the word spread about the Bay Area TransitCamp, I would find out that the message was entirely necessary.

Talk about embracing the chaos! I'm passionate about good public services, but I had no idea how much passion existed in others. As I put together the details and the word spread, I started to receive e-mails and phone calls from both angry citizens and concerned officials. The angry citizens were intent on getting me to add major issues to the schedule, and concerned officials expressed their reticence to attend yet another complaints festival.

I went from being someone organizing an event I hoped would lead to some positive change to being a referee. It was time to implement the wise words of the TransitCamp founders: "This is not a complaints department. This is a solutions playground." The message went up on every piece of material posted on the Web and was relayed to interested reporters covering the event. It was also my standard response to both angry citizens and concerned officials.

I reassured everyone that this would be a productive and interesting event, but in the back of my mind I feared a descent into unproductive arguing and egos. Still, I refused to overstructure anything. I wanted desperately to have interesting projects and conversations emerge. I had a good bevy of ideas on how many of the online tools that we use for ourselves could be used for transit, but I knew I was only thinking within my limited range of ideas from my limited experience. Still, there was no guarantee that the "right" people would show up and the crucial connections would be made.

On the first day of TransitCamp Bay Area, I stood in front of a room of approximately eighty-five people from all sorts of backgrounds, from transit representatives to elected officials to technologists to riders/enthusiasts. They had all heard about TransitCamp through different channels: news articles, blogs, word of mouth, online event-posting sites, and Twitter. With a crowd this diverse, the thing to do is to let them introduce themselves and talk about what they want to get out of the event. So, after a brief introduction of the concept, we went around the room and everyone talked about who they are and what their interest in being there was.

Almost instantly the connections between personal goals was apparent to me. I spent the rest of the weekend making sure those connections were solidified. At the end of the two days of presenting, discussing, and networking, several things emerged and I was ecstatic about the outcome.

TRANSITCAMP BAY AREA BUILT AMAZING BRIDGES

As we went through the introductions on day one, I was blown away at the diversity of the room. Men. Women. People from various backgrounds. Technologists. Elected officials. Transit representatives. Passionate riders. Green activists. There I stood in front of a room of "not the usual suspects" who show up at a BarCamp. It was pretty astounding.

But even more astounding is how everyone adapted to the embrace-the-chaos model of BarCamp. People from all backgrounds took the initiative to pitch sessions, put them on the board, lead discussions, get involved, and help out. There were very rare moments where I had to reiterate the "do-it-yourself" culture of BarCamp.

TRANSITCAMP BAY AREA AVOIDED THE USUAL PITFALLS OF PUBLIC SERVICES EVENTS BY FOCUSING ON NO COMPLAINTS, ONLY SOLUTIONS

Oh, there were touch-and-go moments where I had to step in and be firm, stating, once again, "This is a solutions playground. Please keep it that way." Transit is definitely a hot-button issue, and people get really passionate about it! And yes, there are lots of concerns.

But this weekend quickly avoided getting bogged down in all of those issues and stuck with the exciting possibilities of using collaborative, open technologies, like Twitter, Flickr, and Get Satisfaction, to engage with riders and potential riders . . . and even thinking about doing this *without* the use of technology and just purely being creative. We truly became a solutions playground!

Lots of the ideas were posted on a follow-up Get Satisfaction TransitCamp section.

TRANSITCAMP BAY AREA MADE AN IMPACT

Post-TransitCamp, there was coverage on multiple blogs and in traditional news media outlets. I also received a couple dozen follow-up e-mails asking "What's next?" There was a Transit Data Google Group started that has gone far in convincing the transit agencies not supplying open data to outside developers to supply that data. The same group is hard at work developing a standard markup of transit data so that it can be more easily read by multiple applications. For instance, Ticketmaster may want to advise ticket holders about transit schedules so they can get to the event on time. The standard markup of data allows the Ticketmaster webmaster to easily pull in maps from the various transit agencies across the country without having to reprogram each city. I've also had multiple follow-up meetings with various transit organizations to help them implement the exciting ideas they heard over this weekend, like using Twitter feeds, starting a podcast for people to find out more about their services, and integrating Flickr photos from riders into their materials.

There was also a bit of a reverberation across Twitter regarding TransitCamp. After hearing the tweets coming out of the sessions, several people expressed their desire to throw their own camp in their area outside of the Bay Area.

Several follow-up events in the Bay Area are planned.

TRANSITCAMP BAY AREA EXCEEDED MANY PEOPLE'S EXPECTATIONS

I had several people approach me throughout the event and afterward to tell me that they were not only blown away by TransitCamp, but that they couldn't wait for the next one and they would bring several people with them. To me, that's the hallmark of a great event. Would you tell others? If no, it was disappointing. If maybe, it was okay. If yes, it was awesome. If, as one guy told me, you would drag many people even if they were kicking and screaming, it was kickass.

During the opening talk, I looked around the room to see many skeptics. Those same skeptics were those still hanging around at 5:00 P.M. on the second day, talking excitedly about possibilities. What an amazing sight that was to see!

All in all, everyone involved embraced the chaos of this unstructured event and the results were extremely positive. Since its close I have been told by many attending that they would apply the same model in areas they felt they were getting "stuck" in to see if they could move things forward.

After I helped the transit agencies embrace the chaos, they were able to form more relationships with the developer community as well as engage really enthusiastic citizens who were happy to help in the future. The agencies not only gained a bevy of new ideas, they forged ongoing relationships that continue to this day. They continue to build whuffie in the wider community by implementing these ideas and further opening themselves to more communication, integrating the idea of embracing the chaos into their everyday work. Additionally, by implementing these ideas, they build more whuffie with the people who are using transit every day. BART, the Bay Area Rapid Transit system, announced the release of its estimated time of arrival (ETA) data feed in September of 2008 that made it possible for a third-party developer to build an iPhone application for BART riders. These steady improvements and openness to opportunities that arise through embracing the chaos continue to bring big wins for the whuffie of everyone involved.

HOW TO EMBRACE THE CHAOS

All of the preceding examples require you to not only choose situations to explore but also take advantage of opportunities that emerge from the chaos. Certainly, you don't have endless amounts of time to explore every single avenue, nor should you explore all options. Thankfully, I've tested a few ways to increase my chances of both finding and recognizing good opportunities.

EXPLORE AND EXPERIMENT

When you think you have "the answer," it becomes too easy to get tunnel vision. Many companies are guilty of this. For instance, say a woman owns a small dentistry practice and needs to get the word out and get the interest of new clients. Of course, she realizes that many people are searching for services online, so she does some reading and finds out that having a good Google rank is important for driving new business.

Then she reads a few articles on search engine optimization (SEO) and sends them to her web developer to implement. Every day, she searches for herself in Google to see if her rank gets higher, but it's going slowly, so she hires an SEO consultant. The consultant helps make a few adjustments and she searches again. Now she starts to climb a bit and the traffic has increased to her website, but she still doesn't have too many new inquiries from it. She is puzzled because she is sure that the increased traffic should lead to more inquiries. Now she starts to buy keywords on Google so that when people search for dentists in her area, they are sure to see her ad. The traffic continues to increase, but she still isn't getting many inquiries. She scratches her head and throws in the towel. Back to posting ads with coupons in the local newspaper! The dentist thinks to herself, obviously this web stuff doesn't work for dentists.

What's the problem with this scenario? If you haven't already guessed, the dentist believes that A=B, or, in other words, an increase in website traffic equals more customers. Sometimes this is the case, but not always. This is why I call it chaos . . . there are no clear-cut answers. Sometimes SEO works and sometimes it doesn't. Because the dentist just kept trying to pour time, energy, and money into the same A=B scenario, she did not realize that C could equal B.

The dentist started out on the right foot by researching ways to be successful online. But when driving traffic didn't increase inquiries into the practice, she should have done additional research. Simply stopping and looking at what other similar successful businesses do helps, but not everything that works for others will work for you. It also helps to talk to people from other industries about what they do. Explore, then explore some more. Even if something is working, spend time looking around you for interesting things others are doing that you can learn from.

A dentist in a larger metropolitan center could take a look at services like Yelp.com, a local customer review site, to find out what the customers were saying about her competitors. The top customer-rated dentist in San Francisco, Dr. Allen L. Hasse, has dozens of positive reviews about his hands-on approach to dentistry. Many of the reviews highlight the fact that Dr. Hasse explains procedures thoroughly before performing them and that he doesn't hand off tasks like cleanings to a technical assistant. One of the top dentists in New York, Dr. Jennifer Shim, has rave reviews from multiple patients talking about how they found her to be incredibly gentle, nice, and affordable. Getting listed on Yelp.com is a good first step and the best way to go about doing this is to encourage patients to post their reviews and feedback there.

When sites like Yelp.com drive lots of traffic to your website, search engines take notice organically and your traffic increases. And this traffic is more likely to create conversions with customers as it is real people who are posting reviews and driving this traffic. The whuffie you gain from these types of interactions is real.

This is why I'm fundamentally opposed to creating a marketing strategy several years out. New ideas and approaches are emerging every couple of weeks these days and many of them don't cost any money at all. If something is working, but not fast enough, you may want to tweak your approach rather than abandon it altogether.

BE TRANSPARENT AND OPEN

Not to repeat myself, but when embracing the chaos, you will find answers along the way if you are open with each step you take. You can be like JetBlue and tweet out questions and announcements regarding your next steps. Watching JetBlue's back-and-forth discussions has been really interesting as people are more than willing to offer innovative ideas for the company, like features to add to their flying experience, new cities to add, and what people are enjoying and not enjoying about JetBlue's flights.

Gone are the days of secrecy and intellectual property hoarding. These practices are giving way to openness and collaboration. Is it really an advantage to hold the rights to intellectual property these days or is it more to a company's advantage to put ideas out into the community and get feedback early on, letting customers feel some ownership of it? Sure, your competitors could steal the idea, but you've built the customer relationships. First-mover advantage isn't always advantageous. Loyal, engaged customers are more likely to be your advantage.

The biggest advantage to being transparent and open is that everyday magic opportunities are more likely to present themselves than if you are closed. More people across more social networks will be sharing their whuffie with you if you are open to them.

BE HUMAN

If you want to know what being human has to do with embracing the chaos, just ask Ryan Carson of Carson Systems.

Carson Systems runs the successful Future of Web Apps series of events all over the world. As Ryan knows, big events can often lead to many big, uncontrollable gaffes. To err is human, but how you handle it is divine. And Ryan knows exactly how to handle it: Embrace the chaos and be absolutely human.

At the Future of Web Apps conference in London, Ryan stood in front of an audience of 800 people who were decidedly unsatisfied with the lack of Wi-Fi access that was promised in the program. He'd done his best to hand out individual connection cards to speakers and other people who absolutely need to be connected, but the rest of the audience was restless. He stood up onstage prepared to take the bullets.

"I'm sorry. We f&**ed up. I know it sucks. We paid a bunch for the Wi-Fi and it isn't working," he said. Then he went on to explain that for the rest of the conference, there would be no Wi-Fi, so people could come and ask for their money back, or they could just sit back and enjoy the program. From what I understand very few people asked for their money back. After that honest and open talk, the audience stopped worrying about getting online and just enjoyed the program.

It's the way Ryan handles all business: openly, honestly, and with a human voice. And, because of it, his conferences continue to sell out, his publications continue to attract amazing writers, and he is one of the most well-connected people I know.

REDEFINE SUCCESS

One of the surest ways to open unexpected doors is to approach the world in unexpected ways. I've spent a great deal of time talking about approaching communities from the perspective of building your whuffie instead of the perspective of selling or gathering "eyeballs." When you are approaching community in this fashion, it is natural that your measurements of success will change as well.

When it comes to whuffie, instead of being concerned with quantity, you need to become more concerned with quality of relationships. This doesn't mean that quantitative measurements disappear, it just means they aren't your most dominant measurement.

How do you measure community? I like to think of it in terms of measuring the "health" of a community rather than just measuring community itself. *The health of a community is the gauge of where various qualitative and quantitative metrics lie in relation to the goals you set.*

You need to first set your goals with an emphasis on qualitative measures, and *then* define your metrics, which will include your quantitative measures.

SETTING YOUR GOALS

Setting your goals is a very personal task and not simple to do. It can also lead to an emphasis on quantitative metrics (i.e., I want 500,000 new members by Christmas). To steer goal setting toward a more qualitative, more community-conducive perspective, I like to help my clients frame their overall goal in the following statement: "I want to create a culture of

_____."

The blank space is filled in with a word or a phrase to

describe the kind of community you want to foster. It could be a culture of gaming or a culture of passion. It could be a culture of generosity or a culture of happiness. After you define the type of culture you want to see unfold around your product, site, or service, you can start to define what exactly that means. Let's take a culture of generosity, for instance. What does that mean? How do you want people to act within that community to promote that? What actions should be rewarded? Avoided? What should you build in to encourage this?

Creating a culture of generosity could unfold like this:

- Sharing of ideas openly

- Less competitive, more collaborative

- Encouragement between members for sharing

- Rewards for sharing and collaborating (points? gifts? private kudos?)

- Mentorship program to help new people become well educated on the community

- A higher emphasis on caregiving

When you are designing your product, certain features will help encourage creating the type of culture you desire. As you build the list of the kind of behaviors to encourage, you will also start to understand the kind of metrics you will need to use to figure out whether or not you are successful in creating the culture you desire or whatever game you have chosen.

DEFINING YOUR METRICS

Once you figure out the type of culture you want to create, you can start to define how to measure your success within that goal. The beauty of online communications is that all sorts of metrics are available. Deciding which ones apply to the measurement of your goal is the trick.

For instance, if your goal is to create a culture of generosity, measuring the number of new sign-ups doesn't necessarily mean much. But measuring the number of sign-ups referred by members can mean that people are enjoying themselves enough on the service to invite their friends. Some other types of measurements that are more conducive to showing positive community interaction include the following:

- The rate of member growth and attrition, especially with new members (it is really telling when you drive traffic that doesn't stick around—you will have to really examine whether you are offering something of need).
- The average length of time it takes for a newbie to become a regular contributor.
- Number of referrals (strength of positive word of mouth).
- Multiple community crossover—if your members are part of many communities, how do they interact with your site? Flickr photos? Are they twittering about you?
- The number giving and receiving actions—for example,

people who are only reading are receiving good content, but not necessarily contributing as much to the community as the people who are posting content. PopSugar, an online community for women, has a neat reward system built in for interactions with their gifting for contributions in the community. With more interactions, the members get gifts to give to other members, both encouraging and rewarding members for positive community interactions.

- The quality of the content posted. Was a discussion thread abandoned? Are the posts by community members well thought out and succinct or childish and silly? Are people filling out their profiles? Are people commenting frequently on other people's posts, or is it just staff members? All of these questions can point toward the quality of postings in a community network.

- Community participation in gardening, policing, and keeping the community a nicer place (e.g., people who click on "report this as spam," people who edit the wiki for better layout, etc.).

- Number of apps built off your API (if you have one)—this is a good "number" measure, as the number of apps usually correlates with your social capital.

- The average number of connections/friends that your members have (too high may be as damaging as too low).

- The diversity of your members from various "groups" (measured by the types of interest groups they form, the gender balance, and the geographical areas they sign up from).

- The number of people talking about your site outside of your site.

- The number of messages or interactions, on average, each member receives, low and high numbers, and how many members are in each bracket (this determines how the activity is being spread out).
- The impact of the community interactions on revenue. Does more community interaction equal better ad revenue? Do people upgrade frequently from being a free member to being a premium paid member?

This is in no way a comprehensive list of metrics. These are only some of what I have used quite frequently to determine positive growth on community health for clients.

WHAT ABOUT THE QUALITATIVE?

Most of the preceding metrics are still very quantitative. What about the qualitative? The anecdotal? The measurement of happiness? Love of your product? What of whuffie?

Although the numbers are directly measurable and can be tracked along the way, the truly interesting results (as well as the biggest rewards) come from the stories . . . the human interest pieces. They come from gathering awesome e-mails you receive from really happy community members or running into someone at a party who, when they find out you work for Company A, squeals in delight and tells you how much you rock. Adversely, you may find a forum thread somewhere where someone rants about how awful their experience with you was. Maybe there is a lack of discussion altogether, which is the anti-anecdotal. Maybe you aren't even interesting enough to be talked about. Then you know you are doing something wrong.

One way to start to track the anecdotes is to set up internal cheers and jeers company pages (Zappos.com does something similar). On the cheers page, paste in the happy e-mails, blog posts, and so on, as well as personal stories of positive encounters with customers. On the jeers page, paste in the negative feedback, the angry e-mails, and/or the lack of reaction at all. Don't compare yourself to anyone else, just with whether you have met the goals you set for yourself. And don't get down if the jeers page is full and the cheers page is empty. Think about the jeers as things to work on and customers to win over . . . as opportunities. Think about the cheers page as ideas for ways to create more of that . . . more opportunity.

Once you have enough feedback, then set up anecdotal meetings where everyone shares these stories and brainstorms the opportunities. You will know when you are successful on this end when you have to limit these meetings to people's five favorite cheers and five favorite jeers each so that the meeting doesn't last the entire day.

You can, then, attach a quantitative metric to the opportunities: How many jeers can you turn into cheers? Set a goal there, too. Start simple and add progressively more challenge. Creating more happy customers is always a good metric.

REALLY IMPORTANT STUFF TO REMEMBER ABOUT METRICS

Metrics are rarely useful for the community members themselves. Most of what matters is experience. People may revel in the fact that there are over 25 million people signed up at the same service that they are using, but what matters is that their closest friends are using it and that they are getting value out of it. The 25 million people just have the experience in common.

Who are metrics for then? Investors. Journalists. Outsiders. People who want a number to tell the whole story, mostly because they are not part of the community itself and it's really hard to explain the impact of a great community to an outsider. In the end, it comes down to whuffie. And, as I've discussed, whuffie is incredibly elusive. It is measurable in some respects, but only relative to the source (how do you measure happiness when everyone has a different experience of it?), which probably makes it the loveliest, most perfectly decentralized system in the universe. It is where we are headed, but so many people don't "get it" yet.

Even so, you need to communicate outside of the experienced boundaries of your community, so metrics are very useful. You can use metrics to entice more people to come and experience your community. You can use metrics to try to communicate the pride you have in the amazing things happening in your community. You sometimes have to make comparisons to give others a reference point. But in the end, you know in your heart the real measure is in the experience. The proof is in the experience.

I had the pleasure of hanging out with Biz Stone, cofounder of Twitter. Over and over again, people tried to get him to reveal the "number." "How many people are using Twitter? Must be millions! Tens of millions!" But he wouldn't budge. He would answer calmly, "We don't reveal our numbers."

I really respected that. Twitter probably does have tens of millions . . . egad, could even be pushing 100 million for all I know . . . but by Biz not revealing that number, he made people think harder about their experience of Twitter. He made people think harder about the stories of Twitter. He made people really consider the impact of Twitter. A number would overshadow that really important stuff. I'm glad he doesn't tell, and I hope he and the rest of the Twitter team never do.

LOOK TO OTHER INDUSTRIES FOR INSPIRATION

One of the best ways to open up opportunities for yourself is to create more bridging capital. According to Robert Putnam, author of *Bowling Alone: The Collapse and Revival of American Community,* social capital comes in two forms: bonding and bridging capital. Bonding capital is what we do with good friends and family: We build deep relationships of trust and care. We can count on those we have bonding capital with for our survival. Bonding capital is essential to our individual survival and is what emotionally fulfills us.

Bridging capital, on the other hand, is the type of social capital that helps us grow and builds our careers and businesses. Bridging capital is what you are building when you go outside of your heterogeneous environment (close friends, workplace, etc.) and meet new people. Bridging is what you do when you go to conferences and meet people you don't usually hang out with. It's what you do when you spend time getting to know people across your industry and others online and off. According to Putnam, bridging connections "are better for linkage to external assets and for information diffusion" and provide a "sociological WD-40" that can "generate broader identities and reciprocity."[6]

Therefore, to really open up doors of opportunity and give your whuffie a real power boost, you should be making connections across different industries.

TransitCamp Bay Area was this for me. In fact, I happen to do a great deal of consulting for government services organizations around the world. By taking a risk and connecting the power of Web 2.0 with the need for government services to engage constituents, I opened up a whole new area for my business to expand into. Now I regularly consult with everyone from state chief information officers to municipalities on how to engage their constituents with Web 2.0 tools. I embraced the chaos of collaborating in an area I hadn't previously thought of to connect to the work I was doing and found a great void that needed to be filled.

Doing this has opened me up to multiple worlds of possibility and really expanded my idea of how to apply many of the principles I previously thought only applied to technology. As a result, I am pushing innovation in many areas for my clients.

LET GO OF CONTROL

As I have explained, you really don't have control anyway. Knowing this can be the most freeing feeling of all. Ev Williams from Obvious Corp. (the people behind Odeo and Twitter) realized this and was able to refocus on more important things, like creating applications that spoke to people. He wrote in the inaugural Obvious Corp. blog post: "The consumer web is increasingly hits-driven and increasingly crowded, which makes it more difficult to predict what's going to work." He went on to assert that he "just wanted to create a company that would be as much fun and as fulfilling as possible. Fun in work to me means a lot of freedom, and tons of creativity, working with people I respect and like, and pursuing ideas that are just crazy enough to work. I don't want to have to worry about getting buy-in from executives or a board, raising money, worrying about investors' perceptions, or cashing out."[7] The results of Ev's experimental approach? Twitter, which has now grown to be one of the most beloved online social networks.

In other words, Ev Williams didn't want to run a company with a management team whose focus was on control. He wanted to spend time exploring and figuring out what was going to work. He went as far as buying Odeo *back* from his investors so he could explore new options to expand the business free of external control. The result was astounding. Not only did he turn around after this and sell Odeo for a profit, but he also pursued Twitter, a seemingly crazy idea in the early days of the service that didn't become popular until a year after its launch, but now has become one of the most successful online communities on the web. Ev recognized that he can't predict the market and he can't control outcomes but embraced the chaos and focused on exploring and figuring out what his next steps would be to great success.

HAVE PATIENCE

Success takes time. Opportunities don't always make themselves clear right away. Sometimes the answer to your next step takes more time than you will feel comfortable with. Your success may come as quickly as it did for YouTube, executing an idea that led to rapid growth and being acquired by Google for $1.65 billion, all in under a year. More likely your community build-out and monetary success will be more like it was for Dogster, a strong online community of dog owners. It launched in early 2004 and first became profitable in mid-2006. Even today, it continues to grow steadily by word of mouth and is rabidly (no pun intended) loved by its community members. The owners make a comfortable living and have raised just over $1 million in angel funding (a small amount in terms of a Silicon Valley startup) to expand its development efforts.

THE ULTIMATE PAYOFF FOR EMBRACING THE CHAOS

> Well-behaved women seldom make history.
> —*Laurel Thatcher Ulrich*

I love Ulrich's quote. It's been an inspiration for me all of my life. Really, though, it can apply to everyone. People who make history and truly influence people are those who don't play by the rules. Or play it safe. They take risks and absolutely embrace the chaos. People who make history have an abundance of whuffie. People like Spencer Silver and Arthur Fry, inventors of the Post-it Note, had oodles of whuffie in the science and business communities, not to mention the whuffie they raised for 3M, years after they worked there, because of the millions of people who use Post-it Notes daily. The founders of Google, Larry Page and Sergey Brin, have seemingly boundless whuffie because of the influence of their search engine and multiple online products. Zappos's Tony Hsieh has whuffie coming out of his ears because of his revolutionary approach to customer service; his customers would agree that Zappos has been successful because of this same approach. Companies that have whuffie make history and are led by and made up of people who take risks.

The ultimate payoff for embracing the chaos is not merely innovativeness, agility, and the ability to predict and move with the times and have loads of fun doing it. The ultimate payoff for embracing the chaos is that you become the *ultimate* influencer. You become someone who shapes history and inspires others to shape it alongside you, giving you even more whuffie. Those who embrace the chaos are whuffie spreaders.

This leads me right into the next chapter. Alongside embracing the chaos, the ultimate in whuffie making comes from finding one's higher purpose, that thing that is bigger than you, bigger than just your company. If you want to influence and inspire and you really want people to rally behind you, a higher purpose is necessary.

9

FIND YOUR
HIGHER PURPOSE

A business with a higher purpose not only provides a product or service that people love to use or connect with, but also makes a contribution to the community. These contributions are what I call *gifts* and operate on a level that works alongside the market economy to build whuffie as you build up your bank account. Gifts are to whuffie as money is to your bank account: as gifts are exchanged, your whuffie goes up. The difference between money and gifts is that, in the case of money, as you give it away, the bank account goes down, whereas, in the case of gifts, as you give them away, the whuffie account goes up. Gifts could be the core of the product or service, the gift of choice, an offering of empowerment, the spread of kindness, or the gift of putting your influence behind a passion.

All of the intangible wealth—such as social rewards for solidarity and generosity—that builds whuffie is part of the gift economy. It is the economy where goods and services are given without need for direct payment, such as money or favors. Goods and services exchanged for monetary or equal value are part of the market economy. Gifts create bonds. They create reciprocal connections between individuals, whereas market transactions, including those that are "free," are transactional and impersonal. Gifts, on the other hand, result in interaction between people and thus are highly personal.

A gift creates an unspoken reciprocal bond. Indirect reciprocity makes communities go round. This doesn't mean that the recipient has to scramble to return the gift, though there is an unspoken obligation of the gift receiver to return the generosity at some point in the future in some way, shape, or form. But there is no set date or value for the future interaction, nor does the gift have to be given directly back to the giver. In fact, it is almost better to not have the favors returned at all. Transactions, on the other hand, are immediate reciprocations. When you sell a good or service and get paid directly for it, the exchange loop is completed and there is nothing owed to tie you and the buyer together for future interactions.

In anthropological research about various gift economies, including those in the animal kingdom, it has been found that those who perform the most favors and give the most gifts to others are often the most powerful.[1] Why? Because these individuals have saved up multiple reciprocal favors that they haven't called in yet. Even if they never call in those favors, the gratitude from the recipients of those favors amounts to copious amounts of whuffie.

If you have been widely generous across a community, you

can "spend" some of your whuffie to get things done, to make further connections, and to influence wider decisions that affect the community. Earlier I discussed the deposits and withdrawals from your whuffie bank account. With every way you gift people in a community, you make additional deposits into your whuffie account.

Figuring out what those gifts are—and, thus, finding your higher purpose—is the process of creating a core philosophy for your company, not in the traditional sense of corporate mission statements that are dry as toast and do little to inspire, but in the sense of doing something good for the world, beyond just what you do to make money.

Higher purpose can be directly tied to your company's core business; for example, a company creating environmentally friendly products, such as Stonyfield Farm, an organic yogurt maker with a higher purpose that builds environmental responsibility into the core of everything it does. The CEO of Stonyfield Farm, Gary Hirshberg, talks about *doing well by doing good,* meaning that he ties Stonyfield's success to the fact that his higher purpose is built right into the core business. I will discuss his philosophy on this subject in this chapter as well as show multiple examples of companies who are doing well by doing good.

In addition to doing well by doing good, a higher purpose can also be about *thinking customer-centrically.* Thinking customer-centrically will gain you oodles of whuffie with your current customers as well as the people your customers talk to. Being customer-centric means that you do things like form partnerships with your competitors if it is in your customers' interests. For instance, in this chapter I discuss a group of competing online social networks working together on making the creative content of individual web users portable between their websites. They are doing this because their customers are feeling fatigued by the multiple logins and filling out endless personal information upon sign-up. Having the higher purpose of putting your customers at the center of everything demonstrates that you have their interests at heart and that goes a long way to building trust and loyalty. In other words, a customer-centric company is a very whuffie-rich company.

You can also give the gift of going beyond being a customer-centric business by making your whole business about *helping your customers go further.* Helping your customers go further means that you actually build the tools of empowerment as your core business. For example, before blogging tools like Open Diary, LiveJournal, and Blogger—three of the earlier mass-adopted blogging platforms—came along, only those who could code a website could publish their daily thoughts online. Before YouTube, video distribution channels were limited to those with connections to the entertainment industry. Both blogging tools and video-sharing services allowed anyone to become writer and producer. Affordably priced cameras allowed people to take up photography as a hobby and, for some, take it into a career. Nolo, a company that provides low-cost law books, legal forms, and legal software, gave the gift of helping its customers understand law a little better and allowed them to avoid a few lawyer bills by giving basic tools. These businesses give the gift of helping their customers go further and not only become essential tools, but gain a great deal of whuffie in the process as they help others build their own.

These gifts can go even deeper. How about helping your customers help *others* go further? The gift of *spreading love*—that is, giving your customers the tools to directly affect the lives of others—is ultimately powerful because it creates whuffie times three: You gain whuffie by helping your customers gain whuffie from helping their customers gain whuffie. When your higher purpose feeds into helping others find a higher purpose, the whuffie explodes. For example, you can do this by creating a game like Akoha.com, an alternate reality game played online and offline that I will discuss in this chapter, which gives its members missions to do nice things for others. The missions are passed along through these acts of kindness and so is whuffie. As people introduce one another to the game, connections are made, all traveling back to the originator: Akoha.com.

The final gift I will discuss in this chapter is that of *promoting something bigger than yourself*. All of the other gifts tie directly back to the core of your product, but promoting something bigger than yourself allows companies to get really creative with the gifts they contribute to the community. This isn't the same as donating or offering employees as volunteers, though, which is a long-standing practice for companies. This is about really dedicating resources—ongoing and significant resources such as building a foundation or creating an internship program—to make the world a better place. Sometimes these actions may tie back to your core product or service, but they don't necessarily have to. Dedicating this gift to the community will win your company loads of whuffie as people recognize your significant contributions to the world.

Each of the five of the overarching gift categories—doing well by doing good, thinking customer-centrically, helping others go further, spreading love, and promoting something bigger than yourself—are significant gifts and lead to the kind of whuffie that will drive the kind of positive word of mouth and praise through online communities you could never pay for. You will not only build the word of mouth, but you will build your loyalty and business while doing something positive for the world.

DOING WELL BY DOING GOOD

Doing well by doing good means that you are actually building a product or a service that benefits others and that you make money as a result. Your higher purpose is built right into the core of what you are selling. The gift that you offer is that, through the use or purchase of your product or service, people participate in helping you be a better citizen. Craigslist and Stonyfield Farms are companies that have shown that by doing good, they can do well financially.

Craig Newmark, founder of Craigslist.org, the world's largest online classified system, described his philosophy on doing well by doing good:

> . . . there is nothing pious or anti-commercial about us.
> The decision to make [Craigslist] a business was based on
> values I've been somewhat facetiously calling nerd values.
> The disease of my people—the nerds—is that we are very

literal, which is a real pain in the butt, frankly. But again, nerd values are simple. It's good to make a good living. It's good to do well for your staff.

I feel that one of the best things a person can do for another is to create a job. So you do OK commercially, and then you try to make a difference of some sort.[2]

In other words, what Craig was saying is that he lives by the rule of doing well while doing good, but even more than that he is doing well *because* he is doing good.

Craig started out Craigslist as a hobby and a service to his friends back in 1994; between 1995 and 1998, it became a bona fide business. It was always his goal to offer free classifieds, but at some point he needed to make money to pay his very real employees. So he started charging for people to post jobs. And he made the money he needed.

People have predicted that Craig could make a great deal more money. In fact, multiple suitors have approached Craig about large-dollar ad placements. Craig refused all of them because he didn't believe this was a move that would be accepted by the community of posters on Craigslist. He also refused affiliate programs because they would take the focus away from Craigslist as a tool for everyday people to post and find apartments, goods, and jobs. Several attempts by outside firms to acquire the site were also rebuffed. Craig sticks firmly to his nerd values at all times. Craig decided, instead, to make money to support the site and his staff by charging for certain types of ads in larger centers. Craigslist charges a small fee for job postings in places like San Francisco and New York, where the market can bear the price. I paid $70 for a job posting for a personal assistant, which was reasonable compared with other job listing sites like TechCrunch's job board, which charges $300 per posting.

Craig is an extreme example of sticking to one's principles, since he could potentially make a great deal of money from charging for many of the postings on Craigslist. However, because of his commitment to community, he has gained a great deal of whuffie over the years, which has helped Craigslist grow steadily via word-of-mouth recommendations. This steady growth has meant that years of economic ups and downs since the list launched in the mid-1990s haven't really affected them. Craigslist has stayed true to doing well by doing good, and the customers have stayed true to Craigslist.

Another company that has found success in doing well by doing good is Stonyfield Farm. Stonyfield lays out its higher purpose in a list of five core missions for the company:

1. to provide the very highest-quality, best-tasting all-natural and certified organic products;

2. to educate consumers and producers about the value of pro- tecting the environment and of supporting family farmers and sustainable farming methods;

3. to serve as a model proving that environmentally and socially responsible businesses can also be profitable;

4. to provide a healthful, productive, and enjoyable workplace for all employees—with opportunities to gain new skills and advance personal career goals; and

5. to recognize our obligations to stockholders and lenders by providing an excellent return on their investment.

CEO Gary Hirshberg has been a strong proponent of coupling purpose with product from the launch of Stonyfield in 1983 to the launch in 2008 of his book, *Stirring It Up: How to Make Money and Save the World,* where he talks about turning green ideas into money. Hirshberg doesn't write that his higher purpose *helped* Stonyfield become successful, he writes that his higher purpose is the *reason* for Stonyfield's success. Hirshberg cites companies like Zipcar, the community car-sharing business; Whole Foods, the health food supermarket; and Timberland, the outdoor wear company for finding success through espousing the same values. These companies build their higher purpose into the core of their product, giving back to the community as the core of their business. In a presentation given in Berkeley in early 2008, TriplePundit, an environmental blog, reported that Hirshberg "compared check-writing and volunteering to cutting the leaves and branches off a tree, where the heart of the business and its ability to impact the world positively is the tree itself."[3]

Hirshberg's point is that companies can no longer wreak havoc on the planet or the local economy, then buy back favor by writing a check to a green charity or send their employees to the local community fund-raiser, giving themselves a pat on their own backs for being good community members. Money, once again, cannot buy whuffie. The trust lost in the first place creates a whuffie deficit that does not correspond to a monetary transaction. Monetary transactions belong where goods are exchanged for money and there are no long-lasting relationships intended. When it comes to raising whuffie, a company needs to "walk the walk," and Stonyfield does just that. In 1994, Stonyfield was the first manufacturer to offset its entire carbon emissions. It has built its own machines that use biodiesel and produce very small amounts of sludge. Hirshberg constantly measures the environmental impact of making his product. Paying lip service to a higher purpose, then acting in opposition to that higher purpose, will lose you more whuffie than if you had said nothing at all. Building whuffie through having a higher purpose means you have to live and breathe it.

The returns on whuffie of Stonyfield Farm gifts have been incredible. Its yogurt is the number-one-selling organic yogurt brand and the number-three-selling yogurt overall in U.S. sales. Stonyfield is the world's largest organic yogurt company and has expanded to include products like cultured soy, frozen yogurt, and ice cream. Hirshberg attributes doing well to his longtime loyal customer base who stick with him because he does good.[4]

Both Craigslist and Stonyfield Farm get a great deal of online community love from the whuffie they've raised doing well by doing good. Stonyfield is a sweetheart of the sustainable movement, appearing in hundreds of green blogs, including several appearances on Treehugger, a blog dedicated to environmental issues, and resulting in hundreds of posted interviews and customer reviews on YouTube. The company maintains not one, but two blogs: one dedicated to organic farming and one dedicated to child nutrition. Gary takes time to sit down for interviews with green bloggers and video podcasters. And since 1989 Stonyfield's website reports that hundreds of thousands of people have participated in its "Have-A-Cow" program, where people are introduced to the cows and get to see how they progress along their life cycle.

Craigslist is wound deeply into online communities with mentions everywhere from Flickr, where people post photos of their Craigslist finds, to Facebook, where Craig himself spends time interacting with his nearly 1,000 friends and 1,800 fans. The whuffie both companies have raised through doing well by doing good has led to the kind of word-of-mouth praise in online communities that most companies dream of. All of this is achieved through enacting their higher purpose.

When you do good, you do well, but when you do good by your customers, you are thinking customer-centrically.

THINK CUSTOMER-CENTRICALLY

Without customers, a company wouldn't stay in business very long. That is why I'm surprised that companies aren't falling over themselves to put their customers' happiness at the core of everything they do. What is good for the customer is good for the bottom line, because when your customers are happy, they return to you time and time again resulting in repeat sales. Not only that, but happy customers will let people know in their networks that they should buy from you as well. Happy customers bring copious whuffie.

Customer-centric thinking is more than just providing good customer service. Customer-centric thinking includes things like passing along your savings to your customers instead of putting them in the bank, sending your customers to your competitors if you can't meet their current needs, and under-standing that they are multibrand loyal and giving them the tools to interact between you and those other brands. If you have successfully completed the exercises in chapter 5, you have a pretty good understanding of your customers' desires and what really makes them tick.

Before I go into some examples of companies gaining whuffie because they think customer-centrically, here are some flags that signal you are not thinking customer-centrically:

- You do everything you can to keep your customers on your website.
- You measure number of visitors and time spent on your website to determine whether you are successful.
- You have custom-built tools for posting videos, comments, and/or images.
- When budgets get tightened, you make cutbacks in areas like customer service, marketing, support staff, and design, but you don't make cutbacks in sales.
- You are bothered by customers describing your product in their own words that don't match your brand.
- You have a long list of customer relations policies. Any exception to those policies has to go up the chain of command for approval.
- When you read my suggestion to send your customers to your competitors, you threw the book across the room.
- You need to create multiple instructional videos so that your customers will understand how to use your product.
- You demand social media strategies that win over the "influencers" to blog or tweet about your product.

- You go to conferences and events and return not quite remembering who you met or what they do, and your throat is scratchy from all your talking.
- You constantly go and check the number of fans on your competitors' Facebook page and get upset to see their numbers higher than yours.
- You don't think you *have* any competitors.

If any number of items on this list sounds familiar, you aren't thinking customer-centrically. Why not? Because the behaviors on the list signify that the way you think is centered on your company's needs. When you get the following message, you will know you have started thinking customer-centrically: It's not about you. It's about your customers. It's not about how cool or amazing your product is. It's about your customers. It's not about getting anyone to visit your website or align to your way of thinking. It's about you aligning to the way your customers think. It's about going to *them*.

One example of a company that thinks customer-centrically, even in times of crisis, is Southwest Airlines. Following September 11, Southwest Airlines was the notable exception to the troubled airline industry. Several airlines filed for bankruptcy protection, and most were panic-stricken because of record losses; Southwest hardly felt a blip in its bookings and, moreover, remained profitable and shortly afterward *expanded* its fleet and employees. Why? Because the company has always been committed to giving the customer full value without getting greedy on what it charges: It is focused on being customer-centric. Southwest's marketing strategy is known as *pleasing the customer* and includes points like passing on cost savings through efficiencies to its customers, being early adopters of technologies that help customers gain more control over their travel, and giving a great deal of autonomy to its frontline employees so that they can help customers in any situation. And Southwest isn't operationally efficient from cutting corners, either. It thinks creatively about ways to cut these costs, including opting for satellite airports instead of major ones on some of its stops, like Houston's Hobby airport and Chicago's Midway, cutting down the costs of rent. Southwest also found cost benefits in flying one type of aircraft, which allowed the company to cut back on training costs and maintenance.

Its efficient boarding system and rapid flight turnaround also cuts down costs per flight. Southwest was also one of the early adopters of ticketless itineraries and online booking.

Additionally, because of its open and honest communication with customers, the company has created loyalty and a great deal of whuffie. A great demonstration of the amount of whuffie it has is that not only did the customers of Southwest continue to fly as frequently as ever on the airline post–9/11, but many customers concerned that Southwest would go through hard times actually *sent money to the company* as a show of support.[5] Even during the crunch, Southwest's CEO and vice chairman, Jim Parker, kept his eye on the pleasing-the-customer strategy. On the company's website in March of 2002, he posted: "We are approaching growth opportunities conservatively, but we know our Customers have been anxious for this new non-stop service. Although the airline is still in the recovery process, we cannot forget the wishes of our Customers to continue to bring low fares and affordable travel to more people with more convenient flights."[6] Notice that the word "customer" is capitalized in his communiqué.

Southwest focuses its resources on being customer-centric, keeping its customers happy first and foremost. Because of that, the loyalty will grow and no matter what the financial economy is doing, it will float right through.

Speaking to the point that you may want your customers to only visit *your* website every day and only ever use *your* product, the reality is that, with very few exceptions, customers are loyal to multiple brands. If you recognize this and make it easier for your customers to move between their brand loyalties, they will recognize you as having their best interest at heart.

Narendra Rocherolle, cofounder of start-ups Webshots, a photo-sharing site, and 30 Boxes, an online calendar-sharing tool, attributes the whuffie he has raised with 30 Boxes to the facts that he is focused on sending his customers to other websites and that he didn't build any of his own tools.

With all of the social networks—Flickr, Facebook, Delicious, and Upcoming—that Narendra was taking part in, he found it difficult to keep track of events, photos being posted, and what people were doing. He kept multiple pages open in his web browser, switching back and forth and hitting refresh to try to keep up with everything. This was getting more and more difficult as more social media tools emerged and as he followed more people, and he thought that others would be having the same problem. He came up with a solution focused on the needs of the savvy online social networker: 30 Boxes, a simple calendar that feeds in his friends' information from all of the places they interact online. The calendar was laid out in a monthly view and would show who was posting content on Flickr, blogs, Delicious, and other services on any given day. When users become interested in the activity of one of their friends in this calendar, they can click a link that will take them to the website that the activity is on. Narendra built 30 Boxes to *send people to other websites.* On purpose.

As websites emerged that Narendra found his friends using, he added them to 30 Boxes. Hillary Hartley, one of 30 Boxes's early and devoted users, commented that it was the quick response to adding these new social media tools that really impressed her. She felt that Narendra was working hard to give her a better experience. What Narendra was discovering by focusing on the needs of his customers is the importance of data portability, a hot topic that companies like Google took on in 2008 in launching the Open Social Foundation program. The focus of this program is to work with other organizations to promote the ability to do what Narendra was doing in 2005: allowing customers to easily move back and forth between these social networks.

The result of Narendra's customer-centric thinking speaks for itself. Narendra counts sending users away from 30 Boxes as contributing to

- significantly improving the 30 Boxes product;

- leading to successful marketing on a zero budget;

- resulting in three quarters of a million people registered;

- leading to articles in the *New York Times, Wall Street Journal,* and other large publications; and

- winning multiple user-voted online awards.

More recently Amazon has also taken to the idea of sending people away, creating a universal wish list that its customers can use to add any product off any website to a wish list that their family and friends can follow on Amazon.com. Even though the wish list is stored on Amazon, the products are purchased on the various stores unaffiliated with Amazon. So, for instance, when I add a cupcake bracelet from one of my favorite online stores, Shanalogic.com, which is not affiliated with Amazon, my mom—who is following my wish list—can purchase it for my birthday and Amazon gets no commission. Amazon realizes that its customers are multibrand loyal and by sending people away, they are sure to come back on their own volition. Amazon raises a great deal of whuffie by just meeting the needs of the customer.

Thinking customer-centrically requires you to reverse many of the things on the list of signals that you are self-centric. So here is a list of the signals that you have become a more customer-centric company:

- You send customers to other websites constantly.

- You measure how many people refer their friends as a sign of your success.

- You use websites like Flickr and SmugMug for photographs and YouTube and Viddler for videos, and you allow people to feed in their blogs and their Twitter accounts.

- When budgets get tightened, you get smart about tightening operational costs companywide.

- You are delighted that customers take time out of their busy schedules to talk about your product or service.

- Your only customer service policy is to do right by the customer and do what is fair. You hire people with great, helpful personalities and train them well.

- When you read my suggestion to send your customers to your competitors, you recalled the last couple of times you did that and wondered why that's news.

- Your customers are doing things with your product you never dreamed and are posting videos online to share it with others.

- Influencers are adding you as friends on various social networks and inviting you to speak at their conferences.

- You return from those conferences with a huge stack of business cards, dozens of new Facebook friends, a Moleskine full of great ideas and conversations, and a bit of a hangover from the shots that those bloggers invited you into.

- You meet with your competitors to see how you

can work together toward better customer experiences for all.

- You understand that you compete for your customers' attention with every product, service, and activity out there . . . and you are thankful every day that you have some of it.

If you recognize yourself in that list, you most likely have a wealthy whuffie account. Being customer-centric is an amazing higher purpose to have. Being customer-centric is awesome for making your customers feel like they really matter, and it grows your whuffie. But the next step, helping others go further, actually gives them the power to build their own whuffie, which, as you already know, is whuffie times two.

HELP OTHERS GO FURTHER

Web 2.0 tools such as blogging platforms like Wordpress and Twitter, and Flickr, for photo-sharing, have become successful because they help others go further. They have taken the idea of doing well by doing good, merged it with the idea of thinking customer-centrically, and created tools to help people do things that, previously, were only accessible by experts and the wealthy who could pay the experts to do it. Blogging platforms, like Wordpress and Typepad, democratized journalism so that regular citizens can break news. Many amateur photographers now make a living because of incredible websites like Flickr, where they can showcase their work and get feedback.

When their work gets popular enough, they can sign up on iStockPhoto, where they can sell their work as stock photography without jumping through hoops such as finding a stock image house. It is much easier to grow your reputation as a photographer through these user-generated content websites. Etsy, a website that helps artists, artisans, and crafters set up a shop and promote and sell their goods, helps them connect with people who are looking for unique items. There are even self-publishing sites, like Lulu and Blurb, that provide the tools for budding authors to publish and sell their books—a route I was considering taking myself before I was picked up by a publisher.

Gary Vaynerchuk, the wine guru and host of Wine Library TV (see pages 62–67), owes his success to the tools that helped him easily and inexpensively publish his Wine Library TV pieces through video-hosting sites like YouTube, Vimeo, Viddler, and Facebook video. Gary can upload and host his videos quickly and for free. Social networking tools like Twitter, LinkedIn, Facebook, and MySpace help Gary keep in touch with and make new friends to share his content with. Event sites like Eventful and Upcoming are available to Gary to help him promote events like signings of his book, *Gary Vaynerchuk's 101 Wines Guaranteed to Inspire, Delight and Bring Thunder to Your World,* and wine tastings as he travels from city to city. Even five years ago, the Garys of this world wouldn't have been able to grow themselves to the point of having large audiences and being in control of driving their own brands.

I established my former company, Citizen Agency, to achieve the higher purpose of *helping others go further.* Citizen Agency was a firm that consulted with its clients on how to connect with and empower their own customer communities as well as dedicated time to being part of community projects directly related to assisting individuals achieve more through creating and teaching the tools that connect them to more opportunities.

Having the focus on helping others go further gave Citizen Agency and the people working for it a great deal of whuffie. We worked to achieve our higher purpose by supporting and creating the *building blocks for independents,* a term my adviser and Microformats founder Tantek Çelik coined to describe the online and offline tools that enable any person to carry her voice further. This includes

- teaching blogging and twittering, which gives people a simple online interface for sharing their experiences;

- spreading BarCamp, which provides a simple-to-implement model to gather and share ideas through;

- setting up wikis, which gives individuals a collaborative tool in which to share information and gave birth to enormously successful collaborations like Wikipedia, the free and ever-updated online encyclopedia built by millions of individuals; and

- promoting and spreading coworking, which helps independents find inexpensive collaborative community spaces to work from.

Any tool or framework that is inexpensive or free, open and accessible, and simple enough for a nonexpert to use is considered a building block. These tools and resources are meant to work together with other building blocks to achieve the goals of people wanting to change the status quo politically, personally, or professionally.

At least 90 percent of the time spent at Citizen Agency was spent on achieving our higher purpose. Surprisingly, only about 30 percent of it was paid work. For example, I spent a great deal of my time traveling around helping advise people setting up coworking spaces and speaking at conferences all over the world about supporting and using tools such as Bar-Camp to build locally stronger communities.

Having a higher purpose paid off handsomely in my professional life, and gave me access to all sorts of amazing people, such as luminaries Jimmy Wales, founder of Wikipedia; Arianna Huffington, founder of popular online media site the Huffington Post; and Craig Newmark, founder of the very popular online classifieds site Craigslist—they all have given me incredible insight and opened doors for me. I also received invitations to travel all over the world, to places like Paris, London, Berlin, Bangalore, Vancouver, New York, Seattle, and Lisbon, being paid to speak to large audiences on the knowledge I gained from my "volunteer" journeys.

I find that the more I give to the community in terms of my higher purpose, by continuing to contribute to the growth of building blocks for independents and volunteering my time and expertise to help empower and inspire individuals, the more I get back in reputation, trust, and connections. It all leads to more opportunities and connections and a great deal of actual monetary capital.

A good example is the work I've done with government services organizations. It started with a presentation at an annual GOVIS (Government Information Services) conference in Wellington, New Zealand, entitled Government 2.0: Architecting for Collaboration, a conference I was invited to after my adviser, popular blogger and author Kathy Sierra, had to cancel at the last minute. Through our discussions, Kathy knew my building blocks for independents work well and thought I would be a good fit to replace her presentation on helping citizens "kick ass" through better design. My building blocks fit because they build out the idea of empowering citizens (help them kick ass) through providing the tools necessary to speak out and create change.

In all honesty, this was the first time I thought about applying the building blocks model to government services. But it instantly made a great deal of sense to me. I believed it would lead to more community involvement and more solid relationships between government services organizations and citizens. Sure enough, I found several really strong case studies, including a UK organization—Theyworkforyou.co.uk, a website dedicated to offering tools for citizens to collaborate toward political change—and many examples of developers using government data to create better tools for citizens to access government services. The presentation was very well received and incited much discussion and an invitation to present at another conference for municipal information services representatives.

The opportunities didn't end there. After sharing this presentation openly on Slideshare.net, an online presentation-sharing community, I started to receive many calls and e-mails from U.S. government services organizations, asking me to come and give the same presentation and to consult with them on integrating the building blocks into their offerings. Through this, I continued to develop the presentation and my ideas on how government services could really benefit from using the building blocks. As my ideas became more developed, I continued to be invited to speak and consult all over the United States and Canada. I have also contributed to working documents for governments as well as a book entitled *Rebooting America.*

When I visited New York in the summer of 2008, I had the chance to sit down with Ryan Brack, chief of staff for Mayor Michael Bloomberg's office, where we discussed how these building blocks could improve education. This relationship continues as does the growth of the connections and work I do on government services. It all started with a personal connection formed through my volunteer work for promoting the higher purpose of Citizen Agency. It has blossomed into a balance of lucrative engagements and the continued spread of the idea that we need to empower the grass roots through these tools for helping others go further.

If you can combine the idea of doing well by doing good with customer-centric thinking, and produce a product or service that helps others go further, you, too, will put copious amounts of whuffie in the bank. And, like the companies I mentioned earlier—Flickr, Wordpress, Typepad, Etsy, YouTube, and many others—you will be able to convert that whuffie into cash in the bank. So, then, think about what happens when you go a step further and create something that not only helps someone go further but helps them help someone else go further. The result of that higher purpose is that you create self-replicating whuffie and spread love.

SPREAD LOVE

Earlier, I discussed creating amazing customer experiences by being in the business of happiness. If you create something that helps people achieve freedom and autonomy, helps them feel more confident and competent, and/or helps them connect with others in significant ways, you will not only be popular, but you will be seriously loved. Having your customers love *you* is one thing. But if you empower them personally, it is the first step to them telling everyone they know that they should buy *your product* or use *your service.* Empowering your customers through creating amazing experiences that help them achieve more is a surefire way to create customers who evangelize for your company.

But what if you could go a step beyond you creating happiness for your customers and actually *help your customers create happiness for others*? If you could be the catalyst of the spreading of love between others, you would not only help your customers be happier, but help them help others be happier, which would help you increase your whuffie points significantly. I've already mentioned that when you help your customers gain whuffie, you double your whuffie points. In the case of spreading love, you *triple* your whuffie points because you help your customers help others gain whuffie.

That's what Jane McGonigal dedicated her career to: giving others the tools of spreading love. Her website, Avantgame.com, is about the creation of "alternate reality" games to encourage people to create a better world.

Alternate reality games are played offline instead of in a virtual world. Games are usually designed the other way around, taking ideas from the real world and incorporating them into a virtual world so that people can relate to one another with familiar objects; for instance, in the case of the popular game Halo, military strategy is incorporated into the game. Even board games take cues from real-life scenarios; for example, Monopoly is all about real estate strategy. But in Jane's version, she encourages people to take ideas and elements from the gaming world—be it computer or board games—and incorporate them into their everyday life.

Jane builds high levels of cooperation and collaboration into her games, encouraging participants to form deeper community bonds while they work closely together to achieve their goals. But some of her games take it a step further, like Cruel 2 B Kind. It's a game of benevolent assassination where players become assassins of kind acts and love.

In the game, found at Cruelgame.com, players are given undercover directives to perform random acts of kindness on strangers and other players. To win the game, a player needs to follow instructions to do things like slay by serenade (singing a song to the target) or kill with a compliment. When your target is another player, it is your goal to "assassinate" her, but her role doesn't end there. She can then join with the other killers to help them stalk the survivors. The teams grow until there are two final mobs of "benevolent assassins" attempting to win by killing one another with kind acts.[7]

Jane built spreading love into the core of the game as the players not only learn to kill other people with kindness within the game, they have also taken these lessons back into their day-to-day lives. Jane has received hundreds of notes from current and former players of her games that report a change in overall perspective on how they treat other people in the world. One player, Rose, wrote Jane after only one year of playing, "It is really important to me that you (and other people) understand the differences that these games have made in my way of thinking. It has powerfully affected my attitudes about what is possible. I know that large-scale communities can work and be extraordinarily effective. I am not afraid of the complexities." Sharon, who has been playing Jane's alternate reality games for three years, wrote, "These games change people's conception of human nature. It is like the equal, but completely opposite, power of an atomic bomb being unleashed on the world." Jane has also received the same message from dozens of people saying, "These games have restored my faith in humanity." Other reviews of her research into these alternate reality games at the University of Pennsylvania were, "I am optimistic about the future," "I feel close to most people [now], even if I do not know them well," and "My existence makes the world a better place." By encouraging people to spread love, Jane has changed the perspectives of individuals who continue to spread the message far beyond the game.

In just over one year following launch in September of 2006, the game had spread around the world and had been played in twenty cities in six countries and four continents. All of this spread via word of mouth by bloggers, gamers, and the news media.

Jane speaks all over the world and has won multiple awards for her theories of spreading happiness through the creation of alternate realities such as Cruel 2 B Kind. Jane's alternate reality gaming was named one of the Top 20 Breakthrough Ideas of 2008 in *Harvard Business Review.*

Jane's ideas are definitely breakthrough and she's even brought them to the work world through her involvement with the Institute for the Future's Future of Work program, but one company, Akoha, launched in 2008 by Austin Hill and Alex Eberts in Montreal, Quebec, takes it a step further.

Akoha, derived from the word *"koha,"* which means reciprocal gift giving in Maori, is highly appropriate to how Austin Hill, Alex Eberts, and their team are creating meaningful play through an online game where people win whuffie points through acts of kindness and service to others.

Austin got the idea when observing the level at which people share their experiences to help one another out every day. He wondered if people were encouraged through positive rewards and a bit of a game structure to make it fun, whether the sharing could be taken up a notch more.

Akoha is a "play-it-forward" game played in the real world and online with social action cards that involve real-world and virtual challenges. Akoha players perform the activities on the cards, such as buy coffee for a stranger and share a book with a friend. These actions earn points and more Akoha cards, and increase the players' progress in various game missions. Each card is passed from player to player and even nonplayers, recruiting new players and allowing players to track the path of their actions.

Akoha players receive virtual cards that provide a series of real-world and virtual acts of kindness that, when performed, earn them karma points and kudos, or virtual currency used to purchase virtual items. In addition, Akoha players have a social score (similar to whuffie) measuring positive community participation.

As players complete the challenges on the cards, they pass off cards to the recipients of their acts of kindness. Once the recipient of the card (either existing Akoha players or nonplayers receiving the cards as their introduction to the game) confirms the act has been performed, the recipient has the ability to play that card forward, earning a version of the card for him- or herself as well as being credited for forwarding the original card they obtained.

Akoha, much like Cruel 2 B Kind, is all about spreading love as an intentional act that is rewarded and encouraging people to perform random acts of kindness in the hopes that this "game" will spill out into a general attitude of generosity.

Spreading love isn't just about alternate reality gaming, although I agree with Jane McGonigal that games are powerful because they make it fun to cooperate and collaborate. A corporate example of this is the MINI Cooper community game called MINI Motoring Hearts. The game was launched to MINI Cooper drivers in 2006 to encourage volunteerism. Players download a MINI Motoring Hearts Monitor to their desktop and fill out a form that defines what type of organizations they would like to volunteer with. The monitor then finds appropriate opportunities from the VolunteerMatch database of 37,000 nonprofit organizations that need help and send them to the player. Each time players complete a volunteering gig, they win karma points that lead to MINI Cooper swag and special stickers that players can fasten to their car, showing their participation. There is also the opportunity to win points through a "Good Deed of the Day"; these deeds are smaller and more random acts of kindness such as paying a stranger's toll and starting a carpool. MINI Cooper also shared eighty of its outdoor billboards around North America with the volunteer organizations participating, including Meals on Wheels and the Nature Conservancy.

The impetus to encourage MINI Cooper drivers to spread love through volunteerism and random acts of kindness came from MINI's knowledge of its customer base already. "We know that MINI owners are passionate not only about their cars, but about giving back and this program will give owners the opportunity to channel that passion and energy towards making a real and lasting contribution," said Trudy L. Hardy, marketing manager for MINI USA, in a press release announcing the program on April 26, 2006.

Spreading love is about catalyzing ways for your customers to help other customers and potential customers in positive ways. Helping people do the right thing and help others look and feel good gives you triple whuffie: You get some, your customers get some, and the people your customers help get some. And as I've mentioned time and again, the best way of all to grow your own whuffie is to help others grow theirs.

PROMOTE SOMETHING BIGGER THAN YOU

Promoting something bigger than yourself focuses at least some of your energy on giving back to the community. It is a really simple way to do something good for the community without looking as if you want to sell something. The higher purpose needs to be, in fact, divorced altogether from your sales or any other vested interest. Many of the companies I used as examples earlier, such as Craigslist and 30 Boxes, have one thing in common: They didn't set out with the goal that they were going to get rich or famous or otherwise rewarded for their higher purpose. They just had a higher purpose. Fame and riches often followed.

Promoting something bigger than you may have little or nothing to do with your company or your main product. Nonetheless, you pick up the torch for what you can believe in. We see this all of the time with companies supporting causes like breast cancer and the Red Cross through their donations and volunteerism. However, as Gary Hirshberg of Stonyfield Farm argues, donating and volunteering are nice, but doing this doesn't mean you are contributing to solving anything. You haven't found your higher purpose.

So what would it look like to invest in something bigger than yourself that is only tangentially related to your company? What if, like Timbuk2, the San Francisco bag company, you integrated your passion for something into the company's everyday business?

Timbuk2 can almost be thought of as a staple of San Francisco culture. The company got its start making sturdy, funky

bags for bicycle couriers back in 1989 and pioneered the customizable three-panel bag in 2000. Walking into the offices of
Timbuk2 demonstrates instantly the kind of heart and soul the
company has. Openness is represented by its modular, totally
open floor plan where even most of the meeting spaces are vis-
ible. Its nonhierarchical structure is immediately apparent,
with the CEO indistinguishable from the receptionist in terms
of type of desk and where it is located in the office. Timbuk2's
level of experimentation is shown by its multiple workstations
with piles of fabric, the seemingly endless supply of white-
boards filled with doodles of ideas, and the on-site sewing team
ready to whip up something new.

Timbuk2 is as San Francisco as you get. It still looks and
acts like a start-up, even after being in business for nearly
twenty years. Patti Roll, director of marketing and community, regularly participates in local geek events, like Bar-
Camps and meetups, while Perry Klebahn, the CEO, regularly
participates in the customer service community powered by
Getsatisfaction.com.

Even though Timbuk2 has one of the most community-
driven teams I've ever met, they didn't think they were doing
enough. So Perry and Patti and others came up with the Workshop Timbuk2 program to help support the artist community
in San Francisco.

The Workshop is a partnership with Headlands Center for
the Arts, an international artist residency program. The big
idea is to give the artists hands-on opportunities to create
something unique: in this case a special-edition bag that
might be available for sale via Timbuk2. If a commercial bag is

created, a portion of the proceeds is given to the Headlands Center for the Arts.

Over a yearlong period, the Workshop Timbuk2 hosts one artist per month, giving artists studio space and supporting their projects while they are in residence. The Workshop builds a modular and interactive studio the artist can call his or her own, providing all of the materials needed to create a new project. Each artist has full access to Timbuk2's in-house sewing team so he or she can create a prototype bag at will. The entire staff of Timbuk2 is involved in interacting with the artists, fully integrating them into the company.

This program not only helps out a local art institution and ties Timbuk2 closer to the local artist community, but it also serves, as Patti Roll explains, to "make Timbuk2 rethink many of its assumptions. We can always improve our processes and think more creatively. We don't know what having the artists integrated into our day-to-day [work life] will bring, but it can only help to make us more creative."

This program fits right into the higher purpose of Timbuk2, its core company values of creativity and community, without being directly about the bags.

Google's foundation is another good example of promoting something bigger than a company. From their early days, Larry Page and Sergey Brin have expressed a desire to give back to the community—the world community—by donating resources to making it a better place. In 2004, Google.org was launched to become the branch of Google that concentrates solely on this. The Google Foundation is a hybrid philanthropy that combines investing in nonprofit ventures as well as for-profit ventures that are part of the foundation's five initiatives: green energy; the promotion of hybrid vehicles; education; empowerment and transparency in government; improved health services; and microfinancing. You had better believe that Google not only will benefit from community goodwill, but also will become a leader in innovation in all of these fields while bringing that innovation back into the organization.

At Citizen Agency, we looked at contributions to the wider community as a total win-win situation. By being involved in the championing of BarCamps and coworking, we learned more about communities, our core business, than we ever could have reading books and creating strategic plans. The company was more innovative because of the amount of time we donated to supporting community projects.

Of course, promoting something bigger than yourself can be a win-win situation for everyone. When everyone benefits, it's the ideal situation. Companies grow bridging capital, community goodwill, and innovation while they are giving back to the community. The recipient community benefits by receiving money and energy from an organization that can afford to give it. That being said, totally selfless acts are amazing and admirable and should be done regularly.

THE BENEFITS OF LIVING AND BREATHING
YOUR HIGHER PURPOSE

As I've written this book, one thing I've come to see is the speed at which everything is changing, which is the nature of online business. For example, when I met with Tony Hseih, CEO of Zappos, in January of 2008, he was still pondering making a foray into the wider online community space. Zappos was one of those "1.0" companies that survived the dot-com bust and thrived over the years on totally amazing customer service.

Tony and his team understand that customers are now demanding a different level of engagement. As I videotaped him and his colleague Rachel Brown discussing the core values of Zappos, I was tweeting to my followers on Twitter specific things that Tony and Rachel were saying about Zappos culture. After the interview Tony asked me questions about Twitter.

A couple of months later, I had lunch with Tony and his web team, Alex Kirmse and Lynn Stetson, at the South by Southwest Interactive conference. They had started to use Twitter, but even though Alex was having fun with it, Tony still wasn't totally comfortable with the medium; nevertheless, he tweeted a few announcements and held a contest or two.

A week or two later, I started to see more activity on the Zappos Twitter account. Tony was starting to really get into it, having personal conversations with people, talking about his travels, and really interacting with the people following him. And more people started following him and recommending their friends follow him. Soon enough, he was tweeting out contests for his followers, using Twitter to play games and have some fun with his followers. Alex and Lynn even created a page so that people could follow the conversation back and forth with Tony and people talking with him. As described in chapter 5, Tony has become an example of how to use Twitter for other CEOs.

Tony continues to impress me on many levels, though. He is incredibly experimental and open to new ideas . . . and it continues to benefit Zappos. I really believe that the basis of Zappos culture, their higher purpose, is really what shows through for people who have fallen in love with Zappos.

For those who don't know about the Zappos mission, I'll share it here. The team at Zappos understands that as a company grows, it is more and more crucial that it make its core values explicit. So the Zappos team created ten core values that they follow in their everyday working and living lives:

- Deliver WOW Through Service

- Embrace and Drive Change

- Create Fun and a Little Weirdness

- Be Adventurous, Creative, and Open-Minded

- Pursue Growth and Learning

- Build Open and Honest Relationships with Communication

- Build a Positive Team and Family Spirit

- Do More with Less

- Be Passionate and Determined

- Be Humble

They try to embed all ten of these core values into every-thing that they do, from hiring to training to their personal lives. When I visited the Zappos offices in Las Vegas, Nevada, I met with many employees, but I was blown away by one in particular. She told me a story about how living the Zappos mission has changed her life.

Marcela Coutierrez was at a local restaurant with her family, when she observed a man with four children frantically search-ing through a garbage can. Immediately, she got up and went over to the man and asked him if he needed her help. The man explained to her that he thought he may have thrown his keys into the garbage can. Either way, they were missing. His kids seemed like they were tired and irritated and as they became more agitated, the man grew more frantic. So since they weren't finding the keys, Marcela offered to drive the man home.

"That would be nice," he said. "But nobody is there and my keys to my house are with my keys to my car."

Marcela asked if he had a backup set anywhere and the man explained that he did at work, a ways away on the Las Vegas casino strip.

"Great!" Marcela said. "We'll take you there to get them, then."

The man was floored. Why would this total stranger offer to drive him all over town to help him? What did she have in it for herself? Marcela didn't bat an eye, though, and helped the man get some child care while she took him to get his spare keys.

After the good deed was done and she, her husband, and her

son were on their way home, her husband turned to her and said, "You've totally changed."

"What do you mean?" she asked. "I would never leave someone like that hanging."

"Well," her husband told her, "you would have helped by taking him home. You may have even given him money for a cab. But you went above and beyond."

Marcela thought about it. "I suppose you are right. I wonder what it is that's changed."

Her husband knew. "It's Zappos. Zappos has made you a better person."

After meeting more people at Zappos, I totally believed her. And Tony as the CEO completely embodies these values. This is a company that, despite stiff competition and economic downturns along the way, has continued to double its profits every year. If anyone embodies a higher purpose, it is Zappos.

10

WHUFFIE IRL*

*in real life

Organizations such as Zappos, Timbuk2, Flickr, the Library of Congress, GetSatisfaction, and 30 Boxes have, in a very natural way, turned the bullhorn around, been part of the community they serve, created amazing experiences, embraced the chaos, and found their higher purpose. They have all used a combination of the tools available to really connect with their customers. They've made raising whuffie their core goal and have seen financial and cultural benefits from it.

New powerful tools continued to emerge as I wrote this book. All sorts of interesting communities kept coming to my attention from sources such as TechCrunch.com, CenterNetworks .com, and Mashable.com.

If you have a policy of futzing in your organization—that is, giving people the green light and the time to just wander around the Internet, following links and trying out new tools until they find what is right for your company—you will stay on top of the tools that are emerging online. It's been the "secret sauce" of my successes, giving me a finger on the pulse of what's going on and what new tools are essential to use and how to use them properly.

But it isn't just about the tools. They just help us do the same thing: connect. Nor is it just about building a community, either. It is about recognizing how to find your community and potential community and interact on a level that will benefit everyone. That is the basis of whuffie building.

YOU CAN'T EAT WHUFFIE, BUT IT'S GETTING HARDER TO EAT WITHOUT IT

While writing this book, I heard from a couple of people that they were concerned that whuffie wouldn't pay the bills for individuals. Sure, listening to feedback, being part of online communities, doing great work, embracing the chaos, and giving back to the broader community are all good things to do to become respected and build a network, but how does it affect an individual's bottom line? Well, my personal story is a good example of this, but in addition to that, raising your whuffie is becoming more and more necessary to remain competitive in business as well as your own professional career.

I'm a Canadian citizen on a work visa in the United States. The last couple of times I've come across the border to apply for my visa, the border officers have Googled me. And, to my surprise, they've actually told me that the results were good enough to back up the résumé I handed them. One official actually said, "You should state on your résumé that you are very Googleable!"

This isn't a new phenomenon. It has certainly been the practice for many savvy job recruiters over the years. I have met many human resources professionals who ended up hiring the candidates with the most impressive online presence, especially when it came to more senior positions at organizations. The more results one has that point to professional accomplishments, the easier it is for them to determine if what is in the résumé is accurate. It helps even more if those accomplishments are from websites and blogs other than the candidate's.

Competition is fierce. Billions of people are working to get ahead. Hundreds compete for jobs. And that is just the individual. When it comes to starting a company that provides a service or a product, you will also have to compete for customer attention. Without differentiating yourself somehow, the battle to make ends meet gets tougher.

This is where you figure out that you *can* eat whuffie—just indirectly.

Google is powerful because companies and individuals alike know that if people find them online, they will have a better chance of getting the business or the job. And, if they find them in a positive light reflected through the eyes of other customers and contacts, they will have even a better chance than that. Online tools that help customers voice their satisfaction with your product will help boost your Google ratings and instill a sense of confidence in a potential customer making a decision. This is no different than pinging someone's whuffie, as Cory Doctorow describes it in *Down and Out in the Magic Kingdom.* When you get that new customer or you get that better job because of your positive online presence, the money to buy that food follows.

You can't eat whuffie, but it is getting harder to eat without it, so look for opportunities to raise whuffie where you can cash it in at a future date. Pick events to work on where potential clients or employers can see the good work you are doing. Let your expertise shine through the content you are producing. Others will notice and then you can cash in that whuffie and pay the bills.

THE FOUR STAGES OF SENSE OF COMMUNITY

In 1986, two researchers, David McMillan and David Chavis, published the results of their study on people's stages of connection to a particular community. They defined the connection in terms of a sense of community and defined sense of community as "a feeling that members have of belonging, a feeling that members matter to one another and to the group, and a shared faith that members' needs will be met through their commitment to be together."[1]

Their work was incredibly important in uncovering the levels of commitment that community members have to the community and showed definite patterns of deepening ties. They figured out that the deeper the feelings of membership, the more fiercely loyal the member is to the community.

The four stages are:

1. Feelings of Membership

2. Feelings of Influence

3. Integration and Fulfillment of Needs

4. Shared Emotional Connection

As community members progress through each phase, their bond deepens, until at the level of shared emotional connection, the bond is nearly impossible to infiltrate.

This is a really important study to note. The word "community" means something very different in different contexts. One's "community" is rarely, if ever, attached to one website like Facebook or Flickr, and it is certainly never going to be attached to one particular brand. The commitment lies in the bonds between people who interact around these social catalysts. And those bonds ebb and flow through the stages of sense of community between the particular members and with the social catalysts.

You are tied to your friends and associates, and those friends and associates introduce you to the social catalysts. If your experience with a social catalyst, be it either a brand or a website, is something that enhances your life or deepens your bonds with friends and associates, you will also become bonded with that social catalyst. People fall in love with a social catalyst not because of how cool it is or what it does, but how it has been a tool to help them connect and go further. Social catalysts that help individuals build whuffie with their friends and associates will win their undying affection.

So, understanding the progression of those bonds can make things incredibly interesting and help you, as both a community member and a producer of a social catalyst, move things along.

A feeling of membership is best described as that moment when one reads an article or meets a person and feels instant recognition and connection. Many people come to the Coworking community group and say, "I've had this idea for quite some time, but then I picked up the *New York Times* and there was Coworking and I knew I had to sign up!" The five attributes of a feeling of membership are boundaries, emotional safety, a sense of belonging and identification, personal investment, and a common symbol system.

Featuring member stories is an excellent way to spark a feeling of membership. So is posting the core values and goals of a project. The recognition of shared values and experience creates the safety and identification necessary for a person to take the next step of being part of a particular community. This is also where having member profiles is utterly important. Showing that there are real people whom others can identify with really increases the chances that someone will find a reason to take the leap. And, finally, the story behind the company as well as the founders and employees is crucial to creating those initial bonds of trust.

Feelings of influence happen when community members believe that they are both being heard and learning from the site and their colleagues. It is crucial for members of any given group to feel that they have some say and influence. At this level, the reciprocal nature of information exchange and influence begins to really deepen the members' bonds.

Any ways you can build in to exchange and provide feedback and generally interact around your social catalyst will work to increase feelings of influence. Kathy Sierra, author of the Head First series of books on user-centric design, once suggested that websites put a WTF?[2] button on every page so that when visitors get frustrated, they have the ability to supply instant feedback. The next step would be to acknowledge and act on that WTF? response to your site by working with the person who has become frustrated to improve the user experience.

Integration and fulfillment of needs is where community members begin not only feeling that they can influence others, but can also see their own whuffie rise because of that influence.

So how can you make the whuffie more obvious? Create a VIP or Heroes program. Timbuk2 has a Heroes program that recognizes certain bag owners who post excellent photos and other media around their bags. The company realizes that these customers are influencers and have the ability to drive more people toward shopping at Timbuk2, so it gives them Hero discounts to distribute to people in their network they care about. This, of course, encourages similar behavior: more posting of photos and more talking about Timbuk2 bags to achieve similar Hero status.

This is also where Easter Eggs can come into play. When the expert community members find the Easter Egg, they can teach others, raising their own status within the community as experts.

Finally, shared emotional connections are when a person can't imagine herself without the community. This is how many people feel about Twitter. If it goes down for a day, people start getting antsy. Two days, they get angry. But they don't leave. They have fallen in love with the way that Twitter connects them to the streaming consciousness of others and allows them to be heard. Downtime for Twitter means a loss of voice for many.

This depth of connection is both astounding and frightening. Astounding because you know that if you have created a social catalyst with the power to connect people this deeply, you will secure your longevity as well as continue to attract others to your website or brand. It is frightening, though, because, as Spider Man's uncle told him, "With great power comes great responsibility." With shared emotional connections, you have created a depth of love so deep that even slight changes you make will cause a community outcry.

This has happened every time Flickr has added or changed a feature on the site. Even when it added the ability for members to upload short videos, a group of over 30,000 Flickr community members formed a group to protest the feature: "Flickr is for photos, not video. Keep video off Flickr." Community manager Heather Champ explained at the Web 2.0 Expo in the spring of 2008, "It wasn't a surprise, either. We had talked about adding video since 2005. People knew it was coming."

Flickr and Twitter are two social catalysts with incredibly emotionally connected communities. It is both a blessing and a curse, but most definitely mostly a blessing. Whuffie potential for both the social catalyst as well as the members is strongest in the community that achieves this level of emotional connection.

Other ways you can enhance emotional connectedness is through in-person meetups and other events that allow the members to meet one another as well as the founders and employees.

THE ENTREPRENEUR'S WHUFFIE CHECKLIST

I've presented an overwhelming amount of information and tips throughout this book, so here is a quick checklist of how to get started on your quest for raising your whuffie factor.

STEP 1

First, you need to figure out what you are doing and for whom. This will be your overall strategic pivot point. Sit down with your cofounders, employees, stakeholders, or just yourself, and ask the following questions:

- [ ] Who is our core customer/who are we building this for? List as many as you like but pick one to focus on. Only one. Remember Google focuses on the impatient searcher, not the browser and not the advertiser.

- [ ] Why would they care? Figure out what truly differentiates you from your competition. Are you offering an amazing customer experience? Be brutally honest with yourself.

- [ ] We are creating a culture of _____. Fill in that blank with one type of customer community you'd like to have. This is a very important section as having a strong, positive culture will go a long way to community growth.

- [ ] How do we achieve that culture? Go wild and come up with all sorts of great ideas. Once you have a list of at least twenty ideas, prioritize them and set them in a reasonable timeline. By reasonable I mean that you can work on product development while implementing these ideas.

☐ What is our higher purpose? Take a look at chapter 9 and see how you are going to build whuffie by being part of the gift economy.

☐ Set your qualitative and quantitative measurements of success. Be realistic here, too. You can shoot for the stars, but tie the measurements back to the kind of culture you want to create.

STEP 2

Next you need to apply the right tools for the right jobs. Not all of the online tools will suit you and your customers and you can start simply and gain complexity as you get comfortable. Figure out the tools that you need to use to achieve your goals and set them up.

☐ Collecting customer feedback. Options: forums, Getsatisfaction.com, chat, telephone, comments, social bookmarking, etc.

☐ Market research. Options: Facebook groups, events, social bookmarking, Flickr search, Twitter search, blog search, etc.

☐ Going out to find unsolicited feedback. Options: Twitter tracking, blog search, tag notifications, etc.

☐ Getting transparent. Options: blog, photo sharing, Twitter or other text message alerts, videoblogging, podcasts, etc.

☐ Communicating updates. Options: blog, Twitter or text message alerts, Facebook groups, mail lists, etc.

☐ Meeting your customers. Options: events, meetups, BarCamps, conferences, etc.

☐ Tools for your customers to spread the word. Options: blog badges, sharing tools (such as "share with a friend" to send a link via e-mail), Facebook group, Facebook applications, mobile applications, Twitter integration, etc.

☐ Tracking your progress. Options: analytics, RSS feed of keyword searches, etc.

☐ On-site community (if needed). Options: message boards, group chat, customer-to-customer private messaging, commenting, news feeds, friending/following, sharing tools, etc.

STEP 3

Now is the part where you listen and learn and adjust as necessary. The earlier you start this in regard to your product or service development, the better. Basically, use the tools from step 2 and start listening, interacting, and really becoming a part of your customer community. Keep really great track of feedback and make certain everyone on your team reviews it regularly.

You may have to return to step 2 several times to adjust priorities, add tools, and remove tools. You may even have to return to step 1 to revisit your strategy. This is usually the part where a start-up changes its entire business model or an entrepreneur feels like he or she has to go back to the drawing board. Don't fret. This is a good thing. This is also the part where you become thankful that these tools exist to help you make your company rock.

STEP 4

Wash. Rinse. Repeat. By the time you hit step 4, you have repeated steps 1 to 3 several times, been introduced to hundreds of new communities and online tools, and changed your business model, and your product or service looks quite different than where you started. If not, you were either one of those lucky companies I discussed in the introduction or you haven't realized that you may be in trouble.

The truth is, there isn't one checklist for everyone. I wish there was, but there just isn't. And if I list a tool that I say you just have to use, say Facebook, and a year from now it's yesterday's news, this book will be outdated pretty quickly. What you need to have is a person, either in-house or a trusted consultant, who is on top of what is happening online and can tell you how to achieve your goals of creating that culture of _____. And, as you have read, there are companies who have built a great deal of whuffie without knowing how to use any of the online tools. In the end, what you need to remember is that in Cory Doctorow's future, whuffie is achieved by being nice, networked, and/or notable. It's not about the online tools, they just help you to achieve whuffie faster and further. The secret of effectively using these is in the five principles of building whuffie:

1. Turn the bullhorn around: Stop talking and start listening;

2. Become part of the community you serve;

3. Create amazing customer experiences;

4. Embrace the chaos; and

5. Find your higher purpose.

Integrate as many of these lessons as you can and you *will* build whuffie, and when you build whuffie, you *will* be crazy successful. You will build incredible customer loyalty, spread utterly positive word of mouth, and have the type of business that grows through good times and bad. There is a positive, mutually beneficial relationship to be built between a company and its customers and the most significant thing to know about the online tools is that, as the adoption of them grows, your customers and potential customers will demand that type of relationship more and more.

CAN YOU AFFORD *NOT* TO BUILD WHUFFIE?

No. While writing this book, the stories that came to me from people who have personally and professionally benefited from being part of online communities and building whuffie were endless. In fact, every day, they continue to roll in, so I continue to interview people and have created a regular pod-cast with a website where people can tell their own stories as well.[3]

The fact of the matter is that people are talking more and more, and they are becoming more and more conscious of where they are spending their dollars. When a person has a choice between two similar products and one has only been executing on a traditional branding strategy of advertising and product placement whereas the other one has really connected personally with the shopper, which do you think they will buy?

No matter what industry you are in, no matter how established or early-stage your business is, this shift is going to affect you . . . if it hasn't already. Having a team of people focused on matters of community will be a regular staple in the future. In fact, job descriptions we haven't even thought of today will be a regular staple. Cost centers focused on your customers are not cost centers, they are business development. Designing your product or your company for monetization first and people second will leave you with neither.

The good news here is that this shift is a non-zero-sum game. We all win. Everyone is happier. The customers win because they have more autonomy when it comes to where they are spending their money. They feel more competent in the decisions they make. And they definitely get to connect more with other people who have similar tastes and interests.

Business wins big, too. The monetary costs of building an intensely loyal customer base is way lower. Cost centers like customer service, event planning, and community outreach may go up, but they are nothing compared with the cost of a major media buy. And they are *instantly* rewarding. Anyone executing on a community strategy will feel the results personally and be able to adjust to the needs of the customer on the fly. Not to mention that a community strategy is incredibly enjoyable. Interacting daily with customers and potential customers can win you relationships for life.

And in regard to the pillars of happiness for business? Businesses will definitely feel more autonomy as they receive instant feedback and are closer to their customers daily. Marketing has always been a dodgy industry, full of uncertainty. There is a famous saying that 50 percent of marketing works, we just don't know which 50 percent. This takes the guesswork out. You *will* know what is and isn't working. As Jonathan Coulton told me, "It doesn't cost a lot to try anything and everything available online. You just never know what will work, but when it does, you know where to put more energy."

Competence comes when you are so in sync with your customer community that you are no longer reactive to the changing market; you have anticipated your customers' needs. That competence can only happen when you are close to the community you are serving.

Autonomy, competence, and building social networks all around is what comes from concentrating on raising your whuffie. This is a truly happy marriage between the market and the marketplace. This is the laissez-faire that free-market economists talk about.

And it is already happening. The future that Cory Doctorow envisioned is not science fiction at all . . . it is how online communities operate. If you turn the bullhorn around and start listening, become part of the communities you serve, create amazing experiences, embrace the chaos, and find your higher purpose, you *will* win. And winning means that social capital turns to a long-term gain of financial capital.

Go forth and raise whuffie.

NOTES

1: HOW TO BE A SOCIAL CAPITALIST

1. *USA Today* research, *Adult Video News,* Nielsen/NetRatings, 2004.
2. Cory Doctorow, *Down and Out in the Magic Kingdom*, Tor Books, 2003.
3. "From Major to Minor," *The Economist,* print edition, January 15, 2008.
4. From the Fair Copyright for Canada group page on Facebook, http://www.face
   book.com/group.php?gid=6315846683.
5. Jonathan Coulton, "Over There Again," http://www.jonathancoulton.com/
   2008/04/02/over-there-again.

2: THE POWER OF COMMUNITY MARKETING

1. Barry Schwartz, *The Paradox of Choice: Why More Is Less,* Harper Perennial,
   2005.
2. One of the rules of BarCamp is that organizers cannot collect more than $300
   from each sponsor in order to keep the event centered on the attendees and not
   focus on the sponsors. Lower sponsorship ceilings make it simpler to justify a
   no-banner policy at the event.
3. 2008 Cone Business in Social Media Study, http://www.coneinc.com/
   content1182.
4. Hollis Thomases, *Boomers and Beyond: Targeting the 50-Plus Audience Online,*
   Click-Z Network, April 22, 2008.
5. "Say Anything: Kids, the Internet, and the End of Privacy: The Greatest Generation Gap Since Rock and Roll," *New York*, February 12, 2007.
6. Burt Helm, Brand New Day, *BusinessWeek,* August 20, 2007, http://www
   .businessweek.com/the_thread/brandnewday/archives/2007/08/sorry_wal-mart
   .html.

7. Jeff Jarvis, "Pray Per Post," BuzzMachine, January 31, 2007, http://www.buzz machine.com/2007/01/31/pray-per-post/.

8. Om Malik, "On the Microsoft Ad Campaign," GigaOm, June 22, 2007, http://gigaom.com/2007/06/22/on-the-microsoft-ad-campaign/.

9. Rafe Needleman, "The Obama Presidency, 'It's the Network, Stupid!'" CNet News, November 7, 2008. http://news.cnet.com/8301-17939_109-10086354-2.html.

10. Arik Hesseldahl, Douglas MacMillan, and Olga Kharif, "The Vote: A Victory for Social Media, Too," *BusinessWeek,* November 5, 2008, http://www.businessweek.com/technology/content/nov2008/tc2008115_988160.htm.

11. Jennifer Leggio, "Obama Won the Election—Not Social Media," ZDNet, November 5, 2008, http://blogs.zdnet.com/feeds/?p=305.

12. Umair Haque, "Obama's Seven Lessons for Radical Innovators," Harvard Business Publishing, November 5, 2008, http://discussionleader.hbsp.com/haque/2008/11/obamas_seven_lessons_for_radic.html.

13. Barack Obama, speech, November 14, 2008, http://www.youtube.com/watch?v=Zd8f9Zqap6U.

14. Ryan Lizza, "Battle Plans: How Obama Won," *The New Yorker,* November 17, 2008, http://www.newyorker.com/reporting/2008/11/17/081117fa_fact_lizza.

3: TURN THE BULLHORN AROUND AND CREATE CONTINUOUS CONVERSATIONS WITH CUSTOMERS

1. Michael Phillips and Salli Rasberry, "Marketing Without Advertising: Easy Ways to Build a Business Your Customers Will Love and Recommend," 2005, http://www.nolo.com/product.cfm/objectID/5E5BFB9E-A33A-43DB-9D162A6460AA646A/sampleChapter/5/111/277/#summary.

2. PR Newswire, "Word of Mouth the #1 Influence on Business Buying Decisions," Jack Morton Worldwide, 2007, http://www.prnewswire.com/cgi-bin/stories.pl?ACCT=ind_focus.story&STORY=/www/story/05-14-2007/0004587208&EDATE=MON+May+14+2007,+07:00+AM, and "Word-of-Mouth Phenomenon Spreads Across the Globe According to Worldwide GfK Roper Consulting Study," Gfk Group, 2006, http://www.gfkamerica.com/news/WOMSpreadsAcrosstheGlobe.htm.

3. Sifry's Alerts, "The State of the Live Web," April 5, 2007, http://www.sifry.com/alerts/archives/000493.html.

4. Pew Internet and American Life Project, "The State of Blogging," January 2005, http://www.pewinternet.org/PPF/r/144/report_display.asp.

5. Om Malik, "Vonage's Scary Big Spending Ways," GigaOm, May 28, 2005, http://gigaom.com/2005/05/28/vonage-scary-big-spending-ways/.

6. Om Malik, "Vonage, Slow Road to Nowhere?" GigaOm, August 9, 2007, http://gigaom.com/2007/08/09/vonage-slow-road-to-nowhere/.

7. Om Malik, "Vonage: How Low Can You Go?" GigaOm, September 25, 2007, http://gigaom.com/2007/09/25/vonage-sprint/.

8. See http://www.getsatisfaction.com.

9. Jeff Jarvis, "Dell Lies. Dell Sucks," BuzzMachine, http://www.buzzmachine.com/archives/2005_06_21.html#009911.

10. Louise Lee, "Hanging Up on Dell?" *BusinessWeek,* October 10, 2005, http://www.businessweek.com/magazine/content/05_41/b3954102.htm.

11. "Dell Squeaks Past HP in Customer Satisfaction," *Seattle Post Intelligencer,* August 20, 2008.

4: BUILDING WHUFFIE BY LISTENING TO AND INTEGRATING FEEDBACK

1. Khoi Vinh, "Offending Experts and Pleasing Everybody," March 9, 2007, http://www.subtraction.com/archives/2007/0309_offending_ex.php.

2. From an Internet Relay Chat (IRC) with Ben West of Alexa.com, at http://rbach.priv.at/Microformats-IRC/2007-06-20#T235145.

3. Debora Viana Thompson, Rebecca W. Hamilton, and Roland T. Rust, *Feature Fatigue: When Product Capabilities Become Too Much of a Good Thing,* Marketing Science Institute, 2005.

4. From a workshop entitled "Thriving Under Fire: Responding to Angry and Aggressive Customers," by John Faisandier of Faisandier Associates of New Zealand.

5. Jako Nielsen, "Participation Inequality: Encouraging More Users to Contribute," Alertbox, October 9, 2006, http://www.useit.com/alertbox/participation_inequality.html.

6. See http://www.songbirdnest.com.

7. Burt Helm, "Yelping for Dollars," *BusinessWeek,* December 7, 2006.

8. Pete Cashmore, "Facebook's Face Lift—an Invasion of Privacy?" Mashable.com, September 5, 2006, http://mashable.com/2006/09/05/facebooks-facelift-mini-feeds-and-news-feeds/.

9. See http://www.petitionspot.com/petitions/thenewfacebook.

10. See http://daywithoutfacebook.blogspot.com/.

11. Mark Zuckerberg, "An Open Letter from Mark Zuckerberg," The Facebook Blog, September 8, 2006, http://blog.facebook.com/blog.php?post=2208562130.

5: BECOME PART OF THE COMMUNITY YOU SERVE

1. Marcus Buckingham, *The One Thing You Need to Know . . . About Great Managing, Great Leading, and Sustained Individual Success,* Free Press, 2005.

2. See http://twitter.zappos.com/start.

3. See http://twitter.com/help/lingo.

4. Leisa Reichelt coined the term "ambient intimacy" in her blog post about Twitter written on March 1, 2007, http://www.disambiguity.com/ambient-intimacy/.

6: DEPOSITING INTO AND WITHDRAWING FROM YOUR WHUFFIE ACCOUNT

1. Matt Ridley, *The Origins of Virtue: Human Instincts and the Evolution of Cooperation,* Penguin Books, 1996, p. 137.
2. Ibid, p. 98.
3. Ibid, p. 140.
4. Daniel Lyons, "Attack of the Blogs," *Forbes,* November 14, 2005, http://www.forbes.com/home/forbes/2005/1114/128.html?_requestid=3442.
5. Pallavi Gogoi, "Wal-Mart vs. the Blogosphere," *BusinessWeek,* October 17, 2006, http://www.businessweek.com/bwdaily/dnflash/content/oct2006/db2006 1018_445917.htm.
6. Joe Weisenthal, "Wal-Mart's MySpace Clone Gone, Missed by Nobody," TechDirt, October 3, 2006, http://www.techdirt.com/articles/20061003/074614.shtml.
7. Bryan Gardiner, "Facebook Users Hijack Wal-Mart's Roommate Style Page," Wired.com, August 27, 2007, http://blog.wired.com/business/2007/08/face book-users-.html.

7: BE NOTABLE: ELEVEN WAYS TO CREATE AMAZING CUSTOMER EXPERIENCES

1. Craig Courtice, "The Cult of Moleskine: Memo-Making Mavens Around the World Have Made This Little Notebook a Mandatory Accessory for Artists and Luddites Alike," *National Post,* November 16, 2006.
2. Stephanie Clifford, "26 Most Fascinating Entrepreneurs," Inc.com, http://www .inc.com/magazine/20050401/26-markoff.html.
3. Nichole L. Torres, "Bold Moves," January 2008, http://www.entrepreneur .com/magazine/entrepreneur/2008/january/187696.html.
4. Claire Bushey, "Social Conscience," *Lake Michigan Shore,* Style and Culture section, January 9, 2008.
5. See http://www.myspace.com/vosgeschocolate.
6. Sean Lengell, "Virgin America Woos Public in Quest to Fly," *Washington Times,* January 31, 2007.
7. See http://methodlust.blogspot.com/.
8. "We're Teaming with Danny Seo," People Against Dirty, July 1, 2007, http://peopleagainstdirty.typepad.com/people_against_dirty/2007/07/were-teaming-up.html.
9. "Adam Lowry's Key Move: Taking a Fresh Look at an Old Product Category," http://www.startupnation.com/pages/keymoves/KM_AdamLowry.asp.
10. Mihaly Csikszentmihalyi, *Flow: The Psychology of Optimal Experience,* Harper Perennial, 1991, p. 72.
11. See http://iparklikeanidiot.com/.
12. See http://blogcabin.37signals.com/posts/.
13. Kevin McLaughlin, "Apple's Jobs Gushes over App Store Success," August 11, 2008, ChannelWeb, http://www.crn.com/software/210002313.

8: EMBRACE THE CHAOS

1. See http://www.flickr.com/commons/usage/.
2. See http://boodle.wetpaint.com/.
3. Joel Postman, "Jet Blue Engages in Real Conversation on Twitter," Socialized PR blog, March 17, 2008, http://www.socializedpr.com/jetblue-engages-in-real-conversation-on-twitter/.
4. Stephen O'Grady, Redmonk blog, *Links for April 1, 2008,* http://redmonk.com/sogrady/2008/03/31/links-for-2008-04-01/.
5. Eli Singer, Jay Goldman, and Mark Kuznicki, "Breakthrough Ideas for 2008: Sick Transit Gloria," *Harvard Business Review,* February 2008.
6. Robert Putnam, *Bowling Alone: The Collapse and Revival of American Community,* Simon & Schuster, 2000, pp. 22–23.
7. Ev Williams, "The Birth of Obvious Corp," http://evhead.com/2006/10/birth-of-obvious-corp_25.asp.

9: FIND YOUR HIGHER PURPOSE

1. Matt Ridley, *The Origins of Virtue: Human Instincts and the Evolution of Cooperation,* Penguin Books, 1996, pp. 105–124.
2. Craig Newmark, "CRAIGSLIST: On the record: Craig Newmark," *San Francisco Chronicle,* August 15, 2004, http://www.sfgate.com/cgi-bin/article.cgi?f=/c/a/2004/08/15/NEWMARK.TMP.
3. Ryan Mickle, "What Is Responsible Business, Really? Perspectives from Stonyfield Farms and Clif Bar Founders," TriplePundit: people planet profit, May 1, 2008, http://www.triplepundit.com/pages/what-is-responsible-business-r-003064.php.
4. "Interview with Gary Hirshberg, Stonyfield Farm," Starting up Green, April 2008, http://www.startingupgreen.com/index.php/eco-entrepreneur-profiles/4-eco-entrepreneur-profiles/12-gary-hirshberg.
5. Lisa Roner, "The Big Interview: James Parker—Southwest's Special Sauce," *Ethical Corporation Magazine,* March 11, 2008.
6. Jeremy Raelin, "Southwest Recovers from 9/11 Attacks," BCHeights.com, March 19, 2002, http://media.www.bcheights.com/media/storage/paper144/news/2002/03/19/Marketplace/Southwest.Recovers.From.911.Attacks=218448=page3.shtml.
7. See http://www.cruelgame.com/about/.

10: WHUFFIE IRL

1. David W. McMillan and David M. Chavis, "Sense of Community: A Definition and Theory," *American Journal of Community Psychology* 14 (1986): 9.
2. WTF stands for What The Fuck in online shortcode.
3. Go to http://www.whuffiefactor.com.

ACKNOWLEDGMENTS

This book was made possible because of a series of events and people who used their own whuffie (connections, influence, et cetera) to help me along over the years.

My entire way of thinking was shifted by *The Cluetrain Manifesto* in 1999. I can't recall who on that marketing listserve posted the link to the online version, but thank you. And thanks to David Weinberg, Doc Searles, Chris Locke, and Rick Levine for publishing your radical thoughts on marketing in a way that was free and accessible.

Careerwise, way back in the day, it was Dino Esposito, the founder of Media Dog in Calgary, who introduced a young online marketer to people in the advertising world, where I met Jeffrey Robinson at MGM Communications. Jeff recognized my unconventional approach to marketing as an asset to his team and really took me under his wing. Then it was my client, David Beardsell, the president of Bear Brewing and the genius behind Joe Stiff's Spiked Rootbeer, who gave me a national campaign to dream up that I love to this day. This brought me to Toronto, where I met Beverley Allen at the Human Resources Professionals Association, who encouraged me to push the boundaries of online marketing even in a traditional organization.

Then there is a really key, special person in my life: Shel Israel, who I met through blogging, who introduced me to Munjal Shah of Riya.com, which was my big break in the world of start-ups and brought me to San Francisco. Thanks for pulling for me, Shel, and opening up a whole new world where possibilities were endless and people take chances regularly. Upon moving to San Francisco, I met another key person who helped me hone my way of thinking. Chris Messina became both my business and personal muse over the next two and a half years. He offered up one question that blew open my way of thinking, "Why not?" Chris knows no boundaries and taught me to question my own.

During the time of running Citizen Agency with Chris, I met and read many great books by many amazing thinkers, but the one that really infected my thinking was *The Origins of Virtue* by Matt Ridley (I even named my dog after him, I was so struck). Matt got me to start thinking seriously about the nature of reciprocity and the community ties it binds. With that in place, I stumbled across Cory Doctorow's *Down and Out in the Magic Kingdom,* where he talks about the currency of the future, whuffie, and everything clicked for me. All of a sudden my love of economics, combined with my desire to make marketing more of a customer relationship bridging function, combined with my experience in online communities, all culminated to align my random thinking and experience into this one book.

Aside from that, I wouldn't be anywhere in this world without the people who pay me their valuable attention to read my thoughts and comment back, view my screenshots and photos and share their own, watch and share videos everyday so that our imagination grows together . . . my community. My global, online, fabulous group of friends, colleagues, and lurking interlopers. This includes my 20,000-plus Twitter followers, many of whom supplied me with fantastic examples and feedback while writing this book (as well as heaps of support, love, and encouragement)—your names are acknowledged on thewhuffiefactor.com.

My Flickr friends and contacts who were instrumental in making the jacket of this book happen the way I dreamed it would: Amit Gupta, Eric Kastner, Stef Sullivan, Todd Kalhar, Michael Galpert, Erica G, Drew Robinson, Evan Hamilton, Hillary Hartley, Christine Selleck, Pal Isakson, Tyler Emerson, Erica Douglas, Marcus Nelson, Todd O'Neill, Fred Stutzman, Jeffrey Kalmikoff, Grant Hutchinson, Amie Gillingham, Ed Schipul, Gina Cardzone, Sharon M. McIntyre (Shazz), Dale Larson, Cesar and Angela Castro, Ashley Dryden, Rachel Murray, Alicia Preston, Leslie Chicoine, Jellyfish24 (no real name), Britt Bravo, Joel Hawkins, brhoades245 (no real name), palea2k (nrn), nrobins27, Josh Shipley, Lauren Lee, Brieanna Hattey, chocolatecinderella1 (nrn), lilmisspetrie (nrn), Emily Brock, Mario Paz, Tommy Strong, Gavin Green, mirror_Tsui (nrn), Lilian Mahoukou, Nancy Beaton, Donaldson, Todd Sieling, Matt Harris, Silona Bonewald, Keith Robinson, Kevin Lawver, Robert Steburg, Amy Muller, Jeffrey Zeldman,

Veerle Pieters, Gema Lynn, Paul Annett, Balaji Sowmyanarayanan, Nick Whitmoyer, Nguyet Vuong, Reinier Meenhorst, Neil Ford, Barce, Lisa Price, Chris Tingom, Daniel Miller and, of course, the person who submitted the final cover used, Cindy Li!

All of these people and more are the reason *The Whuffie Factor* exists. Each and every connection here contributed to my own whuffie. Thank you and enjoy.

INDEX